DISRUPTIVE
TRANSFORMATION

NASPA.
Student Affairs Administrators
in Higher Education

◆ NASPA® | Student Affairs Administrators in Higher Education

DISRUP
TIVE
TRANSFORMATION

Leading Creative and Innovative Teams in Higher Education

FOREWORD BY JAIME CASAP, Chief Education Evangelist at Google

Robert D. Kelly, Colin Stewart, AND ASSOCIATES

Student Affairs Administrators
in Higher Education

Published by
NASPA–Student Affairs Administrators in Higher Education
111 K Street, NE
10th Floor
Washington, DC 20002
www.naspa.org

Additional copies may be purchased by contacting the NASPA publications department at 202-265-7500 or visiting http://bookstore.naspa.org.

NASPA does not discriminate on the basis of race, color, national origin, religion, sex, age, gender identity, gender expression, affectional or sexual orientation, or disability in any of its policies, programs, and services.

Library of Congress Cataloging-in-Publication Data
(Prepared by The Donohue Group, Inc.)

Names: Kelly, Robert (Robert Dwayne), 1972- author. | Stewart, Colin, 1984- author. | NASPA-Student Affairs Administrators in Higher Education, issuing body.
Title: Disruptive transformation : leading creative and innovative teams in higher education / Robert Kelly, Colin Stewart, and associates.
Description: First edition. | Washington, DC : NASPA-Student Affairs Administrators in Higher Education, [2020] | Includes bibliographical references and index.
Identifiers: ISBN 9781948213219 (paperback) | ISBN 9781948213226 (mobi) | ISBN 9781948213233 (ePub)
Subjects: LCSH: Educational leadership. | Teams in the workplace. | Universities and colleges--Administration.
Classification: LCC LB2341 .K45 2020 (print) | LCC LB2341 (ebook) | DDC 378.01--dc23

Printed and bound in the United States of America

FIRST EDITION

CONTENTS

Foreword   *ix*

SECTION 1: Historical Context and Best Practices in Creative and Innovative Leadership

Chapter 1   3

Disruptive Transformation in Higher Education:
An Introduction to Creative and Innovative Leadership
Robert D. Kelly and Colin Stewart

Chapter 2   19

In Defense of a System: Higher Education, Change,
and Innovation
Anna Gonzalez

Chapter 3   41

Becoming a More Creative and Innovative Leader:
Pursuing a Different Kind of Professional Development
Joseph P. Zolner

Chapter 4   61

Creating Burstiness
Art Munin

Chapter 5   75

Building a Culture of Innovation in a Division of
Student Affairs
Patrick Love

Chapter 6   89

Creativity in the Hiring Process: Run Successful
Searches by Thinking Outside the Box
Ann Marie Klotz and Vijay Pendakur

Chapter 7   115

Graduate Preparation Programs as a Place to Engage in
Creative Practice
Susana Hernández

Chapter 8   129

Leadership, Creativity, Curiosity, and the Blank
Computer Screen
Cissy Petty

Chapter 9   143

Creative Lessons in Leadership From Both Ends of the
Career Journey
Frank R. Lamas and Amanda Stewart

SECTION 2: Intersections Between Diversity, Inclusion, and Creative Leadership

Chapter 10   163

It Comes From Deep Within: Spirituality and the
Creative Process
Michele C. Murray

Chapter 11   183

Leading Creative and Diverse Teams
Domonic A. Rollins and Kenechukwu (K.C.) Mmeje

Chapter 12   199

"We Out Here, We Been Here, We Ain't Leaving, We Are Loved": Using Creativity in Working With Student Activism and Unrest
Brandon Common and Eileen Galvez

Chapter 13   221

Harnessing Cultural Wealth for Creative Leadership
Bridget Turner Kelly and Natasha T. Turman

Chapter 14   239

The Emergence of Micro-Innovations in Managing Community College Stakeholders
Steve Tyrell

Chapter 15   261

The End Is Just the Beginning
Robert D. Kelly and Colin Stewart

The Authors   275
Index   281

FOREWORD

Creativity and Innovation Have Become Mandatory in Higher Education

I do not buy into the narrative that "both K–12 and higher education are broken," or that "education has remained the same for 150 years." When I hear an "education expert" say such things, I immediately disengage and zone out. Such statements indicate to me that the person doesn't know much about education.

First, I can't say education is broken, because it worked for me. I am a first-generation American born and raised by a single mother on welfare and food stamps in 1970s and 1980s Hell's Kitchen. Education is what broke the cycle of poverty for my family. In my years of talking about education to audiences around the world, I have met thousands of people who shared their story of how education helped them escape poverty. Has education worked for everyone? Absolutely not. However, that is a different conversation involving equity and opportunity. What is indisputable is that education has the potential to disrupt poverty.

Those who say education isn't working in the United States ignore the fact that America has the highest rate of educated residents in its history: More than 90% of Americans have completed high school (Schmidt, 2018), and more Americans have a college degree than ever before (Wilson, 2017).

Saying education hasn't changed in 100 years ignores all the structural and curriculum changes that have taken place. Education has changed dramatically in the past 20 years, let alone the past 100 years. Just take a look at programs like No Child Left Behind or Race to the Top in K–12, or the number of majors that didn't exist 10 years ago in higher education.

If the narrative that education is broken or it hasn't changed is wrong, why is there heightened pressure to "fix" education? The reason is that the world has changed dramatically since the Internet became mainstream in the mid-1990s, especially in terms of the role of information and the skills needed to thrive in a rapidly changing society. In 1995, only 14% of Americans had Internet access, and 42% of Americans had never even heard of the Internet (Fox & Rainie, 2014).

Compare that picture to today, when more than 90% of Americans have Internet access, and 73% of Americans use it every day. Among Americans aged 18–29, usage is 100% (Pew Research Center, 2019). This unprecedented transformation happened in less than 25 years, and really in just the past 12 years, since the release of smartphones that put the Internet in everyone's pocket.

The acceleration of technology since 1995 has seeped into all parts of life, work, and education. We now find ourselves in a new age. Some people call it the "fourth industrial revolution," but I call it the "digitalization economy." By *digitalization* I mean all the technologies that are today shaping the world: machine learning, artificial intelligence, augmented reality, vertical reality, robotics, and automation. We are only at the beginning of the changes that are undoubtedly coming.

The digitalization economy has advanced quickly. So quickly that education hasn't had time to adjust. This is especially true in higher education. For a generation, one of the critical roles of higher education institutions was to create and collect information and distribute that information to students, who spent years processing it. Today, nearly everyone has access to the same information. Thus, information is a commodity with no real value. What is valuable is knowing how to take all that information and create intelligence. This is why higher education institutions need to shift from collecting and disseminating information to helping students create intelligence.

To thrive in the digitalization economy, students will need to develop and master essential skills like problem solving, critical thinking, collaboration, and creativity. They will need to use these skills to solve unstructured, complex problems, and manage and understand an overabundance of information that comes at them at an unprecedented speed. This is where higher education can shine: Higher education is equipped to help students develop and master these skills.

Historically, higher education has been able to adapt and adjust accordingly to what the world requires of it at the time. For higher education to keep pace with the rapid rate of digitalization transformation, it must move away from a system that worked well for a very long time, to one that better reflects the future. Higher education needs a culture of creativity and innovation. This book provides the blueprint for higher education leaders to get on the culture change path.

The other problem facing higher education is cost. At a time when higher education must be accessible to more people, students are facing unprecedented costs to develop the skills needed to thrive in the modern world. In 1979, a student could pay for college by working 2 hours a day at a minimum wage job and cover the entire cost of college; today, a student would have to work 17 hours a day to do the same ("How Many Hours," 2015). The cost of higher education is putting college out of reach for millions of students, adding to the complexities of equity and access.

Higher education leaders must be willing to adapt to undertake these challenges head-on. Reviewing technological advancements from the past—like the personal computer, high-speed Internet access, and the release of the mobile device—reveals that changing the way things are done requires not only new technology, but also behavioral change among those who are doing things the "old way." However, higher education leaders cannot simply be directed to change; they must have the requisite skills to usher in change— namely, problem-solving, critical thinking, creativity, and the ability to manage innovative practices. These are the same skills students need to prosper in a digitalized economy. Thus, higher education leaders must use these skills to not only change institutional practices, but also to model these behaviors for students.

In the pages that follow, the authors lay out the most critical considerations of creativity and innovation. The chapters contain a remarkable collection of examples, strategies, resources, and reflections related to how creativity and innovation can be (and I would argue must be) utilized by higher education leaders and administrators. Transforming the higher education system will require creative and innovative leadership. This book offers a path for higher education leaders to successfully guide their institutions into the digitalized economy.

Jaime Casap
Chief Education Evangelist
Google

References

Fox, S., & Rainie, L. (2014). *The web at 25 in the U.S. Part 1: How the internet has woven itself into American life.* Retrieved from Pew Research Center website: https://www.pewinternet. org/2014/02/27/part-1-how-the-internet-has-woven-itself-into-american-life

Pew Research Center. (2019). *Internet/broadband fact sheet.* Retrieved from https://www. pewinternet.org/fact-sheet/internet-broadband

How many hours would it take you to work off today's college tuition? (2015). *The New Republic.* Retrieved from https://newrepublic.com/article/122814/ how-many-hours-would-it-take-you-work-todays-college-tuition

Schmidt, E. (2018, July 31). *U.S. population more educated than ever before: For the first time, 90 percent completed high school or more.* Retrieved from U.S. Census Bureau website: https:// www.census.gov/library/stories/2018/07/educational-attainment.html

Wilson, R. (2017, April 3). Census: More Americans have college degrees than ever before. *The Hill.* Retrieved from https://thehill.com/homenews/ state-watch/326995-census-more-americans-have-college-degrees-than-ever-before

SECTION 1

HISTORICAL CONTEXT AND BEST PRACTICES IN CREATIVE AND INNOVATIVE LEADERSHIP

1

DISRUPTIVE TRANSFORMATION IN HIGHER EDUCATION

An Introduction to Creative and Innovative Leadership

ROBERT D. KELLY AND COLIN STEWART

olleges and universities are struggling with uncertainty around every corner. No matter an institution's size, student body, affiliation, or type, every campus is facing increasingly complex challenges: enrollment shortfalls, budget deficits, and not to mention faculty and staff who are asked to do so much more with less. Stakeholder demands for increased accountability, shifting student demographics, and confusing governmental policy changes are changing the higher education landscape. Where some see certain doom, the authors of this book see hope, and that hope comes from changing how higher education leaders respond to these challenges.

Creativity and innovation are essential tools for success in higher education. Creative and innovative leaders are present in higher education administration; however, there is limited scholarship,

3

and in some cases no resources, information, or guidance available, on how creativity and innovation can be specifically utilized by higher education administrators. Smith, Blixt, Ellis, Gill, and Kruger (2015) started the conversation on innovation and change within student affairs, and since their book's publication so much has already changed. This book focuses on the process of disruptive transformation along with the intersection of creativity, innovation, and leadership in the context of higher education administration. This text can be utilized by practitioners and faculty at all levels, especially seasoned administrators, to transform a campus culture. Although current resources on generalized leadership and creativity exist, this book stands apart by offering higher education professionals examples, strategies, resources, and reflections on how creativity and innovation can be utilized by academics and administrators. It has been established that creativity brings definition and vibrancy to any professional calling (Treffinger, 2007). The goal of this book is to serve as a broad resource for the higher education administration community while encouraging individuals to engage in disruptive transformation.

The field of higher education is constantly changing and evolving. There is an unquestionable need for professionals and leaders throughout the field to be equipped with creative and innovative skill sets. In a study of 32 competencies identified as necessary for new student affairs professionals, creativity was found to be most crucial for success by mid- and senior-level student affairs administrators (Burkard, Cole, Ott, & Stoflet, 2005). Additionally, in a study examining perceptions of new higher education administrators, hiring managers desired higher education professionals who came equipped with creative aptitudes (Herdlein, 2004). However, there are no guides for developing creative and innovative higher education leaders. Given the need for qualified and innovative leaders in higher education, resources should be readily available for professional development.

There are also implications for how creativity and innovation can be utilized in an institution's overall mission. Evidence shows that students finishing college are not sufficiently prepared for the realities of the world of work (American Management Association, 2010; Wagner, 2008). Wagner's (2008) research on the global achievement gap demonstrated that graduating seniors require adaptability, curiosity, and imagination to survive in the 21st-century workforce. Moreover, the American Management Association (2010) inferred that creativity and innovation were the most critical skills for students to possess upon graduation. With the high demand for professionals at all levels to be equipped with creative skill sets, this book is designed to prepare leaders in higher education to respond to the pressing challenges of today and tomorrow.

Higher education has struggled to keep up with emerging technologies and the digitalization economy. Part of this is due to limited resources, access, and expertise. This text aims to equip those in student affairs with the skills, models, and insights to shift their approach to leadership in order to become creative and innovative leaders who transform the culture of their campuses.

Background on Creative and Innovative Leadership

There is limited training, education, and resources on creative professional development for higher education administrators. Furthermore, there is minimal scholarship on how to incorporate creativity and innovation into the field of higher education administration.

Creativity is difficult to define, understand, track, and measure. Definitions of creativity vary. Singer (1999) inferred that creativity involves replicating an image or concept from an individual's mind—for instance, having an idea for a design and then making the conceptual idea come to life by sketching that design. Kaufman and Baer (2005) shared that while creativity should be thought of "as a construct in abstract, domain-transcending ways, all creative products come into being in some domain or field of endeavor" (p. xiv); thus, creativity is judged by the standards of the current field. From a systems perspective, Csikszentmihalyi (1996) indicated that creativity is something that changes, evolves, or transforms an established framework—for example, the modern cell phone transformed the telecommunications framework. Creativity should also be something of merit, something of significance, or authentic. Researchers agree that there is no one-size-fits-all definition of creativity (Kleiman, 2008). However, there is an understanding among creatives that being creative is more than just a random act, but offers something that is of value and original (Welling, 2007).

The term *innovation* is often used interchangeably with *creativity*, and is even more difficult to define. Innovation is about the process and execution of a creative thought. Dino (2017) stated that although creativity "is the successful generation of an original and potentially useful idea, innovation is the successful implementation of such an idea" (p. 26). For instance, innovation occurs when a professional takes a creative idea from another campus and develops a new program for incoming students based on that idea. Furthermore, innovation includes a process of developing creative ideas followed by application and execution (West, 2002). Others have argued that innovation definitions differ from discipline to discipline and proposed innovation results from a systematic approach rather than merely a random set of actions (Baregheh, Rowley, & Sambrook, 2009). Regardless of how innovation is defined, higher education institutions require innovation to stay viable. The concept of innovation is no longer value-added or a preferred qualification for higher education leaders; rather, it is essential for success (Passig & Cohen, 2014). Innovation and creativity are becoming foundational skills for all leaders.

Both innovation and creativity are also closely connected to the process of *diffusion*. According to Rogers (2003), "Diffusion is the process in which an innovation is communicated through certain channels over time among the members of a social system" (p. 5). This is especially helpful when developing a new product or idea and introducing it to a large group. Creative and innovative leaders in higher education should be equipped with the skill sets to influence change. Puccio, Murdock, & Mance (2007) argued that "to be effective at implementing solutions and introducing creative change, leaders need to anticipate the reaction, both pro and con, to ideas they wish to implement" (p. 172). Several models exist that can be infused into higher education. For instance, design thinking (Kelley & Kelley, 2013), adaptive leadership (Heifetz, Grashow, & Linsky, 2009), and creative problem-solving thinking (Puccio et al., 2007) are all leadership models that incorporate some aspect of creativity and innovation. However, with heightened calls for accountability, dwindling budgets, and more pressure from external forces, creativity can be difficult to implement and assess.

The concept of creativity has many misconceptions and unwarranted biases. For example, Moran and John-Steiner (2004) noted that creatives can be considered by most impatient and unfriendly. Creativity has also long been perceived as a "difficulty" trait due to researchers struggling to develop controlled and empirical studies on the topic (Fink & Benedek, 2013). That raises the question of what specifically qualifies as *creative leadership* in higher education administration. Creative leadership in higher education has no roadmap or model to draw upon. The concept of creativity and effectiveness is often difficult to quantify because developing creative competencies is very different depending on the particular profession or craft (Kaufman & Baer, 2005). Currently, no creative standards exist for higher education leaders. Adding to the challenge, when it comes to assessment of creativity, the evaluator should be aware of the competencies, skills, and standards of that particular craft (Csikszentmihalyi, 1996). Because creativity is so difficult to evaluate and define, it is no surprise that so many higher education professionals do not describe themselves as innovative leaders or feel comfortable leading with creative vision and imagination. However, if higher education leaders had the knowledge and were aware of a set of creative standards, they might aspire to be a more creative leader.

With the varying definitions and challenges of creativity and innovation also come opportunities. Within higher education, there are numerous subcultures and occasions to develop one's identity as a leader. As discussed, creativity is about developing something new, and innovation is about the process and execution. Therefore, *creative and innovative leadership* is the process of developing an original idea combined with the visionary, inclusive, and educational execution of that idea. Creative and innovative leadership is an art form; it takes time and it requires thinking differently about leadership. It requires individuals to gather context, have self-awareness, know the history, and take risks to provide what "could be" for their students.

Disruptive transformation is the process of becoming a creative and innovative leader. It involves an individual not only changing others and organizations, but also themselves. It requires leaders to let go and say "yes, and" to the opportunities that lie ahead. Disruptive transformation can be an uncomfortable process, but it is ultimately necessary for creative and innovative leadership. Leaders may have to disrupt their styles, safety nets, and systems to effectively lead in this way. This process can be used in strategic planning, budgeting, change management, assessment, training, advancement, development, supervision, programming, curriculum development, teaching, service delivery, and resource management. There is great potential for creative leadership in higher education. Even with the endless promise for application, the connection between self-exploration and creativity has not earned the stature it might warrant (Glăveanu & Tanggaard, 2014), although Josselson (1996) argued that the ultimate creative act involves the process of developing ourselves and becoming who we are supposed to be. Ultimately, tapping into a conceptual framework of "yes and" can aid creative leaders in seeing potential solutions to vexing challenges in higher education.

The world is growing increasingly more complex; creativity should be woven into the tapestry of higher education (Gibson, 2010). This text provides practitioners, administrators, and faculty with tools, resources, and strategies for responding to the impending challenges of tomorrow through creative and innovative leadership. The book explores the challenges and tensions that lie within creative and innovative practices. The authors offer best practices for creative and innovative leadership in higher education; explore the connections between diversity, creativity, and innovation; and discuss the barriers for leading creatively. Finally, this text strives to advance a culture that furthers scholarship on creativity and innovation in higher education.

A Guide for This Book

This book includes a total of 15 chapters that draw on the expertise of a diverse array of creative and innovative higher education leaders from various backgrounds and institutional types. Although each chapter is unique, the book as a whole carries a thread of disruptive transformation to inspire readers to reflect, experiment, and evolve their innovative practice in higher education. The text begins with an historical context of innovation and higher education. The first section explores various best practices in creative and innovative leadership in higher education. The second section discusses the intersections between diversity, inclusion, and creative leadership. The book concludes with a presidential perspective on how creativity and innovation are critical at the senior level. At the end of each chapter are questions and activities to unlock readers' inner creativity. The book is designed to be practical and inspiring, and to challenge the way readers think about leadership. To this end, the book includes historical context, best practices and strategies to incorporate inclusive and creative leadership, and reflection questions at the end of each chapter. The following is a brief summary of each of the chapters.

Chapter 2, "In Defense of a System: Higher Education, Change, and Innovation," is written by Anna Gonzalez, vice president of student affairs at Harvey Mudd College. Looking through a historical lens, this chapter examines past practices in higher education and how some of those same practices produced barriers to creativity and innovation. Moreover, the chapter explores the costs to society as leaders draw a line in the sand in defense of a system of higher education that is resistant to change. Finally, this chapter offers strategies and practices to influence and inspire leaders to implement courageous, innovative, and creative changes necessary to meet the needs of today's and tomorrow's society.

Chapter 3, "Becoming a More Creative and Innovative Leader: Pursuing a Different Kind of Professional Development," is written by Joe Zolner, senior director of programs and lecturer at Harvard Graduate School of Education. The chapter offers a set of reflections and recommendations for developing and pursuing a long-term professional development plan designed to increase readers' creative leadership capabilities and capacity to lead innovation and change. This chapter notes that many professional development experiences err on the side of too much informational activity with insufficient attention paid to transformational insights and outcomes. The chapter explains the distinctions between these two forms of professional development and articulates their relationship to creative and innovative leadership.

Chapter 4, "Creating Burstiness," is written by Art Munin, associate vice chancellor and dean of students at the University of Wisconsin. Throughout the chapter, the author provides personal examples of creativity and outlines a strategy that offers specific tools to increase and enhance the moments that produce creativity. The chapter explores the following concepts: cultivating group synergy for high output, determining a unit's meaning or purpose, changing a team's environment, managing structures around creativity, discovering what leaders can do within a creative context, and understanding the effort it takes to master creativity. This chapter bridges the gap between personal acts of creativity and professional practice while providing specific tools and strategies to aid readers in their leadership.

Chapter 5, "Building a Culture of Innovation in a Division of Student Affairs," is written by Patrick Love, vice president for student affairs and director of the Student Personnel Administration graduate program at Springfield College. This chapter focuses on the role of leadership in developing an organizational culture of innovation and the lessons learned from the author's dynamic experiences. The chapter includes a case study from the perspective of the vice president of student affairs, tactics, reflections, and suggested actions for developing a culture of innovation that are grounded in scholarship in innovation. The chapter demystifies creative and innovative leadership through storytelling.

Chapter 6, "Creativity in the Hiring Process: Run Successful Searches by Thinking Outside the Box," is written by Ann Marie

Klotz, vice president of student success at The New School, and Vijay Pendakur, dean of students at Cornell University. The chapter explores the deficits of the current hiring model in higher education and offers solutions to target and attract the type of dynamic practitioners that can help move the needle forward in departments and divisions of student affairs. The chapter also includes innovative strategies for advertising and recruiting for positions, templates for more creative on-campus interview schedules, and a robust onboarding schedule to ensure a strong return on investment in new hires. The chapter points out the creativity gap in recruiting, hiring, and onboarding new talent, and why institutions need to hire creative and innovative leaders to better serve students.

Chapter 7, "Creativity and Leadership: Graduate Preparation Programs as a Place to Engage in Creative Practice," is written by Susana Hernández, associate professor, program coordinator of higher education, administration, and leadership, and department chair of educational leadership at Fresno State. This chapter describes how faculty who prepare graduate students for the field of student affairs can foster creativity in higher education generally, and in the classroom specifically. It clarifies how creativity and innovation can produce opportunities and approaches to address current issues and challenges in the field of higher education and student affairs. This chapter also illuminates the critical role that student affairs faculty play in developing new creative student affairs professionals.

Chapter 8, "Leadership, Creativity, Curiosity, and the Blank Screen," is written by Cissy Petty, inaugural dean of the student experience at The George Washington University. This chapter explores how leaders experience new situations, whether it be writing an annual report, creating a board of trustees presentation, doing a TED-like talk, or taking on an inaugural role. The chapter addresses the process in which leaders take on new challenges by addressing specifically what could stifle creativity when developing new systems, programs, and ideas. Leaders are often expected to take on challenges with little to no direction; this chapter shows readers how to guide their team while not stifling others throughout the creative process.

Chapter 9, "Creative Lessons in Leadership From Both Ends of the Career Journey," is written by Frank Lamas, vice president of student affairs and enrollment management at Fresno State, and Amanda Stewart, coordinator of communications and media for student affairs and enrollment management and a doctoral candidate at Fresno State. The chapter provides context for creative and innovative leadership through a narrative exploring multiple institutions and various professional positions across a variety of divisions of student affairs. The chapter inspires deep thinking to support students in a way that is innovative, energizing, and forward-thinking. This chapter demonstrates how creative professional practice can apply to both young professionals and senior student affairs administrators while best serving the institution.

Chapter 10, "It Comes From Deep Within: Spirituality and the Creative Process," is written by Michele Murray, vice president of student affairs and dean of students at College of the Holy Cross. This chapter explores the concepts of mindfulness, flow, and humility while describing the spiritual dimensions of the creative process. Through a handful of vignettes, the chapter explores the meaning of creativity and innovation in the professional lives of student affairs educators. Student affairs work sometimes requires individuals to carry a heavy burden; this chapter offers readers the chance to imagine, create, and innovate, while giving themselves the freedom to express what they are feeling.

Chapter 11, "Leading Creative and Diverse Teams," is written by Kenechukwu (K.C.) Mmeje, vice president of student affairs at Southern Methodist University, and Domonic A. Rollins, senior director of equity and inclusion at The Dalton School. This chapter highlights topics ranging from inclusive, creative, and innovative practices to leading diverse teams inclusively. It describes how an individual can approach inclusive and innovative practices through self-development, examining structures, culture, and interventions. In this chapter, the authors—a chief diversity officer and a vice president for student affairs—use their professional experience paired with expert interviews to address the need for creative, diverse, and inclusive teams in higher education, and the skills required to effectively lead and support those teams. The chapter explains why colleges and universities needs innovative and creative leadership approaches to engage the diverse students and communities they serve.

Chapter 12, "'We Out Here, We Been Here, We Ain't Leaving, We Are Loved': Using Creativity in Working With Student Activism and Unrest," is written by Brandon Common, assistant vice president of student affairs at Illinois Wesleyan University, and Eileen Galvez, assistant dean of Yale College and director of La Casa Cultural Center at Yale University. The chapter discusses how to utilize creativity when working with campus protests and student unrest. The authors draw on professional experiences, current practices, and academic research in sharing strategies for optimizing student learning and agency, and using creative problem-solving in these situations. The chapter explains that the rapidly changing national landscape of students in the United States and rise in nationalism require creative approaches in centering an institutional commitment to diversity and inclusion. Furthermore, the chapter illustrates that administrators have the capability to amplify the creative forces of students, particularly individuals with marginalized identities, while simultaneously protecting the institution through innovative practices.

Chapter 13, "Harnessing Cultural Wealth for Creative Leadership," is written by Bridget Turner Kelly, associate professor at the

University of Maryland, College Park, and Natasha Turman, director of the Women in Science and Engineering Residence Program at the University of Michigan. This chapter discusses cultivating cultural wealth in order to engage in innovative leadership practice that is nuanced, inclusive, and forward-thinking. Drawing on the authors' own leadership experiences and utilizing Yosso's (2005) community cultural wealth model, the chapter provides case studies and examples of those who were not able to access their cultural wealth due to racism and sexism, which kept them from being creative. This chapter demonstrates the importance of cultural wealth and how oppression at all levels prevents individuals from being creative and innovative leaders.

Chapter 14, "The Emergence of Micro-Innovations in Managing Community College Stakeholders," provides a presidential perspective on community colleges while exploring the creative opportunities that arise from community engagement. Written by Steve Tyrell, former president of North Country Community College, the chapter explains that community colleges across the United States serve many external constituency groups in meeting their core mission in higher education. The chapter points out that these community groups often create both smooth and volatile mixes of opportunities and challenges for community college leaders. As varied as these mixes can be, they are juncture points for where community college leaders can learn to leverage innovation and creativity to recast their institutions' roles in the communities they serve.

Chapter 15, "The End Is Just the Beginning," is written by Robert D. Kelly, vice president and special assistant to the president at Loyola University Maryland, and Colin Stewart, associate dean of student involvement at Fresno State. This chapter provides the conclusion for the book by summarizing models, key findings, and seminal points. The chapter also includes recommendations and considerations for further research and applications of creative and innovative leadership.

Although the book can be read from cover to cover, the editors acknowledge that readers may select key chapters that may best serve them and their institutions at particular points in time. However, each chapter brings value and perspectives that can be fruitful in most contexts. In exploring these chapters, readers should reflect on the questions and participate in the exercises. The editors invite readers to be bold in their approaches to creative and innovative leadership as they integrate these creative practices into their work, life, and organizational culture.

Unlock Your Creativity

Take five slow breaths and reflect on the following questions:

- What are the qualities of a creative and innovative leader?
- What do you hope to get out of this book?

Take another five slow breaths.

References

American Management Association. (2010). *Executives say the 21ˢᵗ century requires more skilled workers.* Retrieved from http://www.p21.org/storage/documents/Critical%20Skills%20 Survey%20Executive%20Summary.pdf

Baregheh, A., Rowley, J., & Sambrook, S. (2009). Towards a multidisciplinary definition of innovation. *Management Decision, 47*(8), 1323–1339. doi:http://dx.doi.org.hmlproxy.lib. csufresno.edu/10.1108/00251740910984578

Burkard, A. W., Cole, D. C., Ott, M., & Stoflet, T. (2005). Entry-level competencies of new student affairs professionals: A Delphi study. *NASPA Journal, 42*(3), 283–309.

Csikszentmihalyi, M. (1996). *Creativity: Flow and the psychology of discovery and invention.* New York, NY: First Harper Perennial.

Dino, R. N. (2017). Comparing and contrasting creativity, innovation, and entrepreneurship. In J. Pluckner (Ed.), *Creativity and innovation: Theory, research, and practice* (pp. 23–34). Waco, TX: Prufrock Press.

Fink, A., & Benedek, M. (2013). The creative brain: Brain correlates underlying the generation of original ideas. In O. Vartanian, A. S. Bristol, & J. C. Kauman (Eds.), *Neuroscience of creativity* (pp. 207–230). Cambridge, MA: The MIT Press.

Gibson, R. (2010). The "art" of creative teaching: Implications for higher education. *Teaching in Higher Education, 15*(5), 607–613.

Glăveanu, V. P., & Tanggaard, L. (2014). Creativity, identity, and representation: Towards a social-cultural theory of creative identity. *New Idea in Psychology, 34*, 12–21.

Heifetz, R. A., Grashow, A., & Linsky, M. (2009). *The practice of adaptive leadership: Tools and tactics for changing your organization and the world.* Boston, MA: Harvard Business Press.

Herdlein, R. J., III (2004). Survey of chief student affairs officers regarding relevance of graduate preparation of new professionals. *NASPA Journal, 42*(1), 51–71.

Josselson, R. (1996). *Revising herself: The story of women's identity from college to midlife.* New York, NY: Oxford University Press.

Kaufman, J. C., & Baer, J. (2005). *Creativity across domains: Faces of the muse.* Mahwah, NJ: Lawrence Erlbaum Associates.

Kelley, D., & Kelley, T. (2013). *Creative confidence: Unleashing the creative potential within us all.* New York, NY: Crown.

Kleiman, P. (2008). Towards transformation: Conceptions of creativity in higher education. *Innovations in Education and Teaching International, 45*(3), 209–217.

Moran, S., & John-Steiner, V. (2004). How collaboration in creative work impacts identity and motivation. In D. Miell & K. Littleton (Eds.), *Collaborative creativity: Contemporary perspectives* (pp. 11–25). London, England: Free Association Books.

Passig, D., & Cohen, L. (2014) Measuring the style of innovative thinking among engineering students. *Research in Science & Technological Education, 32*(1), 56–77.

Puccio, G. J., Murdock, M. C., & Mance, M. (2007). *Creative leadership: Skills that drive change.* Thousand Oaks, CA: Sage.

Rogers, E. M. (2003) *Diffusion of innovations* (5ᵗʰ ed.). New York, NY: Free Press.

Singer, J. L. (1999). Imagination. In M. A. Runco & R. S. Albert (Eds.), *Encyclopedia of creativity* (pp. 13–25). San Diego, CA: Academic Press.

Smith, L. N., Blixt, A. B., Ellis, S. E., Gill, S. J., & Kruger, K. (2015). *Leading innovation and change: A guide for chief student affairs officers on shaping the future.* Washington, DC: NASPA–Student Affairs Administrators in Higher Education.

Treffinger, D. J. (2007). Creative problem solving (CPS): Powerful tools for managing change and developing talent. *Gifted and Talented International, 22*(2), 8–18.

Wagner, T. (2008). *The global achievement gap: Why even our best schools don't teach the new survival skills our children need—and what we can do about it.* New York, NY: Basic Books.

Welling, H. (2007). Four mental operations in creative cognition: The importance of abstraction. *Creativity Research Journal, 19*(2–3), 163–177.

West, M. A. (2002). Sparkling fountains or stagnant ponds: An integrative model of creativity and innovation implementation in work groups. *Applied Psychology: An International Review, 51*, 355–387.

Yosso, T. J. (2005). Whose culture has capital? A critical race theory discussion of community cultural wealth. *Race Ethnicity and Education, 8*(1), 69–91.

2

IN DEFENSE OF A SYSTEM

Higher Education, Change, and Innovation

ANNA GONZALEZ

In an April 2018 interview, former Spelman College president Johnetta Cole said, "In this period in which we are living, many people believe that higher education is not contributing in a positive way to American life" (Yale Insights, 2018, 1:40). Over my more than 25 years in the field of higher education, I have seen a continuing increase in concern for and criticism of colleges and universities. In fact, on the basis of some peer-reviewed and popular articles and books; comments from various constituents, including students and their parents; and queries from my own family members, I might believe that higher education is a broken system (Archibald & Feldman, 2010; Shell, 2018; Strauss, 2012). The questions include: What is the purpose of higher education? Why does it seem to cost so much to have my child attend college? Where are innovations in the structure of higher education? How can higher education provide innovative leadership to help solve some of the world's greatest problems?

As a believer in the tenet that higher education is the most important equalizing factor in a democratic society, I see colleges and universities facing major challenges; for example, affordability, increasingly complex compliance issues, greater challenges in meeting the needs of a changing student body, the need to assess and restructure curricular and cocurricular offerings, and the seemingly insurmountable cost of maintaining aging physical structures. Many people have called on higher education leaders to make transformational changes to the organizational structure and culture in order to create and manage innovative solutions that would elevate colleges and universities to meet the needs of tomorrow's student body (Archibald & Feldman, 2010; Mintz, 2019). However, like most institutions, higher education is slow to change. Many of its leaders came up through the ranks and have a tendency to look to and defend past traditions and practices; in that sense, the very structure of colleges and universities makes innovation and innovative leadership a daunting and near impossible task (Diamond, 2006). One example is the process for introducing new majors or academic programs into the curriculum. This process generally requires that the entire faculty vote on the addition; thus, even if the president or board provides evidence that the new major or program would be a financial and academic benefit to the college, if a majority of the faculty votes it down the proposal fails.

But does this mean that practitioners and scholars should give up on transformational change in higher education? Does the path to meet the needs of our current and future society depend on adherence to leadership bound by tradition? I believe that now is the time for us to examine the history of higher education, with particular emphasis on innovative leadership and actions, and to learn from those brave decisions to forge a new path for the future. As Peter Drucker (1985/2015) wrote, "Innovation by nature is risky, as is all economic activity. But defending what was done yesterday is far riskier than making tomorrow" (p. 171).

The values that have become inherent in colleges and universities—such as upholding traditions, shared governance and decision-making processes, and employment models—are running up against a constantly and rapidly changing world (Diamond, 2006). The general public has questions about the value of higher education, the return on investment that students and their families receive, and the seemingly unending culture wars in colleges and universities. Negative attitudes toward higher education are also informed by the perception that colleges and universities are resistant to change and need to be infused with innovation in order to be relevant for tomorrow's students (Ebner & Pickus, 2018).

Although implementing change in colleges and universities is generally a very slow process, higher education has not always resisted groundbreaking changes. Transformational changes have included curricular reform, the creation of new kinds of schools, and policies and practices that sought to provide educational access to a variety of populations (Thelin, 2004).

In this chapter I examine innovative practices in the history of higher education and how some of these same practices have, over time, become barriers to creativity and innovation. Throughout the history of higher education, people have doubled down in defense of what they believe are the traditional markers of higher education, especially of their college as they experienced it. Society bears a cost when leaders draw a line in the sand in defense of a system of higher education that is resistant to change. However, there have always been those inside the system who have critiqued such resistance to innovation and change. Indeed, colleges and universities, in the act of defending themselves against those who want to tear them down, have produced innovative practices that have created a vibrant system that meets the greatest needs of our society. Through an understanding of what traditional practices were once seen as new, bold, and even groundbreaking, I offer strategies and practices to influence and inspire leaders to implement the courageous, innovative, and creative changes necessary to meet the needs of today's and tomorrow's society.

Back to the Future: Higher Education as Innovation

In his 2018 State of the Union speech, U.S. President Donald Trump referred to higher education only once: "Let us invest in workforce development and job training. Let us open great vocational schools so our future workers can learn a craft and realize their full potential" (Trump, 2018, para. 70). This statement sends a chilling message to those who believe that colleges and universities should be places where students can engage in research and the development of knowledge and critical thinking. The statement seems antithetical to the investment over the past two centuries in creating sites of discovery and learning—a massive growth in the number and type of higher education institutions through initiatives and reforms such as the Morrill Acts, the G.I. Bill, the development of admissions standards, and legislation that expanded educational accessibility for all learners (Thelin, 2004). For U.S. higher education in the 21st century to be relegated to a sentence and a half about training people for jobs suggests a dramatic downward shift in beliefs about the value of colleges and universities.

Never has it been more important to take a backward look at how great institutions of higher education have evolved out of tension and debates about mission and identity. This tension has made possible great societal achievements by students and faculty, because higher education was never perceived as a monolithic system to train the nation's workforce. A backward look will remind stakeholders that colleges and universities have been able to make impactful and forward-thinking changes over the centuries because of innovative and brave leadership (Rudolph, 1990; Thelin, 2004).

Throughout its almost 400-year history, higher education has sought to improve on earlier iterations of itself. One of the motivators for curricular and cocurricular innovations was higher education's responses to questions regarding the mission and purpose of U.S. colleges and universities. At a time when the United States was grappling with its role in the world as a young and powerful nation, its colleges and universities were going through an enduring debate over the role of higher education and how curriculum and infrastructure support that role. The creation of the modern university in the 19th century—led by Daniel Coit Gilman, the first president of Johns Hopkins University, and Harvard president Charles William Eliot— was a truly innovative act (Rudolph, 1990). It created a relationship between the individual acquisition of knowledge and skills and the beneficial effects of educated citizens on the sociopolitical and socioeconomic workings of our nation (Rudolph, 1990; Thelin, 2004).

Leaders like Gilman and Eliot worked to enhance colleges that were originally created in the likeness of the English tradition of higher education so that they were more like the German educational system known as *the university*. A significant change moving from the English tradition, which focuses on the undergraduate student, to the German, which focuses on research, changed American higher education to have a diversity of not just the curriculum of institutions but also their overall mission. American universities emerged as institutions committed to helping students gain knowledge through research and, at the same time, to creating an educated citizenry that would have great societal impact. In addition to the strong commitment to research, the modern American university expected the academic community to develop expertise in subject matter. Eventually, colleges and universities institutionalized a structure that placed the greatest value on developing expertise in a certain area. Fields of study grew stronger and became entrenched as departments, and even those institutions that considered themselves liberal arts schools hired faculty with defined expertise. Not only the faculty but the students themselves—from bachelor's to doctoral—committed to a major field. As the faculty embraced the concepts of expertise and departments, cocurricular life and the creation of student affairs as a practice and professionalized field meant that roles were assigned to specific areas in the university with regard to the education and total well-being of students (Cole, 2016; Thelin, 2004).

At the same historic moment as the creation of the modern American university, the U.S. government began supporting the establishment of land grant institutions to focus on the teaching of practical science, agriculture, military science, and engineering. The emerging industrial era was an opportune time for the development of these institutions, as the government was intent on making the country a global power with a well-trained workforce. The growth of both private and public colleges and universities created a sense of excitement around higher education, but it also created a tension that still exists regarding whom these institutions were intended for and the nature of their role in society. This tension was epitomized in great debates, such as those between the famous educators and public intellectuals Booker T. Washington (1913) and W.E.B. Dubois (1903/1996), both recognized as leaders of the African American community. Like other higher education leaders, they debated whether these institutions should primarily foster the discovery of knowledge and an appreciation of research and the liberal arts or whether they should focus on trade, agriculture, military tactics, and mechanical arts (Dubois, 1903/1996; Rudolph, 1990; Washington, 1913).

Many colleges and universities were built to focus on one or the other of these sometimes competing philosophies. The 19th and 20th centuries were a time of unprecedented growth and diversity in colleges and universities, as women's colleges, historically Black colleges and universities, two-year community colleges, and, in the 20th century, for-profit colleges such as DeVry University and University of Phoenix came into being (Thelin, 2004; Vedder, 2018). Some critics say that many of these institutions—especially the for-profit ones—came into existence because of the inability of traditional colleges to meet the needs of a changing population. In many ways, the purpose of U.S. colleges and universities was lost in the noise of what they will be to future students. The inability of many schools to figure out who may want or require a college degree or some form of higher education in the future has allowed for the growth of different kinds of institutions. Moreover, each year, a growing number of colleges and universities are closing their doors, citing declining enrollment, particularly among private colleges, as one of the main factors (Busta, 2019; Osei, 2019).

We can find many historical examples of innovative and brave leaders who looked to the future and made much-needed reforms and changes, including offering new academic programs, creating the multiversity, and using technology to help students obtain degrees (for example, the online degree program offered at Penn State [McMurtrie, 2018]). The role of higher education as the gateway to upward social, political, economic, and cultural mobility continues to be ingrained in the American psyche. This belief is a driver of the demand for higher education to continue to improve itself and for leaders to make the courageous decisions that will create the colleges and universities of the 21st century.

Unintended Consequences and Barriers to Change

Steve Jobs said, "There are unintended consequences to everything" (Saler, 2019). Some of the primary aspects of higher education (e.g., tenure, admissions standards, evaluation and assessment, the core curriculum, regulations and mandates, the expansion of student support services) were established with a critical lens and well-meaning intentions, although they came with a financial and at times a political cost. And as costs continue to increase in every area—from labor to meeting regulatory mandates to building and maintaining residential and recreational facilities—we find that these important and long institutionalized practices and policies have at times created barriers to managing change.

This section is divided into two parts. The first describes three barriers (traditions and culture, curricular reform, and costs) that make it difficult for leaders to be change agents. The second part outlines three ways leaders can be innovative and take courageous action to meet the changing needs of their institutions.

Traditions and Culture

The culture of a higher education institution is shaped over time by the actions, rituals, and traditions of faculty, students, and staff. The creation of a particular ethos and shared experiences has benefited the majority of those who attended and worked at colleges and universities by encouraging a shared identity and loyalty to their institutions and experiences. Examples of these artifacts include the robes worn at commencement, how new students and their families are welcomed during orientation week, who gets to sit where at faculty senate meetings, statues, mascots, and even the placement of buildings and offices (Kuh & Whitt, 1988).

Traditions, rituals, and artifacts provide a sense of comfort to members of the community. They allow students to get a feel for the institutional culture and gain an insider's knowledge of the values of the institution and how things work. Admissions viewbooks feature photos of students and alumni alike having fun at traditional homecoming parades or participating in decades-old student-run symposia. Buying and wearing a class ring or moving the tassel on a graduation cap from one side to the other are examples of important moments in the lives of college students. They signal the transition from students to alumni and create a common experience that connects one generation of students to the next.

However, rituals, traditions, and artifacts can also create exclusion and division, particularly when they represent dominance or oppression of one group by another. In 2007 the University of Illinois retired its controversial and arguably racially divisive mascot Chief Illiniwek. A few years later the University of North Dakota retired its own racially charged nickname, the Fighting Sioux. At a number of schools, from the University of Virginia to Yale University, students and faculty continue to demand that certain statues be taken down and names of buildings be changed because they honor people who were slave owners or proponents of keeping the institution of slavery intact in the United States (Doerer, 2018; Quintana, 2018).

Curricular Reform

The mission of a college or university determines what is taught there. Liberal arts schools have a particular set of courses and majors, while STEM-based (science, technology, engineering, and math) schools and Research I institutions expect their students to complete a different set of courses. In the shared governance model of higher education, the faculty have the primary responsibility for the curriculum: Not only do they teach courses, but they are expected to provide leadership in reviewing the curriculum and making any necessary changes (Rudolph, 1990).

However, the push to add or eliminate courses and majors has not always come from the faculty. External forces drive some changes to the curriculum. These forces, often influenced by changes in industry, can determine which classes are offered and thus can influence overall enrollment numbers. Currently, the growth in areas related to STEM—especially computer sciences—is shaping the discussion in higher education about which additional programs and courses should be offered. Meanwhile, traditional humanities classes and programs have been slated for elimination as a response to enrollment issues. Sometimes it is the administration rather than the faculty that decides what to keep and what to cut in the academic program. In 2011, the entire theater department at Washington State University in Pullman was eliminated from the curriculum owing to budget cuts. Recently, for the same reason, the president of the University of Montana proposed eliminating 50 faculty positions, many in the humanities. These cuts produced short-term budgetary relief, but it is too early to assess their long-term impact. Institutions are looking at the changing needs of society as reflected in student enrollment in certain academic programs, and they are becoming more willing to prioritize academic programs, consolidating or eliminating old ones and establishing new ones (Gluckman, 2017; Zamudio-Suarez, 2018).

Costs

The flow of public and private funds into American higher education over the years created world-class institutions. Government programs such as the Morrill Land Acts of 1862 and 1890 were responsible for the building and expansion of great public universities, including, for example, the University of Illinois and The Ohio State University. For a long time, it seemed that higher education would continue to receive generous funding from both the public and private sectors.

However, over the past 20 years, more and more questions have arisen about increasing tuition and declining investment by state governments. The creation of such things as climbing walls and lazy rivers at some schools has painted a picture of a system that has excess funds and that does not make fiscally sound decisions about where money should go (Stripling, 2017). Labor costs in colleges and universities also have come under fire: The tenure system and the increase of staff members in a variety of noncurricular areas (including student affairs) are seen by some as unnecessary costs borne by students. One example is the recent battle between Wisconsin's former governor, Scott Walker, and the University of Wisconsin over the issue of tenure (Flaherty, 2016).

Colleges and universities actually do need more funding, not for more lazy rivers but to maintain and improve on the system of higher education. Costs have indeed risen to complete or even just maintain deferred maintenance for buildings and residence halls, to fund the growing number of unfunded government mandates and regulations, and to pay for emerging programs and services that did not exist in the past but are needed now, such as wellness educators, cultural centers, career centers, and tutoring programs. These new programs and services have led to significant expansions in divisions such as student affairs and have affected the institutional budget. At the same time, the huge growth in technology and the development of compliance, accounting, and human resource systems have significantly increased staffing levels in areas such as business affairs and institutional technology (Barr & McClellan, 2018).

On top of all these costs are salaries and benefits. Higher education is labor intensive and depends on a high-quality faculty. Whether they are attending a small college or a very large university, students expect to be taught by and work with faculty members who are experts in their fields. Baumol's cost disease explains the continuing increase in the cost of high-intensive labor industries such as the arts and higher education. An oversimplified explanation of this theory is that in order to keep talent from leaving (and arguably to fairly compensate workers), wages need to rise in people-dependent professions that most likely do not produce "tangible" products (Archibald & Feldman, 2010). What further complicates the issue of labor in colleges is that the labor market in higher education does not work like those of other industries, primarily because many employees have tenure.

Tenure was created by the American Association of University Professors when the organization, along with the Association of American Colleges and Universities, formulated the *1940 Statement of Principles on Academic Freedom and Tenure* to protect academic freedom in the classroom and in research. In many cases, this system ensures lifetime employment at a college; at the very least, it makes it very difficult to fire tenured faculty. Although some institutions are moving to *right size* their faculties on the basis of their academic programs, most continue to retain and even add faculty. Coupled with the need to increase student affairs and student support staff, this approach contributes to the exponential costs of higher education (Barr & McClellan, 2018; Zumeta, Breneman, Callan, & Finney, 2012).

Leading With Courage

A 2017 survey conducted by the American Council on Education found that the average tenure of college and university presidents had dropped from 8.5 years in 2006 to 6.5 years in 2016 (Thomason, 2018).

Surprise departures of chief executives included those of the University of North Carolina's (UNC's) Carol Folt and Earlham College's Alan C. Price. Reasons for the departure of higher education executives include failure to meet the expectations of the board of trustees or the campus community, the inability to resolve financial and other related issues, enrollment woes, political divisiveness on their campuses, and tensions related to a reinvigorated sense of culture wars across the academy. Regardless of the issue, these departures signal the need for leaders who can be both brave and innovative during a very challenging time for higher education (Mangan, 2018; Thomason, 2018).

Innovative leaders in higher education must do three things: (1) manage change; (2) commit acts of courage (i.e., do something different); and (3) think about today's eighth graders when they make long-term decisions. While these three things might not seem innovative or brave in themselves, it takes courage to make change, to use data instead of depending on intuition or what people believe to be the truth, and to avoid doing the same things over and over if you want a different result.

Change Management

For a long time, the term *change management* was embraced only by business and industry. John Kotter's 1996 book *Leading Change*, with its 8-step model, and Spencer Johnson's 1998 book *Who Moved My Cheese?* engaged generations of managers and employees in discussions about why and how to make change. In the meantime, colleges and universities gained a reputation for being slow to make change. However, economic, demographic, and cultural shifts in our society have led to demands for higher education to innovate, create, and build new infrastructures (Kezar & Eckel, 2002). Blended learning, online offerings in areas such as mental health assessment, and the creation of more consortial services among institutions are just a few of the changes we are seeing in colleges and universities (Pittinsky, 2003). And some areas—such as IT and student affairs—are expected to continuously seek new ways to deliver services and programs and ways to shift the institutional culture to meet the needs of an ever-changing student population.

Critical change management skills and practices must be related to the institution's purpose and mission, and strategic pathways are key to ensuring that departments and divisions across academic and cocurricular areas meet not just the desires of current students but the needs of future generations of students as well (Smart, Kuh, & Tierney, 1997). Changes that need to happen include improving student outcomes; increasing access to higher education; creating more efficient and effective operational systems; and recruiting and retaining a diverse faculty, staff, and student population. Innovative leadership as it relates to change management does not mean just making changes; it should also explore resistance to change and develop ways to address groups and individuals who have taken this stance.

An example of innovation and change management is Clark Kerr's coauthorship and strategic leadership on behalf of the original California Master Plan for Higher Education in 1960. The plan set up an ingenious statewide system with defined roles for universities, state colleges, and community colleges in terms of school choice, access, and differentiation of admissions criteria. The journey to implement this transformational change was not easy, but the proponents used key data points, had a clear vision, connected the changes to the University of California mission, and successfully communicated the process and proposal to stakeholders.

Acts of Courage

To be an effective change manager, one must be strategic, thoughtful, collaborative, and data driven. Change management requires a process that looks at constituencies, develops a vision, and includes feedback and communication. This section challenges leaders to take action. For an innovative leader, an act of courage should have a large-scale and long-term effect that transforms the institution and its culture. Courage is required because the leader is taking a great risk, and a significant number of constituencies will probably revolt at the idea. More often than not, everyone understands that a decision needs to be made about this particular issue, but no one wants to or feels empowered to do it. An act of courage is one that boldly challenges the traditions of the institution head-on.

Such decisions are not made lightly. Often the institution experiences the disenfranchisement or separation of one or more constituencies in reaction to the decision. Earlier in this chapter, I cited tradition and culture as possible barriers to innovation. Acts of courage often come up against these barriers, and the initial reaction to a decision can be shock or anger. Yet these acts of courage often result in transforming the college, whether through a fundamental shift in the curriculum or a moment at which the institution charts a new course in defining itself as an inclusive college.

Acts of courage might include overhauling the core curriculum, switching from a quarter to a semester system, or moving from a university-run bookstore to one owned and managed by a for-profit company. In all three cases we should assume that the change management process was data informed. An act of courage that caught the attention of the nation was the decision of former UNC Chancellor Carol Folt to remove the pedestal of the Silent Sam statue. For more than 100 years, Silent Sam stood on the UNC campus as a symbol of the Confederacy, drawing protests as far back as the 1960s. Students finally toppled the statue in 2018, and the university moved it to a storage location. Folt's decision to remove the pedestal symbolized her commitment as the UNC Chancellor to engage with issues of inclusion and move toward a future that does not glorify the Confederacy or the institution of slavery. However, the UNC trustees asked for Folt's resignation. In her willingness to take the risk and accept the consequences of her action, she showed her commitment to shedding the shroud of the Confederacy and the racist past of the institution and envisioning a more inclusive institution.

Thinking About the Eighth Graders

In 2006, when I was conducting a feasibility study of the University of California, Irvine, Student Center and Cross-Cultural Center, one of the architects told me that they conceptualize their buildings for universities by looking at current eighth graders and thinking about what their expectations and needs will be. Being future oriented might not in itself seem particularly innovative, but making long-range decisions based on the needs of future generations can result in a clearer idea of what an institution should do.

Looking at the historical, cultural, and sociopolitical events that have marked the lived experiences of eighth graders can provide clues about how future students will learn and interact, and help college administrators understand and prepare for future students. While members of the college community cannot expect to undergo massive changes from year to year, staff and faculty can engage in innovative and even entrepreneurial thinking to figure out what can be reconfigured or tweaked to keep colleges and universities relevant to the changing student body.

In many ways this third component is the hardest to embrace, because it requires leaders to have a great sense of humility and to accept the fact that they don't know what they don't know. And the data they are mining are coming from eighth graders! However, this is also the component that shows how visionary, forward thinking, and imaginative a leader can be. When colleges and universities plan for changes in their curricula, the normal practice is to look at who is on the faculty and build the program around them. The eighth-grade method encourages leaders to instead use predictive data analysis or predictive modeling, make decisions based on the needs of future students, and then begin making the needed changes to current curricular and cocurricular programs and services.

Milton's 2019 article in *Forbes* gave compelling examples of innovation in higher education and the use of predictive analysis. The article provided examples of creative solutions to issues such as declining enrollment, retention, and the student experience. It cited schools such as Georgia State University and Cornell University that have made changes with the student as the primary stakeholder. Leaders who use predictive analysis can push their institutions to be more aware of what is changing in the world around them rather than just what is happening now.

Conclusion

Traditional brick-and-mortar colleges and universities face the daunting task of proving that they are relevant in an ever-changing world. These institutions are faced with the challenge of celebrating their long-held traditions—some even centuries old—and meeting the changing needs of current and future students. This challenge becomes even greater when both on- and off-campus stakeholders are aligned to resist change and innovation. However, innovation in higher education is possible, even at the oldest and seemingly most traditional institutions. Tenure, faculty sabbatical, the core curriculum, and the division of student affairs were all considered innovative and even revolutionary when they were first envisioned and established. The infusion of technology and the Internet into teaching and conducting research is another example of innovation, of great ideas that allow the discovery of knowledge to flourish. Now, in the 21st century, higher education faces critical questions from inside and outside the academy. Constituents demand that faculty and staff explain the purpose of higher education to society. Do we as institutional leaders continue to defend the system we know in order to save it? I believe that to save higher education and make it better, faculty, staff, and even students must face the part of ourselves that resists change.

Innovation in higher education should not be constrained by using only tools from inside institutions; rather, leaders should be open to a combination of practices and theories from other industries. Some of the most important changes occurring in higher education come from partnerships between colleges and universities and outside people and organizations. The Bill and Melinda Gates Foundation's Millennium Scholars Program is an innovative partnership that transforms the lives of students from traditionally disenfranchised communities. The program has changed the lives of individual students and their families as well as the colleges and universities they attended.

Transformational change in higher education is facilitated by a combination of boldness, strategic planning, and an eye to the future. These are also key attributes of innovative leaders. A quote attributed to Mahatma Gandhi, "If we could change ourselves, the tendencies in the world would also change. . . . We need not wait to see what others do" (Morton, 2011, para. 5)—is relevant to innovative leadership and higher education. This chapter has offered a few examples of individuals and groups who created transformational change, but American higher education, in its 400-plus-year history, has continually brought forth innovation. Administrators and faculty members must strive to remember this and not be afraid to make the changes necessary to create institutions that 21ˢᵗ-century students and society need.

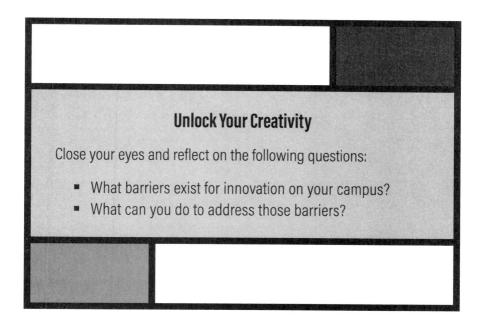

Unlock Your Creativity

Close your eyes and reflect on the following questions:

- What barriers exist for innovation on your campus?
- What can you do to address those barriers?

References

Archibald, R. B., & Feldman, D. H. (2010). *Why does college cost so much?* New York, NY: Oxford Press.

Barr, M. J., & McClellan, G. S. (2018). *Budgets and financial management in higher education.* San Francisco, CA: Jossey-Bass.

Busta, H. (2019, March 29). How many colleges have closed since 2016? *Education Dive.* Retrieved from https://www.educationdive.com/news

Cole, J. R. (2016, September 20). The triumph of America's research university. *The Atlantic.* Retrieved from https://www.theatlantic.com/education

Diamond, R. M. (2006, September 8). Why colleges are so hard to change. *Inside Higher Ed.* Retrieved from https://www.insidehighered.com

Doerer, K. (2018, September 23). How colleges confront their racist pasts. *The Chronicle of Higher Education.* Retrieved from https://www.chronicle.com

Drucker, P. F. (2015). *Innovation and entrepreneurship: Practice and principles.* New York, NY: Routledge. (Original work published 1985)

Dubois, W. E. B. (1996). *The souls of Black folk.* New York, NY: Penguin Random House. (Original work published 1903)

Ebner, K., & Pickus, N. (2018, July 25). The right kind of innovation. *Inside Higher Ed.* Retrieved from https://www.insidehighered.com

Flaherty, C. (2016, December 7). What remains of tenure. *Inside Higher Ed.* Retrieved from https://www.insidehighered.com

Gluckman, N. (2017, April 18). 6 years ago, this department got the ax. Where are the faculty and staff now? *The Chronicle of Higher Education.* Retrieved from https://www.chronicle.com

Johnson, S. (1998). *Who moved my cheese?: An amazing way to deal with change in your work and in your life.* New York, NY: Putnam.

Kezar, A. J., & Eckel, P. D. (2002). The effect of institutional culture on change strategies in higher education: Universal principles or culturally responsive concepts. *Journal of Higher Education, 73*(4), 435–460.

Kotter, J. P. (1996). *Leading change.* Boston, MA: Harvard Business School Press.

Kuh, G., & Whitt, E. (1988). *The invisible tapestry: Culture in American colleges and universities.* Washington, DC: Association for the Study of Higher Education.

Mangan, K. (2018, July 2). Questions swirl as Earlham College's president will leave after just a year. *The Chronicle of Higher Education.* Retrieved from https://www.chronicle.com

McMurtrie, B. (2018, September 18). U. of Pennsylvania says it will be the first Ivy to offer online bachelor's degree. *The Chronicle of Higher Education.* Retrieved from https://www.chronicle.com

Milton, J. (2019, January 8). Transform or perish: Innovative tech key to higher ed survival. *Forbes.* Retrieved from https://www.forbes.com

Mintz, S. (2019, February 6). Higher education needs to innovate. But how? *Inside Higher Ed.* Retrieved from https://www.insidehighered.com

Morton, B. (2011, August 29). Falser words were never spoken. *The New York Times.* Retrieved from https://www.newyorktimes.com

Osei, Z. (2019, April 5). Hampshire president resigns suddenly, citing campus pulled apart. *The Chronicle of Higher Education.* Retrieved from https://www.chronicle.com

Pittinsky, M. S. (Ed.) (2003). *The wired tower: Perspectives on the impact of the Internet on higher education.* Upper Saddle River, NJ: Prentice Hall.

Quintana, C. (2018, June 6). As hard as it tries, Illinois can't move on from its Native American mascot. *The Chronicle of Higher Education.* Retrieved from https://www.chronicle.com

Rudolph, F. (1990). *The American college and university: A history*. Athens, GA: University of Georgia Press.

Saler, T. (2019, April 19). Technology, like earlier developments, has unintended consequences. *Journal Sentinel*. Retrieved from http://www.jsonline.com

Shell, K. R. (2018, May 16). College may not be worth it anymore. *The New York Times*. Retrieved from https://www.nytimes.com

Smart, J. C., Kuh, G. D., & Tierney, W. G. (1997). The roles of institutional cultures and decision approaches in promoting organizational effectiveness in two-year colleges. *Journal of Higher Education, 68*(3), 256–281.

Strauss, V. (2012, December 6). Why everyone shouldn't go to college. *The Washington Post*. Retrieved from https://www.washingtonpost.com

Stripling, J. (2017, October 20). The lure of the lazy river. *The Chronicle of Higher Education*. Retrieved from https://www.chronicle.com

Thelin, J. R. (2004). *A history of American higher education*. Baltimore, MD: Johns Hopkins University Press.

Thomason, A. (2018, May 1). Is college president the toughest job in the nation? *The Chronicle of Higher Education*. Retrieved from https://www.chronicle.com

Trump, D. (2018, January 30). *President Donald J. Trump's State of the Union address* [Transcript]. Retrieved from https://www.whitehouse.gov/briefings-statements/president-donald-j-trumps-state-union-address

Vedder, R. (2018, December 17). Needed: A revival of for-profit higher education. *Forbes*. Retrieved from https://www.forbes.com

Washington, B. T. (1913). Industrial education and the public schools. *Annals of the American Academy of Political and Social Science, 49*, 219–232.

Yale Insights. (2018, January 30). Johnetta Cole interviewed at the Yale Higher Education Leadership Summit [Video file]. Retrieved from https://insights.som.yale.edu/insights/what-s-the-value-of-higher-education

Zamudio-Suarez, F. (2018, May 3). 4 months into his tenure, a flagship's president proposes 50 faculty layoffs. *The Chronicle of Higher Education*. Retrieved from https://www.chronicle.com

Zumeta, W., Breneman, D. W., Callan, P. M., & Finney, J. E. (2012). *Financing American higher education in the era of globalization*. Cambridge, MA: Harvard Education Press.

BECOMING A MORE CREATIVE AND INNOVATIVE LEADER

Pursuing a Different Kind of Professional Development

JOSEPH P. ZOLNER

For two decades, I had the honor and privilege to oversee a portfolio of professional development programs for higher education leaders at the Harvard Graduate School of Education. The unit for which I was responsible, the Harvard Institutes for Higher Education (HIHE), serves, in effect, as the School of Education's executive education division for college and university administrators. HIHE is responsible for planning and delivering multiple convenings, seminars, programs, and institutes for higher education leaders from a wide array of institution types, administrative areas, functional responsibilities, and geographic locations in the United States and abroad. In fact, HIHE believes that the eclectic, "Noah's Ark" makeup of its participant cohorts is a critical component of the overall professional development experience, one that creates powerful opportunities for important peer-to-peer learning and long-term networking.[1]

HIHE offerings vary in length from brief two- and three-day gatherings to intensive, two-week, retreat-like, full-immersion institutes. In all instances, however, HIHE espouses a commitment to providing what it describes as a "transformational learning experience." Although that phrase may qualify as compelling marketing copy (and is certainly used by multiple purveyors of higher education professional development services), what does it mean in practice and why is it important? What's the case for having transformational learning occupy a prominent place on the professional development agendas of higher education leaders? And, perhaps most important, what connections might exist between transformational learning experiences and creative leadership? Drawing on my work with countless cohorts of higher education leaders who have attended one or more HIHE programs, this chapter will address these questions and consider ways that college and university leaders might continue to improve both themselves and the institutions they serve.

A Transformational Learning/Creative Leadership Connection

My central thesis is that transformed leaders (i.e., leaders who routinely and intentionally pursue a *transformational learning* agenda, as I will later define that term) are more creative leaders. They continually exhibit what Kanter (2000) long ago called "kaleidoscope thinking"—a leadership orientation that analyzes situations from multiple angles and perspectives; embraces new

---

[1]   See https://www.gse.harvard.edu/ppe/harvard-institutes-higher-education-programs for additional information about HIHE and its program offerings.

and disconfirming data; and identifies novel combinations, patterns, and future possibilities, all while keenly appreciating that personal development is a nonnegotiable prerequisite to institutional improvement.

As Schwartz (2018) rightly noted, far too many organizations single-mindedly focus on matters of strategy and execution, thereby giving short shrift to the thoughts, perspectives, mindsets, and feelings of the individuals who will inevitably be affected by organizational change and innovation. In light of this imbalance, he argued that organizational transformation must depend on and emanate from individual transformation. Such a perspective, however, is rare among leaders. As Schwartz (2018) wrote,

> Few [senior leaders and influencers] have spent much time observing and understanding their own motivations, challenging their assumptions, or pushing beyond their intellectual and emotional comfort zones. . . . All this explains why the most effective transformation begins with what's going on inside people—and especially the most senior leaders, given their disproportionate authority and influence. Their challenge is to deliberately turn attention inward in order to begin noticing the fixed patterns in their thinking, how they're feeling in any given moment, and how quickly the instinct for self-preservation can overwhelm rationality and a longer-term perspective, especially when the stakes are high. (pp. 2–4)

Given its potential to inculcate more nuanced thinking, more sophisticated acting, and more creative leading, transformational learning needs to become a central and ongoing part of one's professional development plan.

Confusion or Insight?

At the close of HIHE's two-week residential programs, I often tell a favorite story that I suggest might reflect what program participants are thinking as they approach the finish line of an intensive, introspective, and "all-in" learning experience designed to help them reconsider assumptions and challenge routine ways of thinking and leading.

The story, first told by now retired HIHE faculty member Dan Fenn, is about a formal lecture that Fenn delivered years ago. After Fenn had completed considerable preparation on a complex topic, he was introduced, approached the podium, and began his speech. Almost immediately, Fenn noticed an individual seated in the first row who, every time Fenn made what he felt was an important or incisive point, seemed to be in full agreement with and was clearly appreciating his commentary. The person's enthusiastic nods and other nonverbal cues confirmed to Fenn that he was locked in to his line of argument and reasoning. It was, therefore, no surprise to Fenn that, after completing his presentation and acknowledging applause from the crowd, this person made a bee-line to the podium.

"Thank you, Professor Fenn, for your wonderfully thoughtful and cogent remarks," the person said excitedly. "I thought your thesis was right on the money, and I can't imagine a better way to have made your argument. Your remarks were chock full of valuable insights and thoughtful detail. The speech was really terrific." As Fenn expressed appreciation for these kind words, the person shared a final—and somewhat perplexing—thought about the speech: "I was confused about this topic before you spoke. I'm still confused, but at a higher level. Thank you!"

More times than not, this punch line elicits at least a few knowing chuckles among the group of soon-to-be HIHE program alumni. After having worked with thousands of higher education leaders, I believe this laughter is rooted more in a keen appreciation for the dynamic (and fundamentally different) learning experience they have completed rather than any inherent humor contained in the story, regardless of how adroitly it may have been delivered.

In my view, truly valuable professional development—the kind that leads to transformational learning outcomes—should confuse people at higher levels. Put differently, effective leadership development should, by explicit design, seek to challenge existing assumptions about oneself and one's institution; create a "safe space" (a setting that provides equal measures of challenge and support) that enables personal introspection via the receipt of meaningful feedback from concerned and caring colleagues; and, informed by the insights gained through such a process, enable the leader-as-learner to adopt new perspectives, understandings, and behaviors that reflect a more nuanced understanding of themselves and the institutional context in which they lead. Although these are the key ingredients of transformational learning, my experience suggests they are not routinely imbedded in the design and delivery of many professional development experiences.

Two Important (and Complementary) Forms of Learning

Throughout the course of my HIHE work, two equally important and mutually reinforcing forms of learning—informational and transformational—have served as important shapers of the professional development curricula and experiences offered to college and university leaders.[2]

---

2   Robert Kegan (the William and Miriam Meehan research professor in adult learning and professional development at the Harvard Graduate School of Education) has identified and articulated the key features of informational and transformational learning. For those interested in learning more about the informational/transformational learning framework, Kegan's work was developed further by Jennifer Garvey Berger (2012) in *Changing on the Job: Developing Leaders for a Complex World* (note pp. 17–24 in particular).

Informational forms of learning strive to impart new information and knowledge that are unknown or unfamiliar to the learner. Under this formulation, if one were to think of a metaphorical "vessel of the mind," informational learning is designed to pour new content into the existing vessel, ideally filling it to the brim with new ideas, perspectives, insights, and other useful information that adds to one's existing inventory of knowledge and competencies. Informational learning focuses on receiving and understanding new concepts, ideas, approaches, theories, do's and don'ts, lessons, rules of the road, and the like—even better if the new information incorporates contemporary research findings, includes readings with recent copyright dates, and explains newly emerging theory, all of which reflect a natural human desire to be aware of the most current ideas in areas of personal interest and professional practice.

At its core, informational learning strives to make the unfamiliar more familiar, more comfortably accessible, and more practically useful. Whether it's learning the key components of blockchain technology, better understanding the rules for giving and receiving performance feedback, confirming how to change the GPS coordinates in your automobile, or learning the latest changes to regional accreditation standards, informational forms of learning and professional development impart important, valuable, and often intricate data in ways that strengthen one's skills, enhance one's confidence, and build one's competencies.

By contrast, *transformational* forms of learning are designed to have the learner think in new and different ways about information the leader already "knows." It strives to challenge traditional assumptions, long-standing frames of reference, and views of the world. It seeks to inspire new possibilities rather than convey established, tried-and-true ways of thinking. With this form of learning, one's orientation is the exact opposite of the informational mode—one strives to make the familiar less familiar through introduction of new ways of considering and understanding the world and experimenting with alternative ways of acting on and influencing intellectual mindsets and institutional cultures. Rather than pouring new content into the existing vessel of the mind, transformational learning seeks to alter the shape of the vessel in ways that yield new understandings and insights about oneself and the contexts in which one lives and leads. The learner changes their mind about key ideas, points of view, and frames of reference. At its best, transformational learning raises more questions for the learner than provides answers. It strives to both expand one's conceptual repertoire and, in the process, increase the volume and capacity of one's "vessel" to accept a greater number of future opportunities for informational learning. Table 3.1 summarizes key characteristics of and distinctions between informational and transformational forms of learning.

Table 3.1. Key Characteristics of and Distinctions Between Informational and Transformational Forms of Learning

Informational Learning	Transformational Learning
Fill the existing vessel of the mind with new facts, insights, and information.	Alter the shape of the vessel of the mind in ways that accept new insights, different understandings, and increased capacity for subsequent informational learning.
Make the unfamiliar more familiar.	Make the familiar less familiar.
Download new apps.	Install a new operating system.
Focus on short-term knowing.	Pursue lifelong growing.
Learning defined as mastering extant processes and protocols; understanding current ways of knowing.	Unlearning defined as considering alternative mental models and paradigms; adopting a "beginner's mind."
Analytical reasoning that preferences "top-down," logical ways of thinking and understanding.	Elastic thinking that lets go of comfortable ideas; welcomes ambiguity and contradiction; reframes questions asked of oneself and the world; uses imagination; experiments and tolerates failure.
Manage information efficiently and effectively—process, store, recall, pattern-match, and produce robust alternatives.	Exhibit higher quality thinking, listening, relating, collaborating, and learning. Be open minded and learn to update beliefs in light of new data. Overcome limits imposed by one's ego and fears.

A quote attributed to Albert Einstein is relevant here: "If I had an hour to solve a problem and my life depended on the solution, I would spend the first 55 minutes determining the proper question to ask, for once I know the proper question, I could solve the problem in less than five minutes" (Tervooren, 2015, para. 1). Transformational learning recognizes that problem shaping is as important as problem solving. In an interview with *Inside Higher Ed*, Southwestern University President Edward Burger nicely illustrated this point when he argued that the focus of learning should not be on "what to think, but rather how to think more effectively, how to understand more deeply, and how to be more creative while making meaningful (and, ideally, original) connections" (Jaschik, 2018, para. 6). In other words, learning is best served by enhancing one's facility to identify and pose more thoughtful questions of oneself and others. In light of this perspective, Burger drew an important distinction between short-term knowing and lifelong growing. Harvard colleague Daniel Wilson described this same circumstance as a need to create conditions for "help seeking." In his professional development work, Wilson urged the adult learner to imbed a range of routines and protocols (e.g., prebriefing, debriefing, tail-boarding, instructional rounds) into their leadership practice that foster what he called "situational assessment in performance"—that is, real-time opportunities for stock-taking and conscious, deliberate reflection on how the shape of one's "vessel" may be changing in the face of new, potentially transformative information and experiences (D. Wilson, personal communication, June 26, 2017).

Eminent transformative learning scholar Jack Mezirow (1997) argued that a necessary precondition for transformational learning is being confronted with "disorienting dilemmas"—experiences that do not fit one's preexisting mental models and meaning structure. Such dilemmas can be epochal (all at once) or incremental (a gradual recognition over time of a disconnect between one's meaning structure and one's environment; "Mezirow's ten phases," n.d.). Either way, one is faced with an imperative to question traditional modes of thinking and understanding, and to act in light of new, nonconforming information and experiences.

Articulated differently, Bonchek (2016) described what I call *transformational learning* as a series of "unlearning" opportunities and challenges. He explained that unlearning is not about forgetting or discarding existing knowledge. Instead, it's about actively, consciously, and deliberately choosing to consider alternative frameworks and paradigms. When individuals learn in an informational sense, they add new knowledge, skills, nuance, and sophistication to what they already know. When they unlearn, they eschew familiar, comfortable, and well-practiced ways of understanding, influencing, and acting in the world, thereby opening themselves up to new approaches and possibilities. Finkelstein (2019) described this kind of learning as rediscovering what the Buddhists have long called a "beginner's mind"—a perspective on the world designed to counteract a type of overconfidence that he called the "expertise trap" (pp. 1–2).

Mlodinow (2018) covered this same intellectual territory by arguing for more of what he called "elastic thinking":

> the capacity to let go of comfortable ideas and become accustomed to ambiguity and contradiction; the capability to rise above conventional mind-sets and to reframe the questions we ask; the ability to abandon our ingrained assumptions and open ourselves to new paradigms; the propensity to rely on imagination as much as on logic and to generate and integrate a wide variety of ideas; and the willingness to experiment and be tolerant of failure. (p. 6)

Within the emerging artificial intelligence (AI) and machine learning context, Hess and Ludwig (2017) called for a form of transformational learning that is rooted in humility. They argued that no human will ever be able to compete with AI in terms of knowledge. AI will always "win" in terms of being better able to process, store, recall, pattern-match, and produce more robust alternatives than any mere mortal. As a result, a new definition of "being smart" is required within the AI environment. Hess (2017) posited, and I concur, that

> the new smart will be determined not by what or how you know, but by the quality of your thinking, listening, relating, collaborating, and learning. Quantity is replaced by quality. . . . We will spend more time training to be open-minded and learning to update our beliefs in response to new data. We will practice adjusting after our mistakes, and we will invest more in the skills traditionally associated with emotional intelligence. The new smart will be about trying to overcome the two big inhibitors of critical thinking and team collaboration—our ego and our fears. Doing so will make it easier to perceive reality as it is, rather than as we wish it to be. In short, we will embrace humility. (p. 3)

The Hess and Ludwig (2017) articulation of future leadership competence is a powerful endorsement of the value and importance of transformational modes of learning.

Reflections on Informational and Transformational Learning

When striving to incorporate both informational and transformational forms of learning into the leadership development experiences offered by HIHE, I have been guided by multiple inclinations and insights:

- **Although different, informational and transformational learning experiences are equally valuable and important.** To achieve a balance of good professional development, both informational and transformational forms of learning need to be acknowledged, understood, and actively engaged. Leadership development experiences should consciously incorporate both forms of learning. As part of their routine assessment practice, professional development providers should "audit" curricula and other program content to determine the extent to which both forms are present and actively encountered by the learner.

- **Too much professional development preferences informational learning at the expense of transformational learning opportunities and outcomes.** Too many professional development experiences focus on transmitting information and function as passive (from the learner's perspective) opportunities to hear the wisdom of others. I've attended too many events where "death by PowerPoint" seems to be the operative form of instruction. Invariably, when the instructor realizes that only a few minutes remain in their session, the typical response is to plow through all remaining slides to prevent the audience from "missing anything." The reason often cited for poor time management is that "too many" questions were asked during the session or that instructor interaction and idea exchange with the audience ran too long. This phenomenon reminds me of something that Chris Christensen (the legendary scholar of discussion leadership and master of case study pedagogy) once told me: "Efficient teaching does not always equate with effective learning. Appreciate the constructiveness of inefficiency" (personal communication, January 19, 1994). Inert delivery of instruction unfolds way too often and represents a classic illustration of trying to achieve transformational learning ends through informational learning means.

- **Effective transformational learning requires sustained connection to salient professional development needs over time, ideally in collaboration with peers.** A successful transformational learning experience will yield next steps that require substantive, ongoing, and often profound changes to the beliefs, behaviors, and practices of the learner. These kinds of learning outcomes do not lend themselves to quick-fix solutions or routinized, formulaic, and/or excessively-structured "check-the-box" kinds of developmental activities. As the earlier Einstein quote suggests, in transformation learning, the learner will often identify a particularly "juicy" and meaningful set of questions that require considerable time to consider, understand, and act on fully. As a result, the professional development provider should take steps—via both face-to-face and distance learning modalities—to offer an ongoing opportunity for the learner to stay connected to what I call a "learning edge" set of follow-up activities. In other words, next steps are needed that enable the learner to continue confronting disorienting dilemmas, fostering unlearning, encouraging elastic thinking, and inculcating humility and emotional intelligence in the learner's personal life and professional practice.

- **In addition to fostering both informational and transformational forms of learning, the best professional development provides meaningful peer-to-peer interaction, collaboration, and colleagueship.** From the learner's perspective, meaningful pursuit of transformational learning requires both acknowledging one's weaknesses, blind spots, and inadequacies and actively pursuing new and "foreign" ways of thinking, understanding, and acting. For many, this is a formidable and often scary proposition. As a result, concerted attention must be paid to creating a supportive, collaborative, diverse, and respectful learning environment—one that adult learning and development expert Bob Kegan (personal communication, April, 17, 2016) described as providing equal measures of challenge and support. To best attain this delicate balance, I attempt to create synergistic opportunities for interaction. I also try to achieve what I call "relaxing the performance constraint" among the participant group, particularly when engaging in small-group reflection and introspection. This orientation seeks to instill a sense of shared responsibility among all participants to support one another's learning rather than seek to "impress" HIHE program faculty or fellow program participants.

- **When creating optimal conditions for transformational learning, the little things are big things.** Regardless of the setting, multiple curricular, operational, financial, and organizational details must be handled adroitly to create the optimal conditions for transformational learning. From my experience, however, there is all too often a discernible split between the "academic" and "operational" sides of professional development planning and execution. Typically, the faculty address program objectives and learning outcomes, and the optimal curriculum to achieve them, while planners on the marketing, admissions, operations, and finance teams worry about their respective responsibilities in a siloed way.

To produce the most powerful learning results, I have found that all members of the operation must know about, understand, and support the work of the overall enterprise. Much has been studied and written about the "Disney experience" (see, e.g., Gallo, 2011; Grebski, 2018)—a comprehensive and coordinated set of customer service activities designed to provide a powerful and unforgettable entertainment experience. Although Disney's corporate setting may not translate directly to leadership development work in higher education, I believe that much more can and should be done within our context to bring all professional development functions together in a more intentional, strategic, and collegial way in order to create a powerful and unforgettable learning experience.

- **The best professional development strives to leverage leadership strengths and identify leadership weaknesses, limitations, and blind spots.** In my view, effective professional development should both accentuate the positive and identify and act on the negative. Given the growing complexity, volatility, and uncertainty of organizational life and leadership, each leader must bring all that they can to institutional leadership. The best outcomes—both individual and institutional—are not achieved by outsourcing select leadership capabilities or responsibilities to someone with, say, a different or better Myers-Briggs personality type designation or a CliftonStrengths theme that complements one's own. Instead, through the educative power of transformational learning, it is every leader's duty and responsibility to take fullest advantage of their demonstrated competencies while also working to improve deficiencies and eliminate blind spots. In many key respects, my thinking squares with the argument made by Chamarro-Premuzic (2016) that leadership development work should focus in equal measures on mitigating weakness and leveraging proficiency.

Creating Conditions for Transformational Learning

Given the importance (and relative paucity) of transformational learning experiences for higher education leaders, it may be helpful to note steps taken within HIHE programs to foster transformational forms of professional development. Multiple components of the HIHE learning environment and curriculum are designed to achieve this objective:

- **The four frames of leadership**. Bolman and Deal (2017) and Bolman and Gallos (2011) presented four frames for understanding and exercising leadership within organizations. These four frames—structural, human resource, political, and symbolic—function as lenses through which to understand and analyze organizations and determine how to exercise effective leadership within them. These frames are particularly robust and powerful tools due to their ability to foster both informational and transformational forms of learning. In HIHE programming, the frames are introduced early on as a foundational concept, thereby enabling institute faculty to highlight the presence and salience of these leadership perspectives within multiple content areas (e.g., strategic planning; assessment; diversity, equity, and inclusion; financial management; team effectiveness). Participants are encouraged to pursue a particular learning arc: first, developing awareness and understanding of each frame, followed by identifying "default" frames on which one relies during times of leadership uncertainty or stress, followed by developing greater comfort and facility with "weaker" frames. The ultimate goal is to produce a four-frame leader capable of drawing on multiple (and more nuanced and sophisticated) forms of analysis when making and executing challenging leadership decisions. Recent research (Rishi & Farley, 2014) articulates a "circular framing model" that applies the Bolman and Deal (2017) four-frame construct to the distinctive leadership challenges present within the student affairs administration context.

- **The immunity to change framework.** Kegan and Lahey (2009) developed a powerful diagnostic that enables individuals and collectives to identify and act on the sources of resistance to change. Often, major reasons for leaders' inability to achieve their most compelling improvement goals have more to do with an intricate and elegant personal psychological dynamic—what Kegan and Lahey (2009) called an "immunity to change" (ITC)—than to resistance exhibited by other parties. Identifying and acting on long-held personal understandings of the world (one's "big assumptions," in ITC terms) are experienced as an intensely inward-looking form of professional development. Kegan and Lahey (2009) believed that "without a better understanding of human development— what it is, how it is enabled, how it is constrained—what passes for 'leadership development' will more likely amount to 'leadership learning' or 'leadership training'" (p. 6). ITC's introspective focus and methodology are the stuff of true transformational learning. During HIHE programming, an interactive workshop (very similar in content and design to the process that Kegan and Lahey described) is completed that yields an ongoing ITC "partner" with whom the participant is encouraged to stay in touch as tests of his or her big assumptions are created, executed, debriefed, and analyzed.

- **Deliberately developmental organization thinking.** Extending the ITC framework more deeply into organizational life, Kegan, Lahey, Miller, Fleming, and Helsing (2016) developed the concept of a "deliberatively developmental organization" (DDO)—that is, an organization with a core purpose and central strategic orientation to function as an "incubator of capability" (p. 5) that engenders genuine trust, palpable openness to exposing personal weaknesses in ways that enable colleagues to support efforts to overcome them, and a true commitment to accelerating personal growth and development. Efforts to become more "DDO friendly"—whether the unit of analysis is an entire institution, a college within the larger university, or a department within a college—are explored within HIHE curricula. The kinds of changes implicated through this framework beg multiple kinds of interesting and important transformational learning questions.

- **Active use of personal minicases.** As prearrival homework, participants in HIHE's intensive residential institutes are required to complete a "personal minicase" assignment. In no more than two to three pages, all participants identify and describe a leadership challenge in which they are currently involved that is not unfolding in the way they would like. Participants write the challenge in a case study format that, by design, positions the author as the protagonist in their own leadership drama. The minicase concludes with questions that the learner considers of greatest personal relevance and value. The primary venue in which these questions are considered is a small, confidential discussion group. Throughout the institute, personal minicases provide an important bridge to practice and serve as meaningful touchstones to encourage real-world introspection and foster supportive peer-to-peer feedback—critical ingredients to achieving transformational learning outcomes.

Toward Greater Transformational Learning and More Creative Leadership

Whether a higher education leader is confronting disorienting dilemmas, unlearning long-standing mental models and paradigms, thinking in more elastic ways that welcome ambiguity and discard convention, or embracing humility and exhibiting greater emotional intelligence, informational and transformational learning represent two sides of an important professional development "coin" that, when combined thoughtfully and managed carefully, will produce more creative and innovative leaders and will improve institutional performance.

As Shea, Smith, and Gilmore (1998) so aptly noted when describing the path to more effective organizational outcomes (whether in higher education or elsewhere), "The primary task of the educator is to create conditions where others can make their own discoveries" (p. 23). This overarching goal should function as the North Star in an ongoing quest to design and deliver the best possible professional development to future generations of higher education leaders and aspiring leaders. May we all maintain a steadfast commitment to this important work.

Unlock Your Creativity

To sustain creative and innovative energy, make sure you stay hydrated throughout the day. Reflect on the following questions:

- If you were to participate in a class, course, or professional development experience that would challenge the way you think, what would that include?
- What support would you need to make that happen?

References

Berger, J. G. (2012). *Changing on the job: Developing leaders for a complex world.* Stanford, CA: Stanford University Press.

Bolman, L. G., & Deal, T. E. (2017). *Reframing organizations: Artistry, choice and leadership* (6th ed.). Hoboken, NJ: Jossey-Bass.

Bolman, L. G., & Gallos, J. V. (2011). *Reframing academic leadership.* San Francisco, CA: Jossey-Bass.

Bonchek, M. (2016, November 3). Why the problem with learning is unlearning. *Harvard Business Review.* Retrieved from https://hbr.org/2016/11/why-the-problem-with-learning-is-unlearning

Chamarro-Premuzic, T. (2016, January 4). Strengths-based coaching can actually weaken you. *Harvard Business Review.* Retrieved from https://hbr.org/2016/01/strengths-based-coaching-can-actually-weaken-you

Finkelstein, S. (2019, May–June). Don't be blinded by your own expertise. *Harvard Business Review.* Retrieved from https://hbr.org/2019/05/dont-be-blinded-by-your-own-expertise

Gallo, C. (2011, April 14). Customer service the Disney way. *Forbes.* Retrieved from https://www.forbes.com/sites/carminegallo/2011/04/14/customer-service-the-disney-way/#32ebab7478f8

Grebski, J. (2018, September 27). Disney: A case study in customer service perfection. *Medium.* Retrieved from https://medium.com/@jgrebski/disney-a-case-study-in-customer-experience-perfection-1053bacfb431

Hess, E. (2017, June 19). In the AI age, "being smart" will mean something completely different. *Harvard Business Review.* Retrieved from https://hbr.org/2017/06/in-the-ai-age-being-smart-will-mean-something-completely-different

Hess, E. D., & Ludwig, K. (2017). *Humility is the new smart: Rethinking human excellence in the smart machine age.* Oakland, CA: Berrett-Koehler.

Jaschik, S. (2018, November 8). Author discusses new book on problem solving and creative thinking. *Inside Higher Ed.* https://www.insidehighered.com/news/2018/11/08/author-discusses-new-book-problem-solving-and-creative-thinking

Kanter, R. M. (2000). Kaleidoscope thinking. In S. Chowdhury (Ed.), *Management 21C, someday we'll all manage this way* (pp. 250–261). Upper Saddle River, NJ: Financial Times Prentice Hall.

Kegan, R., & Lahey, L. L. (2009). *Immunity to change: How to overcome it and unlock the potential in yourself and your organization.* Boston, MA: Harvard Business Press.

Kegan, R., Lahey, L., Miller, M. L., Fleming, A., & Helsing, D. (2016). *An everyone culture: Becoming a deliberately developmental organization.* Boston, MA: Harvard Business Review Press.

Mezirow, J. (1997). *Transformative learning: Theory to practice.* In P. Cranton (Ed.), Transformative learning in action: Insights from practice (New Directions for Adult and Continuing Education, No. 74, pp. 5–12). San Francisco, CA: Jossey-Bass.

Mezirow's ten phases of transformative learning. (n.d.). Retrieved from https://sites.google.com/site/transformativelearning/elements-of-the-theory-1

Mlodinow, L. (2018). *Elastic: Flexible thinking in a time of change.* New York, NY: Pantheon Books.

Rishi, S., & Farley, J. H. (2014). Circular framing: A model for applying Bolman and Deal's four frames in student affairs administration. *Journal of Student Affairs, 23*(1), 103–112.

Schwartz, T. (2018, June 25). Leaders focus too much on changing policies, and not enough on changing minds. *Harvard Business Review.* Retrieved from https://hbr.org/2018/06/leaders-focus-too-much-on-changing-policies-and-not-enough-on-changing-minds

Shea, G. P., Smith, K. K., & Gilmore, T. N. (1998, April). *Mindfulness and executive education.* Retrieved from Center for Applied Research website: http://cfar.com/sites/default/files/resources/Mindfulness_and_Exec_Ed.pdf

Tervooren, T. (2015, April 21). How to solve problems like Henry Ford and other genius inventors. *HuffPost.* Retrieved from https://www.huffpost.com/entry/how-to-solve-problems-lik_b_7103986

4

CREATING BURSTINESS

ART MUNIN

The process of creating music is awe-inspiring. Pulling together a group of musicians draws together different personalities, styles, backgrounds, and passions. Each musician brings a different instrument—or their own voice. These instruments each make unique sounds, with each musician seeking to find a harmony and rhythm with one another in the hopes of a combined effort of worth. Although musicians may fall short of their musical goals, the successes experienced are so euphoric that it draws them back for more.

Some of the most creative times in my life have been when I played in musical groups. I have played guitar for over 25 years, and I started college as a music major. Early on, I learned there is a significant difference between a true musician and someone who plays an instrument; I am the latter. Nonetheless, music has been formative to how I view the world and the creativity of teams.

Many factors inspire creativity in a team. Much forethought, planning, and practice goes into setting the stage for creativity. For a musical group, each member must prepare for countless hours before he or she can contribute to the group. There is trying, failing, and trying again. Skill must be matched with perseverance, and talent matched with patience. This should also be true for student affairs leaders. The ability to create, foster, and contribute to the creativity of a team must be intentionally cultivated and developed.

Most of us have experienced moments of synergy within a group when creativity is at its peak and outputs are high. The energy is heightened, the mood is light, and the group is striking a delicate harmony. In the podcast *WorkLife*, Adam Grant (2018) described these moments as having "burstiness." He went on to say, "Burstiness is like the best moments in improv jazz. Someone plays a note, someone else jumps in with a harmony, and pretty soon, you have a collective sound that no one planned. Most groups never get to that point, but you know burstiness when you see it" (Grant, 2018, 5:03).

When we experience burstiness in a team, the phrase "catching lightning in a bottle" comes to mind. We are often unaware of how such a magical moment was created. It is as if a series of random events caused lightning to strike the room and spark the creativity. However, this magical thinking engenders the belief that such moments are purely random. They do not have to be. Any leader, from a graduate assistant to a president, can create environments that foster creativity. We can engender spaces where teams freely explore. We can cultivate environments where catching lightning in a bottle is not necessary because the electricity is already in the air. This chapter will cover topics and tools to assist leaders in cultivating burstiness within their teams.

Start With Why

I was first introduced to the notion of "Start with Why" at the NASPA–Student Affairs Administrators in Higher Education AVP Institute in 2015. This adage, penned by Simon Sinek (2009), dramatically reframed how I challenge my teams to think about their work. This overarching philosophy is surmised in The Golden Circle, a series of three concentric circles (see Figure 4.1). The outer circle is the "What." This is the easiest level to identify because it tangibly describes what your unit does. It is concrete and measurable. The next circle in is the "How." This level is a bit more difficult; it describes what makes your unit different from others. For instance, all student affairs departments foster student development. That is a defined What. The differences between the dean of students office and the career center is the How. The methods, tactics, and tools each department employs are different even if the outcomes they seek are the same. Finally, the innermost circle is the "Why." This is "your purpose, cause or belief" (Sinek, 2009, p. 39). It is the reason your unit exists, and the greater meaning behind what the unit adds to the environment.

Figure 4.1. Sinek's (2009) The Golden Circle

WHAT
Products sold, services offered, or your role at work

HOW
Your strengths, values, and guiding principles

WHY
Your purpose, cause, or belief

When communicating a vision for their work, most leaders start from the outermost circle and work their way in. They describe what they do and how they do it, and, through those descriptions, they hope internal and external agents discern why they exist. This process may adequately describe a product if it is a simple output. Student affairs units, however, seek to inspire and motivate beyond simple outputs. That is the reason naming our Why is so critical.

I once witnessed an organization's failure to address the Why cause the demise of a new initiative. A leader sought to build greater connections between first-year students and student affairs staff as a method to increase retention. In this plan, each student affairs staff member would be assigned 10 first-year students to connect with throughout their first year. This would have meant an additional workload that would be difficult to manage. However, the leader did not sell the division on the greater purpose of this work—the importance of retention and fostering student success. He merely shared that, for this work, if the assigned students were retained for their second year, that staff member would receive a financial bonus.

The failure to address the Why for student affairs practitioners' work was this leader's unmaking. By attempting to, in a directly linear fashion, monetize work with students, he lost nearly all buy-in for this initiative. A financial bonus (unless substantial, which it was not) was not going to motivate the staff members to take on this new endeavor and be invested in the outcome. The leader's failure to understand and speak to the Why ultimately led to the demise of the idea.

Being able to recite and rally around a Why will drive a unit further ahead than any top-down edict. This is at the core of effective leadership. Sinek (2009) wrote, "Leaders never start with what needs to be done. Leaders start with WHY we need to do things. Leaders inspire action" (p. 228). Such inspiration is the reason Sinek challenges us to always start with Why. Starting with What, which is the first step of most organizations and leaders, fails to capture the imagination of those involved. It is rudimentary and simplistic. However, starting with Why speaks to the core of the unit and those involved. "For great leaders . . . they are in pursuit of WHY, they hold themselves accountable to HOW they do it and WHAT they do serves as the tangible proof of what they believe" (Sinek, 2009, p. 182).

Starting with Why is foundational to creating a climate that sparks creativity. It gives the professionals of that unit ownership over their work, helps them identify how their service accomplishes a greater vision, and engenders an environment where ideas are welcome. Furthermore, when a unit has a defined Why, "anyone within the organization can make a decision as clearly and as accurately as the [leader]" (Sinek, 2009, p. 168). This allows creativity to occur seamlessly throughout the unit at any point in time. When everyone knows the Why, those unique creative moments can take hold and flourish.

Change the Environment

For me, one of the primary benefits of social media is the near-constant stream of snarky, sarcastic memes regarding work life. One of my favorites includes the phrase "I just survived another meeting that should have been an e-mail." This statement should resonate with almost anyone who has ever worked in an office. The fact is that leaders often do not reflect on the experience of those who attend their meetings. They carry on assuming everyone is engaged and contributing.

Most of us are hardwired with our expectations about what a meeting should constitute. If this meeting is attended by a recurrent group of colleagues, the norms extend much further. Often, part of the pattern even includes where we sit in the room. Such confines can drastically reduce the potential for creativity in that space. Colleagues are merely going through the motions, following their patterns, changing nothing. To spark some creativity a leader needs to change the normal mode of operation. Here are some ideas to consider.

Change the Location

Every so often, your group will benefit greatly from taking your show on the road. We all get into routines because they are comfortable; and with the random stress that can arise throughout the day, having something to count on is reassuring. Routines do serve a purpose. However, for those times when we want to spark some creativity, moving a meeting location can be an asset. It changes the dynamics of the meeting, how people interact, and the energy they feel from the space.

Moving the location can have the added bonus of those involved interacting with different segments of the university. Many of us work at institutions with all different types of buildings spread throughout campus. Students traverse these buildings all throughout their academic career; yet, administrators may live their whole work life moving between two or three buildings. Getting out and about on campus by moving your meeting helps you see what your students are seeing in their daily lives.

Change the Seating

I once did a guest lecture in a graduate higher education course with a group of students whom I had taught in a different course the semester prior. I walked into the room and had a significant déjà vu experience. It took me a few moments to realize what I was feeling, but then it hit me: Although we were in a different room, all the students were sitting in nearly the exact same seats from the semester prior. After that experience, whenever I have taught courses, I have had students change seats throughout the semester. This allows students to interact with different people in small-group conversations and therefore be confronted with different ideas.

I believe the same holds true for the meetings we host. Just like the cafeteria in high school, many people tend to gravitate toward likeminded individuals. That can have its benefits, but if we stay in that silo, we are less likely to be challenged. Challenge and conflict can foster creativity if used appropriately. So many of us attempt to minimize conflict, treating it like a fire to be extinguished immediately when it sparks up. However, for creativity, sometimes we need a spark.

I work with a professional, Greg Batten, who oversees the outdoor adventure initiatives at University of Wisconsin–Oshkosh. As an avid rock climber, he uses the idea of friction as a discussion topic to understand pain points that can be beneficial. Rock climbing requires friction between the climber's hands, feet, rope, and carabiners and the rock. That friction can cause blisters, cuts, and scrapes, but it is also what keeps the climber on the rock. Those pain points are part of the experience and necessary to summit the rock.

As it relates to friction, a common joke among my staff involves my StrengthsQuest results. What is humorous to people is not my top 5 strengths, but rather, my lowest-rated strength: harmony. Every time I challenge the group to lean into an uncomfortable reality that causes friction among staff members, they are reminded that my strengths do not push me to maintain group cohesion as a central driving force. That does not mean that I do not value harmony within a group. But sometimes well-managed discord can be helpful to achieve the best possible results within a team.

As such, challenging your staff to disrupt their patterns and interact with other colleagues may elicit some of those same pain points.

Nevertheless, if managed appropriately, it can also jolt a group toward considering new and different ideas that would not have emerged if the silos were perpetuated.

Change How You Start

Through social conditioning, we are taught from a young age to operate our lives in a protective shell. We shield ourselves from real or perceived threats, creating a sense of real or perceived safety. Taking away someone's sense of safety can leave that person feeling too vulnerable to positively contribute to a group. However, that armor can also significantly inhibit creativity.

Thompson's (2017) article in *Harvard Business Review* reported a simple method to lower people's inhibitions to spark their creativity. Two groups were given a paperclip and asked to brainstorm possible uses for it. Prior to starting their brainstorm, one group's members were asked to share a time they felt proud. The other group was asked to share an embarrassing story from the past six months. The results were nothing short of remarkable. "On average, the embarrassing stories group well outperformed their counterparts" (Thompson, 2017, para. 4).

The takeaway from this article is simple: When group members lower their inhibitions, they open themselves up to greater creativity. It breaks the script of what a typical day at the office looks like, or what a typical brainstorming session entails. It pushes individuals to operate differently and, in turn, garners different results.

Of course, it is not feasible to start every single meeting by having people share embarrassing stories. However, there are a plethora of other ways to engage a group to obtain the same results. I have used everything from card tricks to useless trivia tests to prompt staff members' minds to operate differently at the outset of a meeting. This creates a more enjoyable work atmosphere, helps colleagues get to know one another in different ways, and helps spark creativity.

Manage the Stress

Stress is an evolutionary necessity hardwired into the human brain to ensure survival. The triggered stress response is meant to assist in "helping you run faster, jump higher, see better, and think quicker" (David, 2016, para. 5). On a day-to-day basis, many of those responses are not helpful in an office setting. Nonetheless, there is no getting away from two simple facts: Stress in our lives is inevitable, and our bodies and minds are capable of managing stress.

Leaders need to create climates that manage and mitigate stress for their teams. A figure often used to explore this topic is based on the Yerkes-Dodson law (see Figure 4.2). This bell-shaped curve exemplifies how stress affects performance. On the left side of the curve is low stress, where the performance of staff may be increasing, but not optimal. As stress increases, there is a peak at the top of the bell curve, where an optimal performance level is reached. From there, if stress continues to mount, performance deteriorates and staff members become impaired in their ability to do their job (Gino, 2016).

Figure 4.2. Yerkes-Dodson Law

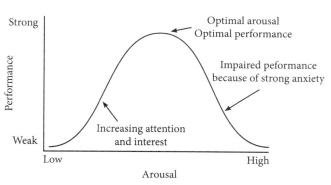

Note. From "The Temporal Dynamics Model of Emotional Memory Processing: A Synthesis on the Neurobiological Basis of Stress-Induced Amnesia, Flashbulb and Traumatic Memories, and the Yerkes-Dodson Law," by D. M. Diamond, A. M. Campbell, C. R. Park, J. Halonen, P. R. Zoladz, 2007, *Neural Plasticity, 33,* p. 3 (http://doi.org/10.1155/2007/60803). CC BY-3.0.

Creating a stress-free environment should not be the goal. Fighting against our very nature is a losing battle. Instead, leaders need to find ways to keep a team in that optimal performance range. For instance, deadlines can be helpful to increase energy and creativity. However, such stress is helpful only up to a point. If deadlines are unreasonable, leaders can push stress beyond the limit where it is useful. Leaders must stay attuned to the needs of their team members and the ways in which each individual manages and experiences stress. Whether it is meeting individual needs through permitting time for exercise and time away or meeting group needs through fostering teambuilding and camaraderie, being mindful to not exceed that optimal level of stress is required to forestall staff dissatisfaction and burnout. Finding that sweet spot of just enough stress to spur your team's creativity and performance is an art form that takes practice and experience.

Recommendations for Leaders

This chapter has introduced several topics and resources to assist leaders in fostering a climate of creative burstiness for their teams. Remember that, ultimately, the burden of cultivating this climate falls on you as the leader. You carry a responsibility to challenge yourself to think and act differently if you desire a new outcome. As the saying goes, if you always do what you have always done, you will always get what you always got. As such, in summation, here are a few final tips for leaders.

First, create safety for your team. It can feel risky for a staff member to bring a new idea forward or offer a divergent opinion. How can you create a climate that invites staff to think differently, and where they feel safe enough to speak up? Not all new ideas will be good. Take the good with the bad so as to spur the group to think creatively and generate new ideas. That less-than-stellar idea might be the key to spur another team member to suggest the idea that will take your team forward. Creativity is about progress, not perfection. It can be a messy process, but staff who feel safe and secure in their leader and team will be far more likely to lean into that discomfort and take the risk inherent to being creative.

Second, along those lines, staff members who offer new ideas are taking a risk. Remember to praise those who step forward. Obviously, it is easy to praise those who bring forward the stellar idea that is going to transform your office's work. However, those ideas are rare, and often a long process of bad and mediocre ideas must be formulated to set the stage for the breakthrough. Leaders need to remember to praise the process and not just the outcome. We succeed because of the teams we work alongside and the road we have journeyed together. Leaders who fail to recognize the process that led to a great idea run the risk of making a team feeling disenfranchised. Often, praise is given at the end of a process and is focused on the singular individual who brought forth the final idea. However, the praise needs to be spread to all involved to recognize the team's contributions in that process.

Third, as a leader, you need to exemplify a professional who is forever growing and developing. Great ideas come from the experiences an ever-expanding life offers. Find ways to experience life in new ways—for example, by traveling, reading, engaging your community, or picking up a musical instrument (I personally recommend the guitar!). It is disingenuous for leaders to ask something of people that they are not willing to do themselves. Take the leap, challenge yourself, share your experience, and encourage those you work with to do the same.

Last, and certainly not least, cultivating creativity within a team takes practice. This is truly a journey and not a destination. At some point, you will experience success in cultivating a creative environment with a team. Then you will attempt to replicate that process with a different group of people only to see your efforts fail. The same inputs do not necessarily generate the same outputs when the people or the environment changes. All of this takes practice.

At the start of this chapter, I likened building creativity to musicians learning their craft. Previous success lays the foundation for future success, but it is not inevitable. It is a constant work in progress. Put another way, Malcolm Gladwell (2008) wrote that it takes 10,000 hours to become proficient at any task or skill. If we assume that we have 8 hours to work a day, 5 days a week, for 52 weeks a year, it would take nearly 5 years to reach 10,000 hours. Realistically, the capability to cultivate creativity is developed throughout one's entire career. The best you can hope for is, upon your retirement, to have experienced more successes than failures. The successes spur us on and the failures provide worthwhile learning opportunities for our next chance to cultivate creativity.

When cultivating creativity in your team, remember that the status quo is not an option. We already know where that road leads. Higher education needs something different. When in doubt of the right next step, do not be afraid to take a risk. It may take several attempts to find the tool or tactic that will work best for your team. In referencing Gladwell's (2008) work, the hip-hop artists Macklemore and Lewis recorded a song titled *Ten Thousand Hours* that includes the following lyrics: "The greats weren't great because at birth they could paint. The greats were great because they paint a lot" (Macklemore, Lewis, & Mansfield, 2012, track 1). Whether it is painters, musicians, sculptors, or higher education leaders, a part of creativity and cultivating those moments of burstiness is a numbers game. The more attempts we make, the greater the likelihood of success.

Unlock Your Creativity

Stop what you are doing and go for a 10-minute stroll to somewhere you never have been. Be keenly aware of your surroundings and keep note of things you have never seen. Afterward, reflect on what stood out to you.

References

David, S. (2016, August 8). How to use stress to your advantage. *Harvard Business Review*. Retrieved from https://hbr.org/2016/08/how-to-use-stress-to-your-advantage

Gino, F. (2016, April 14). Are you too stressed to be productive? Or not stressed enough? *Harvard Business Review*. Retrieved from https://hbr.org/2016/04/are-you-too-stressed-to-be-productive-or-not-stressed-enough

Gladwell, M. (2008). *Outliers: The story of success*. New York, NY: Back Bay Books.

Grant, A. (2018, March). *The Daily Show's secret to creativity* [Audio podcast]. Retrieved from https://www.ted.com/talks/worklife_with_adam_grant_creative_burstiness_at_the_daily_show?referrer=playlist-worklife_with_adam_grant

Macklemore, Lewis, R., & Mansfield, C. (2012). Ten thousand hours [Recorded by Macklemore and Lewis, R]. On *The Heist* [MP3]. Seattle, WA: Self-recorded.

Sinek, S. (2009). *Start with why: How great leaders inspire everyone to take action*. New York, NY: Penguin Group.

Thompson, L. (2017, October 2). Research: For better brainstorming, tell an embarrassing story. *Harvard Business Review*. Retrieved from https://hbr.org/2017/10/research-for-better-brainstorming-tell-an-embarrassing-story

5

BUILDING A CULTURE OF INNOVATION IN A DIVISION OF STUDENT AFFAIRS

PATRICK LOVE

The purpose of this chapter is to share the efforts, tactics, and lessons learned from one instance of attempting to build a culture of innovation in a division of student affairs. A culture of innovation is one in which members of an organization accept that an expected aspect of their job is to come up with frame-breaking ideas and attempt to put those ideas into action in order to address challenges and obstacles to accomplishing the desired outcomes of their work. The organization reviewed is the Division of Student Affairs at New York Institute of Technology (NYIT).

I began my role as vice president for student affairs at NYIT in 2013. The division I inherited was staffed with good, hard-working people dedicated to serving their students. However, I could see that there was not a lot of new thinking going on, and the notion that innovation should be a part of one's professional practice was absent. I knew that would be something I would seek to change given the myriad challenges facing the division and the institution.

The day I began my new job, I sent a letter to everyone in the division introducing myself. I included a document listing and describing my core professional values, one of which was innovation. Here is what I said about innovation:

> In order to be excellent and continually improve our services, we must encourage creativity and innovation throughout the organization. Innovation is not merely incremental improvements. Innovations are qualitative changes that transform people, programs, and services. We will set aside time for staff to be creative and generate new ideas. We all need to forage for new ideas beyond the boundaries of NYIT, our subfields (e.g., counseling, athletics), student affairs, and higher education. (P. Love, personal communication, August 15, 2013)

I was intent on building a culture of innovation in the division. Individually, people were very open and attracted to the notion of innovation; however, before I could effectively build a culture of innovation, I learned that I would need to dismantle aspects of the current divisional and institutional culture that were working against innovation.

Undoing Anti-Innovation Cultural Elements

In my initial observation and assessment of the organization I had come to lead, I quickly realized that in addition to there being no culture of innovation, there were two main anti-innovation aspects of the prevailing organizational culture: One I labeled a "culture of fear," and the other I labeled a "culture of no."

Several factors contributed to the culture of fear, including the fact that the Division of Student Affairs had lacked significant leadership for almost two and a half years, meaning that there was neither encouragement of new ideas nor protection to afford staff members the opportunity to take the kinds of risks innovation requires. It was also clear that the dominant source of fear was the president and, surprisingly to me, he was aware of it. He told me that he believed that generating fear was one aspect of effective organizational leadership. I suppose fear can be used to motivate some expected behaviors in staff; however, in this case it clearly diminished the likelihood of staff being willing to attempt or propose innovative, status-quo-challenging ideas.

My primary means of dealing with the culture of fear was to assure the staff that I would support them when they took steps to implement innovative programs or activities, especially if they were afraid that they might generate disapproval from people outside our division, including (and perhaps especially) the president. I had to be their shield to nay-sayers and resisters. For example, I remember a meeting during which one of my more senior staff members said, when talking about an unusual promotional idea for a program, that "the president won't like that." I responded by saying if you think that the best way to promote something is to go on the academic quad in a chicken suit, then I want you to go on the academic quad in a chicken suit. If the president happens to stop you and asks you why you are in a chicken suit, you can tell him, "Because Patrick wants me in this suit," even if I don't know you are there in a chicken suit. Of course, if I don't know, please call me immediately after the president leaves to give me the heads-up.

I wanted staff to know that I would take on the risk of their innovative ideas. Working to reduce staff fear was fairly straightforward;

it took continual effort, but the leadership actions I needed to take were clear.

Dealing with the culture of no was a much more complex effort. Organizations are conservative entities. Even in the most innovative organizations, there will be resistance to change and the subconscious embracing of inertia and the status quo. We are all programmed to take the easier way, and in organizations often that easier way is to say "No"—to requests, to changes, to exceptions, to ideas. Saying "No" means less work, less adjustment, and less stress. It takes strong leadership and intentionality to create an institutional culture that embraces the open and careful consideration of requests, changes, and new ideas.

At NYIT, I came to understand that the institutional culture was a faux helpful culture in which the default answer was 'No." People expressed a desire to help, but when someone made a specific request, too often the answer was "No, we can't do that," or "No, we can't afford that," or "No, the president wouldn't like that." This attitude was culturally entrenched and subconsciously accepted by the members of the entire organization, including those in student affairs.

Such a strong culture of no is an insidious and dangerous thing, because it infects virtually every person. When a person hears "No" enough times, several negative things happen. One is that the person stops asking for things (e.g., making requests, suggesting changes). Worse is that the person stops conceiving of things to ask for (e.g., coming up with ideas).

Evidence of the loss of ability to come up with innovative ideas was clear in my early days at NYIT. I was specifically told by my staff that people did not innovate in the division because there was no money. I decided to publicly test my assertion that money is not necessary for all innovative ideas. During my first semester, I established a $5,000 Innovation Grant program. I created a one-page application, announced it to the division, and repeatedly encouraged staff to apply. At the deadline one month later, I had only a single application. Clearly, lack of money was not the only reason why people were not innovating. People had learned to not come up with ideas.

One of the other things people in a culture of no start to do is to become part of the "no-saying"—that is, they tell people "No" about things they are not even responsible for. For example, when I started my job I wanted to include my Twitter handle and cell phone number on my business cards. I was told by several people that was not possible. However, none of those people worked for the unit that produced business cards—they worked in student affairs. I fully recognize they were trying to be helpful and have me avoid the pain of hearing no; however, they were also doing the job of the culture of no.

I discovered that combatting this culture was a longer term and more complicated project than dealing with a culture of fear. This was because changing the culture of fear mainly affected only my staff, but trying to address the culture of no caused us to butt up against other units and divisions in the institution. Organizational culture is not easy to change. It will bend to efforts at altering it and initially look like it has changed, but soon it will return to its original shape. It takes awareness, intentionality, and persistence—as well as the cooperation of other units in an institution—to permanently change a culture of no. What follows are some of the action steps my division took to try to combat the culture of no.

Make the culture of no visible. Organizational culture often exists outside our conscious awareness (Schein, 2010). To make a culture of no visible, one must collect and share examples of the culture and then discuss their impact with other colleagues. I shared stories with my leadership team of eight deans and directors about the number of times I was directly or indirectly confronted with a "No" in my first several weeks on the job. I also pointed out instances of when I noticed this happened to them. In addition, I shared these stories at larger divisional gatherings where the entire staff was present.

Do not blame people for being part of the culture. People cannot help being a part of and influenced by a culture of no. It is up to the leader to try to help staff see the culture and overcome its effects.

Encourage people to persist and "stand strong in the face of no." This was the key message to division staff. Standing strong does not require people to be argumentative or combative; it can start with people asking for rationale for a "No" they receive—for example, "Can you help me understand why we can't do that?" or "Is there someone I can speak with to request an exception to that practice?" This stance was encouraged among staff immediately, but even more than a year and a half into this effort, staff had to be reminded because it was easy to fall back into old prevailing cultural habits. It is important to consistently reinforce the message and discuss with new staff the existence and influence of the culture of no.

Expect and plan for resistance. The resistance will come from both within your unit or division and especially from those beyond it. A mistake I made was not educating colleagues beyond my division early enough in our efforts. Although most divisions were either pleased with the innovative and collaborative efforts or not impacted by our efforts, some felt negatively impacted. Some of our efforts led to misunderstandings and resistance from some leaders and their units. Being strong in the face of no does not mean refusing to take no for an answer, as several of my senior colleagues assumed it to mean. This led to conflict or perceived competition. It is vital to try to get other leaders on board with a culture change effort. It is also important to plan for how you might experience resistance, what form it might take, and how to best address it.

Share positive results of standing strong in the face of no. Recognizing the importance of celebrating success, we created and shared with members of the division a poster of about a dozen examples from our first year of "standing strong." We wanted to reinforce to staff that standing strong could change some no's to yes's. Examples included me getting business cards depicting both my Twitter handle and my cell phone number, the Counseling Center getting an administrative assistant even though it had been told for several years that it could not, the athletics department getting needed travel money it had been told it could not get, and my senior staff getting computer system access we had been told was restricted to vice presidents.

Celebrate "yay-sayers." Through our various divisional award programs, we specifically identified people and units outside our division and publicly thanked them with awards for actions made to internationally counter the culture of no. The awards celebrated people and units who challenged the status quo. Although the awards did not specifically mention the culture of no, it was an important underlying reason for making these awards. The pervasiveness of these efforts changed the conversation within the division, and "standing strong" became part of the lexicon helping to reinforce the changes being made to the overall culture.

Building a Culture of Innovation

In addressing the culture of no, the staff was also building a culture of innovation. We took idea generation and innovation very seriously. I communicated that generating new and creative ideas to address the many challenges that faced our division was an important skill to develop and to use. Acquiring and enhancing that skill took time and practice for some. We shared techniques that encouraged staff to challenge their assumptions, find connections between apparently disconnected issues and ideas, generate new ideas, and consider problems and challenges from new perspectives.

One of my first actions at NYIT was to institute a mandatory weekly "idea generation" hour, an idea I got from Tony Doody, my colleague from when we were both at Rutgers University. During that hour, everyone was to individually do nothing but generate innovative and creative ideas for their work. We removed or turned off distractions, and made it clear to others that, aside from emergencies, we were not to be disturbed.

When we started this process, we primed the pump by sharing some of the things that we needed ideas about. These included the following:

- Engaging commuters in out-of-class life
- Meeting the needs of various student subpopulations (e.g., first-year students, transfer students, graduate students, veterans, athletes, post-traditional students, part-time students, working students, international students, LGBTQIA students, students of color, students of faith)
- Assessing the work of student affairs
- Connecting academics and student affairs and the in-class and out-of-class experiences of students
- Meeting the needs of students challenged by disabilities, mental health concerns, or financial burdens
- Finding new ways to teach, coach, and train essential skills
- Making better use of divisional resources
- Finding better, more efficient or effective use of space
- Finding ways to generate additional resources

We also shared basic techniques for generating ideas. These included the following:

- Reading an article or blog post from outside the field, then reflectively writing about how that might relate to the challenges we faced or the problems that we had
- Listing challenges and then trying to combine them in a creative way and writing about them
- Listing difficult tasks and obstacles, then picking one and identifying all of one's assumptions about it, and then writing down what would happen or what one could do if these assumptions were not true
- Choosing a word from a dictionary, website, or article and looking for novel connections between the word and one's problem
- Creating a mind map of possible ideas: writing a key word or phrase in the middle of the page, writing whatever else comes to mind on the same page, and then seeing if one can make any connections with the challenge at hand
- Choosing a picture from a magazine and considering how it could relate to a situation, challenge, or problem
- Taking an item from a colleague's desk or office (with permission!) and asking questions such as "How could this item help in addressing the challenge?" or "What attributes of this item could help solve the challenge?"
- Free writing about one's job, stresses, challenges, successes, frustrations, and failures, and accompanying any identified problems with suggestions on how to address or improve them
- Downloading a creativity or idea generation app, such as Ideas, Whack Pack, Oflow, Idea Factory, Brainsparker, and Simplemind, for one's phone or tablet
- Watching a TED Talk

At the end of the idea generation hour, staff recorded up to three of the best, weirdest, or funniest ideas they came up with and sent them to their supervisor. The supervisors compiled them for their unit and sent them to my office. After six weeks, we had generated a 25-page document of ideas—some crazy, some sane, some impossible, some doable, some expensive, and some that cost little or nothing. Early on, virtually everyone and every unit participated in the practice. Over time, the practice evolved as some units started to incorporate idea generation into their staff meetings and others encouraged staff to meet in groups. After about a year we stopped emphasizing the activity; the change in behavior had been made and people were generating ideas on their own without the need for the structure of a specific idea generation time.

After the lack of response to the initial attempt at an Innovation Grant program, we tried something different: A staff member came up with the idea of having a Pitch Day in October. Staff and units spent September and early October generating ideas. Then, every functional area developed a three-minute pitch of one innovative idea for their work to present at Pitch Day. Following each pitch, the rest of the staff provided feedback on their idea. After Pitch Day, the Innovation Grant applications were again distributed, and individuals and groups were encouraged to apply. Of the 12 ideas pitched at the first Pitch Day, six were submitted for grant applications. The division leadership team, which served as the selection committee, ended up funding three proposals. The following year saw 22 pitches and 21 applications (six were funded by the divisional grant program, but a few more were funded by the units themselves). The higher quality of the presentations in the second year (several even included video productions) clearly indicated the degree to which staff were taking the process seriously.

The division continued to focus on innovation until I departed in 2017. From my four years at NYIT I have gleaned seven lessons:

- **Lesson 1: Innovation is not just for dreamers and creative types.** Innovation is for people willing to take the time (or, as in our case, being required to take the time) to generate ideas about how to address the challenges and needs in their work. Everyone can contribute, as was the case for our idea generation hour.

- **Lesson 2: The mere act of taking the time to generate ideas can lead to innovation action.** The expectation of idea generation was to brainstorm ideas, not to produce innovation. The ideas were to be gathered and discussed by the division's leadership team. However, what we discovered was that the act of generating ideas was enough motivation for some staff to try to implement some of the ideas.

- **Lesson 3: The greatest obstacles to innovation are the perceptions, beliefs, and internal resistance that exist within individuals.** As I mentioned earlier, the shared belief across the division was "we don't have enough money." However, the lack of response to the first Innovation Grant program established that lack of money was not the reason for the lack of innovation. Rather, staff beliefs, perspectives, and internal resistance, coupled with the culture of no, were the obstacles.

- **Lesson 4: Creating a culture of innovation takes persistence.** To combat the persistent culture of fear and the culture of no, we had to continually engage in efforts to bring these cultures to a conscious level so that people could "see" them and to engage in conversations and actions to overcome their effects.

- **Lesson 5: Innovation does not have to be expensive.** The first year we funded three ideas: a career services video series, a residence life senior spirit program, and a counseling and wellness initiative to bring in psychologists who spoke Mandarin, Hindi, and Arabic to talk with new international students about counseling services. The total spent was less than $5,000.

- **Lesson 6: An organized program of innovation can encourage innovation beyond ideas and proposals.** After our efforts around the idea generation hour, Pitch Days, and Innovation Grant program, staff grew to understand that innovation was an expectation of their jobs. Innovations began popping up in virtually every unit.

- **Lesson 7: An innovating division puts pressure on other divisions.** As new ideas and new and larger programs began to emerge throughout student affairs, this put pressure on other units, specifically facilities and security. Facilities had to contend with multiple programs in spaces during weekends, when before no more than one program ever was held in a particular space on a weekend. Students and staff also began to advocate for expanded building hours. Facilities did not have the money to fund so many staff working on the weekends. The same thing happened with security: The department needed more people for events and burned through its budget. This created resistance and, in some cases, backlash from these units. As I mentioned earlier, that is why it is important to alert and educate leaders outside your unit or division to solicit their support and endorsement.

Recommendations for Leaders

Just as someone doing a home renovation often has to demolish existing structures before constructing new ones, so does someone who is attempting to build a culture of innovation in an organization. A leader interested in building such a culture must be sensitive to the cultural obstacles to innovation that exist and take the necessary steps to dismantle them. Additionally, leaders must look beyond the boundaries of their own unit: An active and intentional program of innovation can unleash the innate creative talents of individuals and groups throughout an entire organization.

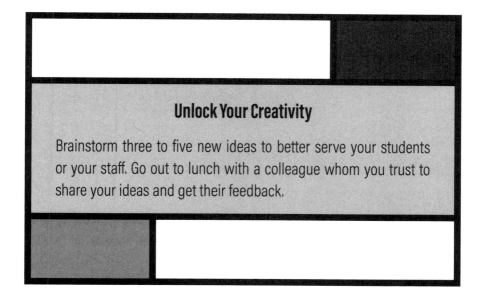

Unlock Your Creativity

Brainstorm three to five new ideas to better serve your students or your staff. Go out to lunch with a colleague whom you trust to share your ideas and get their feedback.

Reference

Schein, E. H. (2010). *Organizational culture and leadership* (4th ed.). San Francisco, CA: Jossey-Bass.

6

CREATIVITY IN THE HIRING PROCESS
Run Successful Searches by Thinking Outside the Box

ANN MARIE KLOTZ AND VIJAY PENDAKUR

As higher education continues to grapple with national policy changes and substantial challenges to funding and enrollment, it is critical that administrators hire talented, innovative, solutions-focused self-starters to fill professional staff positions. Higher education has traditionally suffered from a creativity gap in recruiting, hiring, and onboarding new talent. Colleges and universities spend substantial resources to attract prospective students but lack the same savvy and strategy for securing talented professional staff. Studies by the Society for Human Resource Management (SHRM) and Glassdoor reported that the average cost to hire a new employee was $4,129 (SHRM, 2016) and $4,000 (Glassdoor, 2019). This chapter explores the deficits of the current hiring model in higher education and offers solutions to target and attract dynamic practitioners who can help move the needle forward in departments and divisions of student affairs. Strategies for advertising and recruiting positions are suggested, and templates are provided for more creative on-campus interview schedules. The chapter concludes with a robust onboarding schedule that will ensure a strong return on investment for the new hire. The chapter focuses on developing innovative search processes for the director level and above, but nearly all these strategies also work for entry- and mid-level positions. If you are looking for a practical approach to search processes that will result in securing top talent to join your team, this chapter is for you.

The Hiring Challenge on College Campuses

Higher education is often at the forefront of innovative learning strategies and new resources to streamline services for students; however, it is notoriously antiquated in its recruitment and hiring practices. Consider the following three scenarios. Have you personally experienced one or more of them, or know someone who has?

1. You apply for a job, participate in the first-round phone interview, then don't hear anything for weeks or months, if at all.

2. You are invited for an on-campus interview and do not receive an itinerary until a couple days in advance; you have to scramble to put together a presentation at the last minute.

3. You attend the on-campus interview and (a) you are asked an illegal question; (b) you are asked the same questions in each interview session; or (c) the interviewers do not seem to be prepared.

Sound familiar? Before writing this chapter, we reached out to higher education community members and asked them what missteps they have encountered in the interview process. Our inboxes were flooded with story after story of being stranded at the airport because someone forgot to pick them up, being put in a residence hall room with no linens or air conditioning on a hot summer night, being alone at an interview because the itinerary listed the wrong room number, botched negotiations because the hiring manager offered an unapproved (out of budget range) salary, and many, many more.

The recruiting and hiring process is a chance for an institution to showcase the best of what it has to offer prospective candidates. If done correctly, it can have a positive impact on the campus culture and ultimately enhance student success. If done poorly, it can create a toxic culture staffed by underperformers and can decrease overall retention and satisfaction for both staff and students. We wanted to write this chapter because we have seen firsthand how strong search processes that result in recruiting top talent can enhance the culture of departments and divisions of student affairs—it is the ultimate difference-maker when it comes to building high-performance teams.

The following sections are structured chronologically to mirror the search process, from writing the job description through onboarding the new employee. While there is no one-size-fits-all approach for recruiting and hiring, we provide some practical tips that can be tailored to your own institution.

Step 1: Maximize the Job Description

Hiring (owing to a resignation, restructuring, or the creation of new position) is a prime opportunity to ask, "What are the gaps in our organization that this job will seek to minimize?" The job description should be a clear road map that outlines the scope of work, the specific duties, and the metrics by which the work will be evaluated. It is critically important to think about what you are really looking for in the position. Too often, people simply use the same job description each time the position comes open, with few or no changes. What does your organization really need right now? How can this position contribute to achieving your departmental and strategic goals? Each hiring process can be seen as an opportunity for organizational improvement, rather than just filling a vacant seat.

If your area is going through a reorganization, this can be an excellent opportunity to identify the essential duties that need to be covered or aren't currently assigned to a particular person and craft a job description based on those needs. It can be a chance to start fresh and reimagine the position in new ways.

In crafting the qualifications, we suggest having very few *required* qualifications and focusing on a comprehensive list of *preferred* qualifications instead. This will enable viable candidates who have non-traditional experience to apply and be considered. For example, you might be hiring for a marketing director in the division of student affairs. Some institutions might require candidates to have a master's degree or two to four years of higher education experience, but what if the position attracts strong candidates from the corporate sector who are highly skilled in marketing but do not have any experience in higher education or do not have an advanced degree? If you put these *preferred* qualifications in the *required* section, potentially strong candidates might not be eligible for a phone interview, and your pool might suffer as a result.

Look at job descriptions outside higher education but within a specific industry (e.g., marketing, communications) to understand how they are structured, and wherever possible replicate the language to attract non-higher-education practitioners. Also, avoid higher education jargon in your qualifications list. If you are interested in specific skills and experiences that you deem vital to success in the role, name them. But lists of higher education acronyms or professional societies in the qualifications section of a job posting might simply turn away top talent from other industries who are looking to apply their skills in a campus setting.

Step 2: Build a Timeline With Deadlines at Certain Milestones

One of the biggest challenges search committees face is filling open positions in a timely manner. Many of the professionals we spoke to in doing the research for this chapter told us that it was common for searches to take six to twelve months. If the hiring manager prepares before the job is posted and creates a timeline with milestones, nearly any search can be completed in 90 days. Each institution has its own processes and challenges when it comes to moving a search along swiftly, but a precise and ambitious timeline can mitigate some of the delays. The following is a sample timeline.

- **September 1.** A staff member submits their resignation. The hiring manager informs human resources (HR) of the intent to post within the next week.

- **By September 5.** The job description is reviewed and updated to reflect the needs of the unit. The final version is sent to HR to post. A search committee is appointed and the first meeting is set up for the following week. A save-the-date post (see Figure 6.1) goes out on social media and to selected listservs to let people know about the vacancy.

- **By September 12.** The hiring manager and the search committee chair review expectations and the proposed search timeline. The search committee is convened and the hiring matrix is reviewed. The job posts on the university website and on several other targeted websites.

- **September 12–30.** The search committee chair reviews applications every day. Anyone who meets the minimum qualifications is passed on to the committee for review. After the first week, the chair begins scheduling web meeting interviews for the highest ranked candidates.

- **September 19–October 12.** Web meeting interviews are conducted with 8–15 candidates. On-campus interviews are offered and scheduled on a rolling basis, based on the committee scores and recommendations. Each finalist is informed of the salary range and the reimbursement process for travel expenses to the interview. Finalists are also told that their references will be contacted before the interview. Each finalist is assigned a host to help them navigate the on-campus interview.

- **October 5–20.** References are checked, and on-campus interviews are conducted. The search committee compiles the evaluation comments and scores, and lists the strengths and weaknesses of each candidate for the hiring manager to review.

- **By October 25.** The hiring manager reviews the search committee recommendations and calls the top candidates to answer any questions they might have.

- **By October 30.** An offer is extended to the top candidate, and negotiation conversations are convened. If the position is declined, it is offered to the number 2 candidate. If there is no number 2 candidate, or if the number 2 candidate says no, it may be necessary to restart the search.

- **By November 10.** The offer is accepted, paperwork is finalized with HR, and the news is shared with the search committee and the larger campus community.

Step 3: Advertise the Opportunity—Go Beyond Post-and-Pray and Your Institution

Some HR departments have tight parameters regarding position descriptions, but there are several ways to get the word out, including the formal description on the HR website, a more approachable advertisement on various job placement sites, and a shortened, more direct description via social media. The more details you can put into the description of the campus, culture, and department, the more likely you are to cultivate a talent pool of people who are interested in the opportunity and have the skills to successfully navigate the role.

As soon as the position posts, the marketing plan should go into effect. Too often, institutions post a position with a wait-and-see mentality toward garnering candidates. A targeted marketing approach limits the chance for a failed search and often produces a more experienced and talented candidate pool. The following are a few approaches to consider in marketing open positions.

Advertise the opportunity to target markets by creating a save-the-date announcement—a targeted memo that can be shared with professional listservs and social media before you actually post the job (see Figure 6.1). Creating a save-the-date announcement helps spread the word and gets people thinking about whether this could be the right opportunity for them. It also gives prospective candidates the chance to reach out to the contact person with any questions before applying.

Figure 6.1. Sample Save-the-Date Announcement

Coming Soon!

[Insert institution name] will be posting a dean of students position next month!

Description of [insert institution name]: We are a fast-paced, innovation-focused institution with a commitment to student success. The ideal candidate possesses excellent critical thinking skills and strong problem-solving abilities, and enjoys working with students. Our office environment is collegial, supportive, and forward-thinking.

What we are looking for:

- 10 years post master's degree
- Experience with crisis management and student conduct
- Previous experience supervising professional staff
- Commitment to diversity and inclusive practices

Want to learn more about our division? Check out our website at [insert URL].

For direct inquiries, please contact [insert name and contact info].

Sometimes an institution's location can be a barrier to achieving recruiting goals. For example, it can be challenging to create a diverse candidate pool for a position at a rural institution. Vijay worked at urban institutions for more than a decade before moving to Cornell University, where he had the opportunity to make 16 hires in his first 18 months on the job. Many of these positions were in specialized diversity areas, such as LGBTQIA campus centers, Asian American resource centers, or working with undocumented college students. Cornell's main campus is in Ithaca, New York, a town of 30,000 people that is a four-hour drive from any major city. Garnering a competitive, diverse candidate pool in these searches was deeply challenging for Vijay, so he had to enact some strategic shifts in the way he advertised the opportunities.

First, he made extensive use of colleague networks to ensure that the posting reached passive candidates—people who might not be actively searching but who might consider applying for the right position. Second, he used social media to describe the positions not simply as jobs that needed filling but as opportunities to join a growing and changing institution. Many student affairs professionals might be willing to consider a geographic move that is outside their normal comfort zone if they think the result will be significant professional growth. The language in the position descriptions and the social media postings emphasized the impact these roles would have on the campus, what the person who got the job would learn and be able to speak about after several years in the role, and the team culture at Cornell. Third, and most important, when candidates came to campus for final interviews, they had several experiences that had historically not been part of recruitment at Cornell. Candidates were brought in for two nights instead of one, which gave them time to explore the city and see how they could make a life for themselves there. They were given a rental car and a list of places to check out, to help them overcome apprehension or stereotyped ideas about small-town life and to see some of the amazing aspects of living in Ithaca. Vijay's team built a small social gathering into the interviews, in which a diverse group of divisional staff members were invited to have a beer or a glass of wine with the candidate. This experience was particularly effective, as candidates began to see the breadth and depth of their potential collegial community at Cornell. Each of these strategies was designed to address barriers to hiring diverse talent to work in rural locations; they resulted in more competitive and diverse candidate pools and more successful completed searches.

Step 4: Use Social Media and Video Promotion

Both the save-the-date announcement and the actual posting can be shared via social media and should be part of a larger strategy of publicizing the opportunity. The following are a few options:

1. Promote the position through the institution's social media channels.
2. Share the position through divisional and departmental social media outlets.
3. Post the job on your personal social media platforms.

When Ann Marie found herself leading a division with 15 vacancies in key staff roles, she listed every job opportunity with a blank line next to it. She headlined the list "Now Hiring—Join Our Team!" and flooded this image on Twitter, Instagram, LinkedIn, and Facebook. The posting received more than 28,000 unique views. Her LinkedIn post about the open jobs was shared with a much larger audience than if it had been simply posted on a website. As a result of this marketing approach, her division was able to successfully hire for all 15 positions within 85 days. To congratulate the new team, she posted the same list with names beside the jobs.

At a previous institution, Ann Marie was charged with leading the search for a new dean of students. After creating and distributing a save-the-date memo (but before the position posted), the division made a 60-second commercial posted to YouTube in which the vice president for student affairs and other members of the staff explained what they were looking for in a candidate and outlined the exciting opportunities that came with the position. This commercial received more than 20,000 unique views. A big challenge in the recruitment process is simply letting people know about an opportunity. By using social media, spreading the word about the vacancy before it is actually posted, and flooding the industry with information about the position, you are increasing the chance that you will attract a large, diverse, and talented applicant pool.

Consider using career placement services such as The Placement Exchange (TPE). These services aren't just for entry-level roles, and they maintain a year-round posting database that job seekers can access at any time. When Vijay found himself with numerous vacancies in several diversity-related departments, he used TPE to generate buzz and increase the number of applications. Vijay and his team also hosted a reception specifically for these diversity vacancies. All applicants who were attending TPE were invited to a reception at which they could meet with hiring managers and staff from the diversity departments and ask any questions about the positions. The team received feedback from numerous visitors that the reception not only enabled them to get answers to important questions but also gave them a glimpse of the fun, healthy, team-oriented culture they might join if they were to apply. Overall, the reception increased the quantity and quality of the pool, resulting in greater success in these important searches.

Finally, consider how you train your team to talk about the institution, the division, and the geographic location. Don't assume that people know how to be diplomatic, honest, and professional when they are asked direct questions about areas that need improvement. For example, when staff answer questions about the racial diversity of a campus community, it's possible to both share that the numbers are small, but also that the community is quite strong and tightly knit. Remember, people don't just change jobs; they change their whole life. Your current team should be prepared to highlight the areas of the campus and community that support the health, well-being, and happiness of your prospective applicants and, if applicable, their families.

Creatively managing the hiring process also entails thinking about it even when you don't have a vacancy. Keep a detailed spreadsheet with a list of talented people you meet at conferences, industry events, and online. This spreadsheet can help you in two ways. First, when you have a sudden vacancy, you will have a potential short list of talented people you can attempt to recruit. Second, you can use the list to help spread the word about your vacancy by asking the people on it to cross-post your job advertisements and social media strategies.

Step 5: Strategically Build the Search Committee

In building the committee, determine who the primary stakeholders are and whose input you truly need. Most important, identify people who will prioritize the time to be productive members of the search committee, especially in time-intensive processes like conducting applicant reviews. Administrators often stack these committees according to political considerations rather than thinking about who would be a strong contributing member of the team. Hiring managers frequently feel pressure to fill their committees with various stakeholders who represent interest groups, political factions, and community partners—to manage people's emotions and agendas rather than simply getting the search completed in an expedient manner. Institutional politics matter, but balance one or two political appointments with several committee members who will work hard, model compromise in the decision-making process, and keep the best interests of your department or unit in mind. We recommend keeping your committee small: six or fewer people, if possible. An overly large committee can make it difficult to schedule meetings at which everyone is present or to reach a compromise on a tough decision. Finally, consider selecting at least one student to serve on your hiring committee. A student who is familiar with the role or department for which you are hiring and who has a high level of maturity and professionalism can add a critical perspective to your search process.

The hiring manager should attend the first meeting of the search committee to review the job description and charge the group with finding a successful candidate. Committee members should be encouraged to ask questions about the goals for the position and to deepen their understanding of the specific talents and skills that are needed in this role. If you are trying to run a search process that differs from the norm at your institution, your search committee needs to be on board and supportive of this vision. As hiring manager, you can use the charge meeting to energize the search committee, help them see the value of the type of search you are trying to run, and ensure that they participate in ways that further your goals.

Step 6: Develop a Detailed Matrix to Screen Candidates

Reviewing résumés can be a subjective process; therefore, a matrix is necessary to ensure that each reviewer is critically evaluating the candidates in a fair and inclusive manner. To create a matrix, the hiring manager must thoughtfully determine what characteristics and experiences are needed in this role. All marketing materials and information regarding the position will stress the importance of these requirements, and each candidate will be evaluated on them. This approach ensures that candidates know the requirements for the role and that reviewers are evaluating each applicant on the same critical skills. The return on investment is high when the applicant pool reflects the needs of the role. In crafting a matrix, list each required qualification on a spreadsheet; this will be the primary document the search committee uses to conduct its initial review. The following are a few items that could be on the matrix:

- At least three years of professional staff supervisory experience
- Demonstrated experience with strategic planning
- Experience working in an urban setting or with a diverse population
- Evidence of positive collaboration with faculty and academic affairs

Depending on the scope of the role, a matrix could have anywhere from 6 to 12 categories. For each applicant, each member of the search committee must evaluate each category; the use of a common rating scale helps minimize subjectivity. Table 6.1 illustrates a sample matrix with two example categories and a rating scale.

Search committee members will use the résumé and the cover letter as the basis for their review. After looking over the categories and the guidelines listed for each category, they will rank the candidate based on a rating scale such as the one provided in Table 6.1. The search committee chair can create a Google document or a shared folder to which committee members submit their scores. In the case of ties or if more discussion is needed, the chair can convene a meeting to review the rankings.

Table 6.1. Sample Candidate Résumé Evaluation Matrix

	1 No Experience	2 Poor	3 Needs Improvement	4 Average	5 Good	6 Excellent
Demonstrated experience with strategic planning. Candidate demonstrates evidence of experience with the strategic planning process in a unit, department, or organization. Other qualifying experiences could include the development of an organizational or restructuring plan. Higher marks should go to individuals who have led the strategic planning process with a team.	❏	❏	❏	❏	❏	❏
Experience working in an urban setting or with a diverse population. Candidate demonstrates evidence of engagement with student communities of difference. Evidence of this could be development of sustained dialogue programs, cross-community programmatic events, or research projects involving intersection of identity. Higher marks should be given to collaborative educational program or policy development that focuses on inclusion, equity, social justice, or cultural competence.	❏	❏	❏	❏	❏	❏

Rating Scale

6 = Excellent. Candidate shows evidence of a significant amount of demonstrated experience and success.

5 = Good. Candidate shows evidence of experience and success.

4 = Average. Candidate shows evidence of some experience and some success, but not significant.

3 = Needs Improvement. Candidate indicates having had some experience but provides no evidence of success.

2 = Poor. Candidate shows very little evidence of experience and no evidence of success.

1 = No Experience. Candidate shows no evidence of experience or success in this category.

Step 7: The Phone Interview Reimagined

Once the results of the screening process are tabulated, the committee determines who will move forward as semifinalists for the phone interview. We suggest using a web meeting application, because it allows the entire committee to interact in a more authentic way with the candidate. Also, we believe that phone interviews advantage extraverts, who tend to think and respond quickly. The web meeting interview allows the active listening and nonverbal communication cues typically exhibited by more introverted candidates to be visible; thus, it provides a more level playing field for diverse learning and leading styles.

The strategy for the web meeting interview is to determine whether the candidate has the skills and experience to be successful in the role and to convey information to the candidate about the culture and expectations of the department. Most important, the committee must decide whether this candidate can fill the current talent gap on the team and whether this person would be a good fit for your campus. The following sample questions are innovative in their approach and can shed a lot of light on who the candidate is and how they think through complex problems.

1. What is one thing about your leadership style that we might not know from your résumé and cover letter?

2. What is one thing that student affairs does not do well nationally, and what would be your solution to improve it?

3. Talk about a time when you created something new despite limited financial or staff resources. What was the impact of your innovation on the campus, department, or student experience?

The web meeting interview is a critical piece of the process: It determines who will move forward to the on-campus finalist stage.

Any candidate who advances past the web meeting interview should have the full confidence of the committee. By focusing the web meeting interview on whether the candidate has the experiences and skills necessary to do the job you're hiring for, you can use the on-campus interview to go deeper and engage the candidate on characteristics that are harder to assess, such as specific workplace attitudes, thinking on one's feet, and how this person would fit into your overall organization.

Step 8: Reference Checks

One of the most overlooked yet critically important parts of the search process is conducting thorough reference checks. Often they are conducted in a rush at the tail end of the search process instead of at the midway point, where the information gleaned can add value in face-to-face conversations with candidates.

The best approach is to conduct reference checks after the phone/web meeting interview for all the candidates you are bringing to campus for the final round. This allows you to ask questions of the references that you can follow up on with the finalists during their on-campus interviews. For example, if you learn that a certain finalist struggles with administrative tasks, you can make that an area of discussion in your meeting, providing a space for honest dialogue about how you could support this person if they were to get the job.

The following are some sample reference check questions that go beyond "What are the strengths and weaknesses of the candidate?"

1. What is this person like on their worst day?
2. How does this person manage stressful times and challenging situations?

3. In what kind of professional environments have you seen this person thrive? What conditions enable them to perform best?

4. Discuss the person's ability to execute and deliver results. What is their project management style? Do they typically need a lot of direction, support, and input?

5. How does this person use financial acumen to strategically think about financial priorities to support the goals of the division and the university?

6. Please tell us about a time that you saw this person manage a difficult conflict with another employee.

Whether you do reference checks before or after the on-campus interview, we suggest two innovations to squeeze all the value out of them. First, don't simply ask for three references from candidates. Think about what you are trying to learn and ask for very specific kinds of references. For example, for a mid-level hire, you might ask candidates to give you the name of someone who has supervised them, someone they have supervised, a student they have mentored, and a colleague with whom they have collaborated on a major initiative. If you are specific about the kinds of relationships you want references for, you will receive much richer data from the reference check process. A second innovation is the *reverse reference check*. Offer your finalist candidates a list of references of people who have worked with or for you. The finalists can reach out to people on your list and ask them what it is or was like to work for you or with you. The manager–supervisor relationship is a critical one; any additional insight can help ensure that it is a good mutual fit and can help with staff retention down the road.

Step 9: A New Model for the On-Campus Interview

Not all positions in higher education are the same, but the on-campus interview follows a similar format. Typically, the interview lasts a day to a day and half, with several interview panels that might include the search committee, students, campus stakeholders, and direct reports. It often includes a campus tour and an open forum or presentation. Candidates go through a 7- to 10-hour interview process in which they often are asked the same questions repeatedly. Methodologically, this process is more a test of a candidate's stamina than a process to uncover truly precise and valuable information about the candidate that will help you make the right hiring decision. In this section, we propose an innovative approach with fewer interview panels and more practical exercises.

First, we strongly suggest that hiring managers have a phone conversation with candidates before offering them an on-campus interview. This conversation should cover the salary for the position and other potentially limiting particulars. In fact, both Ann Marie and Vijay disclose a very narrow salary range to candidates *before* the phone interview stage of the process, as we have lost too many candidates late in searches because of a mismatch between their expectations and our compensation realities. Similarly, if you have unusual limitations in relocation support, no temporary housing support, or other similar challenges, tell the candidates early in the search—and definitely before the on-campus interview—so they can select out before the laborious and costly final interview.

In a recent search, Ann Marie asked the candidates to do two presentations and one practical exercise, meet with the search committee, and connect with students on a campus tour. The revamped interview day eliminated at least three hours of traditional interviews, and the presentations enabled any campus stakeholder or direct report to have two chances to see the candidate in action. The first presentation followed a 15- to 20-minute TED Talk style that allowed candidates to present on a topic of their choosing—one in which they had subject matter expertise. Attendees had the opportunity to learn about a variety of topics and hobbies—such as music, running, cooking, and even knitting—that were important to the candidates. The talks made them seem more real and approachable and made it easier to assess overall fit. The second presentation connected to a key value of this particular university: retention. In this session, candidates presented a 30-day plan to develop a strategy for student retention, and attendees were able to ask questions during a Q&A period. It was a tangible and action-oriented experience for all.

As part of the interview day, the candidate was given a private office, a laptop, and an hour to read over a case study and submit a one-page memo with action items. This activity allowed the hiring manager to assess each candidate's problem-solving skills and written communication style. It also assessed the candidates' ability to think on their feet, which was a key requirement for that specific job.

For more senior-level roles, we suggest having each finalist meet with a university photographer for a headshot that can be used in a press release shortly after the contract is signed. If you are recruiting from an underrepresented or minoritized community, building in a chance for candidates to interact with a diverse cross-section of your staff in a casual setting can help them assess whether they would thrive in your climate.

These aren't the only ways we can reimagine the interview day, but they are some alternatives to simply meeting with campus stakeholders and repeatedly answering the same questions. Innovations in the interview process can provide greater insight into the working style, personality, and abilities of each candidate.

Hiring managers must be as thorough as possible in doing their due diligence on each finalist. During the wrap-up meeting with the candidate, they can follow up on questions or concerns that arose in the reference checks and discuss other issues that might affect a move for the successful candidate. Candidates often have partners (with jobs), children (school districts), homes to be sold/leases to end, pets, hobbies, faith communities, and cultural implications—all of these play a role in whether a candidate will accept a position. Make the wrap-up meeting an opportunity for the candidate to talk openly about the personal needs and concerns they are weighing, and provide whatever insight, clarity, or support you can.

This end-of-day conversation can also be the time to bring up any concerns about fit. Vijay was once interviewing a candidate for a director-level role at an access-focused, regional teaching institution. The candidate was coming from an Ivy League institution and had mentioned a few things over the course of an otherwise stellar interview day that concerned the search committee. The candidate did not appear to understand the difference in resources between the Ivy League and this university. Vijay used this conversation to candidly address the concerns of the committee and to give the candidate a chance to mull over the resource realities of the teaching institution. He did this from a place of honesty, compassion, and transparency, rather than communicating any sense of frustration or disappointment in the candidate. The candidate was able to dispel the confusion by rearticulating a strong feeling about the access mission and an understanding of the fundamental budget realities. With this issue cleared up, both the candidate and the employer could proceed with clarity and trust.

Step 10: The Offer

If reference checks are completed earlier in the process, an offer can typically be extended shortly after the final candidate visits campus.

We suggest having the search committee compile a list of strengths and weaknesses for each finalist within 48 hours of the last visit and reviewing every evaluation form to look at common themes in the feedback.

Because of the due diligence you have given to the process, you should be aware of any hot-button needs for your top candidate. For example, will they need temporary campus housing until a house sells? Will a partner need assistance in finding suitable employment? Your comprehensive offer should acknowledge any issues that need to be resolved so you can get to "Yes."

Step 11: Onboarding and Beyond

You put in the work and you got your first-choice candidate. Congratulations! Institutions spend thousands of dollars posting a job, marketing, and recruiting top-tier applicants, but they tend to spend much less time and effort to onboard the new hire. An onboarding program that builds loyalty will ultimately have a positive impact on staff retention.

In *The Five Elements of Well-Being*, Rath & Harter (2010) posited that everyone seeks harmony in five areas: career, social, community, physical, and financial. We suggest building an onboarding program that addresses these areas. For example, when we take the time to set up appointments for our new hires with retirement plan representatives or connect them with local banks, we are investing in their financial well-being. When we set up meetings for them to tour local gyms and recreation centers, we are demonstrating care for their physical well-being. When we connect them with a realtor or rental agent, we are showing support for their community well-being. Take the time to ask your new hires what is important to them and, if applicable, their families. Yoga studio? Faith community? Cultural opportunities? When we have a better understanding of the priorities of the new employee outside work and we demonstrate that we want to help them get connected so they can meet those needs, we are investing in the long-term success and happiness of the employee. The return on investment for your time and effort in this endeavor will be high.

Build new employees' calendars for the first two weeks by pre-scheduling appointments for them to meet with key stakeholders across campus. Include opportunities for them to get connected to the campus community, including lunch with students, tours of local area businesses, and a meeting with HR to review insurance and benefit options. When you hire underrepresented staff, be intentional about connecting them with allies and in-group colleagues, so they can begin to form a community of shared experience. As the hiring manager, set up appointments on your own calendar at the 30-, 60-, and 90-day marks to check in with your new hire on each of the elements of onboarding. Many managers focus on the new employee's mastery of the job duties, but challenges in other dimensions of the transition—such as finding a community or navigating schools or health care—can lead to rapid turnover. We see a thoughtful, holistic onboarding strategy as a critical component of creative hiring: How someone starts out at your institution will have significant bearing on their success and longevity on your team.

Recommendations for Leaders

The following are a few suggested takeaways to apply to your own search processes.

1. The entire search process, from the minute you post the position description, is a recruitment process and an advertisement

for your organization. Every step of the process reflects on the institution.

2. You have to recruit the whole person, which may include family, pets, and hobbies. When you are in the finalist stage, ask candidates about their priorities outside the job. Do they have a partner who is also seeking a job? Will they need child care? Connection to a faith community in the area? To show your investment in their candidacy and who they are as a whole person, find answers, resources, and opportunities before the on-campus interview.

3. Focus on detailing the required skills for the position and the challenges and opportunities of the role, then create a selection process that evaluates a candidate's skills and ability to succeed in your campus culture.

4. Shorten the timeline of the search. Most searches can be developed, posted, and completed in 90 days. Plan accordingly and set target dates for each milestone of the process. For example, conduct reference checks before the on-campus interview, so you won't be trying to finish them at the very end of the process.

5. Once you have a successful candidate, the real work begins. Many institutions invest a lot of time, effort, and money in finding the right hire but do not plan beyond Day 1. Create an onboarding program for the first week; the first 30, 60, and 90 days; and the first year.

Unlock Your Creativity

If you are a hiring manager, design your ideal timeline and job search process. What does that process look like?

Set up a meeting with HR and discuss a strategy to improve the process for your prospective candidates.

References

Glassdoor. (2019, July 5). *How to calculate cost-per-hire.* Retrieved from https://www.glassdoor.com/employers/blog/calculate-cost-per-hire

Rath, T., & Harter, J. (2010). *Wellbeing: The five essential elements.* New York, NY: Gallup Press.

Society for Human Resource Management. (2016, August 3). *Average cost-per-hire for companies is $4,129, SHRM survey finds* [Press release]. Retrieved from https://www.shrm.org/about-shrm/press-room/press-releases/pages/human-capital-benchmarking-report.aspx

7

GRADUATE PREPARATION PROGRAMS AS A PLACE TO ENGAGE IN CREATIVE PRACTICE

SUSANA HERNÁNDEZ

F aculty play a critical role in the development of students who pursue a graduate degree in higher education and/or student affairs. Faculty are able to expose students to salient and relevant scholarship, foster a network of peers interested in a similar profession, and engage in rich reflection and discussion on professional practice.

When I was approached by one of the editors to contribute to this volume, we sat down to discuss student affairs—our passion for the work—and he brought up this idea of creativity. I was intrigued, but in no way did I think of myself as creative. I don't draw—well, nothing beyond stick figures and happy faces anyway. I lack the artistic talents that I initially believed would classify me as creative. Until our conversation, I didn't realize how as a scholar, an educator, and a Latina woman, I am creative, daily.

This conversation spurred me to think more critically about my role as an educator and faculty member who prepares higher education professionals to join or advance in the profession. I am reminded of NASPA–Student Affairs Administrators in Higher Education President Kevin Kruger's call for change efforts in higher education to be rooted in student affairs (Smith, Blixt, Ellis, Gill, Kruger, 2015). Student affairs professionals are uniquely positioned to advance innovative practices to support students in reaching their personal, professional, and academic goals.

The compelling need for student affairs and higher education professionals to engage in creative practices could not be more urgent. The constant challenges student affairs professionals face— tightening budgets, supporting students who are juggling multiple roles and responsibilities, and being asked to do more beyond the job description—create an environment where doing business as usual is no longer the case.

Creativity and innovation are becoming compelling enterprises for chief student affairs officers (Smith, et al., 2015). Vice presidents for student affairs are fostering environments in which professionals feel empowered to think more creatively about organizational goals. How does student affairs preparation mediate creativity as a way for higher education professionals to think differently about their practice? How can creativity be adopted to support supports? How can creativity be leveraged to lead organizations and staff?

This chapter describes the nature of graduate preparation programs and offers examples of how creativity can be integrated into both the profession and the classroom. The chapter will also describe various understandings of creativity and how these concepts can apply to higher education broadly and student affairs practice specifically.

Student Affairs Preparation: A Brief Overview

Student affairs work is central to the mission of higher education. Although student affairs began as a profession, it has evolved to encompass more than just holistic student development. Student affairs professionals are navigating dynamic campus environments; as such, their roles now require a higher level of competence as well as skills in multiple areas.

The scholarship on the practice of student affairs has grown, and so, too, has the pursuit of an advanced degree in higher education and student affairs. Graduate preparation programs play an integral role in introducing students to the higher education literature, a space for reflection of professional practice, and an opportunity to think deeply about one's sense of self (both personal and professional). There is a growing body of literature on the nature of graduate preparation, and the following section offers a brief review of some of the salient scholarship in this area.

In 2008, Renn and Jessup-Anger conducted a national study of new professionals in student affairs to understand their transition into the field of higher education and learn how well their graduate program prepared them to be effective and satisfied new professionals. Although the study is now more than 10 years old, it offers some insights into how graduate preparation, as a space, is important to the transition and preparation of professionals in higher education. The researchers found that the relationships new professionals formed prior to employment and the orientation phase of employment formed the basis for their transition to their new roles. More salient to this chapter is the role of competence. Participants described issues of job training, skills, and knowledge as relevant to their competence in performing their job.

Recent work by Cooper, Mitchell, Eckerle, and Martin (2016)

found several skill deficiencies among student affairs graduate preparation programs. Their work described the studies that have explored the degree to which graduate programs prepare entry-level professionals from the perspective of senior student affairs officers, supervisors of entry-level professionals, student affairs professionals themselves, and faculty responsible for graduate preparation. The authors identified seven common skill deficiencies among entry-level student affairs professionals: (a) budgeting and fiscal management; (b) strategic planning; (c) research, assessment, and evaluation; (d) legal knowledge and standards; (e) supervision; (f) technological competence; and (g) institutional and campus politics. Cooper and colleagues examined the graduate program directories from both the NASPA and ACPA–College Student Educators International websites and reviewed 138 master's-level graduate programs in student affairs. Through their qualitative content analysis, they were able to determine how graduate programs were addressing the seven skill deficiencies identified in the literature. Scholars have explored how advocacy work and social justice integrates with graduate preparation in student affairs as outlined in the following section.

Advocacy Work and Social Justice

Harrison's study (2014) found that coursework in student development theory and administration prepared students to do well in performing their jobs; however, coursework did not prepare students for advocacy work. The findings suggest that study participants relied on informal networks, such as mentors, to fill in the gaps on how to advocate and that participants' informal advocacy education came from outside of student affairs preparation programs—that is, from negotiating institutional contexts, navigating the limitations of numbers-driven assessment cultures, and managing the dynamics from hierarchal structures (Harrison, 2014).

More recently, Boss, Linder, Martin, Dean, and Fitzer (2018) looked at how new student affairs professionals engage a social justice lens in their work. Adopting a critical consciousness framework, the authors examined the ways in which student affairs professionals use theory in practice to enact their social justice perspectives. Their findings highlighted how participants struggled with the incompatibility of theories with the students with whom they worked—particularly regarding the hegemony of theories taught in their graduate programs and the inability to discuss theories with their colleagues. These findings confirm how new professionals navigate social justice in their practice and attest to the challenges they face in having sufficient theories to account for the complexities of student experiences, development, and identity.

Student affairs professionals who pursue graduate preparation are often encouraged to adopt a scholar–practitioner identity. Kupo (2014) explored the meaning of "scholar–practitioner" and the ways in which research can be used to demonstrate its impact. Evidence is key to understanding a program or unit's effectiveness—and it is particularly necessary now, as programs are under increasing pressure to demonstrate success. Kupo raised important questions on which scholar–practitioners can reflect, such as: What should I be doing to stay on the cutting edge of my field? How is the role of scholar-practitioner important on my campus? How is it important to me professionally? What resources do I have access to that help me integrate scholarship into my practice? What are successful strategies for scholar–practitioners, and how do I incorporate scholarship/ research/evidence into professional practice? Kupo's questions also help to identify and explain professional values. Kupo raises critical understanding of the agility needed not just to know but also to do. In other words, bridging theory to practice.

Generally, creativity has not been understood or framed as a competency within the student affairs profession or in relation to social justice work; however, creativity offers an opportunity to leverage new ideas, innovative practices, and alternative ways of doing student affairs work. The next section gives a brief overview of the standards and competencies adopted by leading higher education professional associations and how creativity can foster growth in these areas.

How Creativity Fits Within the ACPA and NASPA Professional Competency Areas

Professional competency areas for student affairs educators have been adopted by ACPA and NASPA, and a body of literature has identified the role of standards and competencies in higher education and student affairs graduate programs (Cuyjet, Longwell-Grice, & Molina, 2009; Dickerson et al., 2011; Eaton, 2016; Iverson & Seher, 2017; Liddell, Wilson, Pasquesi, Hirschy, & Boyle, 2014; Muller, Grabsch, & Moore, 2018).

Initially developed in 2009 and updated in 2015, *Professional Competency Areas for Student Affairs Educators* (ACPA & NASPA, 2015) constitutes a common set of 10 core areas in which student affairs professionals should be proficient: (a) personal and ethical foundations; (b) values, philosophy, and history; (c) assessment, evaluation, and research; (d) law, policy, and governance; (e) organizational and human resources; (f) leadership; (g) social justice and inclusion; (h) student learning and development; (i) technology; and (j) advising and supporting. These competencies are intended to set out the essential knowledge, skills, and dispositions expected of all student affairs professionals, regardless of functional area of specialization.

Eaton (2016) contended that the development of a competency-based movement in student affairs can be understood as a response to forces outside of education, such as societal and political pressures. Eaton raised critical questions about the linearity, fragmentation, and standardization that competencies can have on the field of student affairs, ultimately leading to reduction of complexity and watering down of concept. Creativity is a way to think critically about how to elevate student affairs practice beyond sheer competency. Creativity lets us think differently about the work we do, how we manage and respond to situations, and how we lead and encourage staff. Creativity allows for the complexity of student affairs practice of which Eaton (2016) encouraged, and it enables professionals to think critically and differently about how we achieve competence. Creativity fosters constant growth: How we work is being modified to address the situations we face. Creativity then enables us not just to sharpen our competency in professional areas but to do it in a way that fosters intellectual and professional growth.

A recent study by Iverson and Seher (2017) captured the impact that graduate programs had on the development of multicultural competence; participants included graduate students enrolled in two programs. The study adopted the Multicultural Competence for Student Affairs-Preliminary 2 Scale, which was developed by Pope and Reynolds (1997) to measure multicultural competence in a higher education context. The study authors wanted to assess the impact that diversity curriculum had on the graduate students when they entered the program, in the middle of their two-year program, and shortly after completion. Iverson & Seher (2017) suggested that diversity curriculum aids in the development of multicultural competence. Scholars have been interested in exploring how advocacy work and social justice is adopted by graduate students and early career professionals.

Creativity can be a way to embed social justice into the graduate curriculum. Creativity affords the opportunity to complicate how multicultural competence is achieved as well as how it is practiced. What are some innovative ways to support students of color, LGBTQIA students, student-parents, and other populations? The answer to this question is not stagnant and one that requires constant reflection and attention.

Creativity: How Does It Fit Within Higher Education?

You may be asking yourself, "But how does creativity fit into student affairs?" Or maybe even think, as I did: "I'm not creative." In many ways, creativity is not something we as student affairs professionals tend to think about when we identify our strengths, skills, or traits. However, we must allow ourselves to consider all the *many* and *daily* ways in which we engage in creative practice. When I reflected on this question, I realized that I am very much indeed creative. For example, as a first-generation student, I have used creativity to navigate myriad situations. As a first-generation college student, I constantly navigated unfamiliar spaces that required me to make sense of new situations and experiences. As a student affairs professional, I have developed new student programming and creatively problem-solved to stretch some funding. As a faculty member, I am constantly thinking of new ways to engage with my students, design assignments that are relevant to their professional practice and identities, and stay current in the field.

If there is one constant in higher education, it is change. The evolving landscape of higher education offers ample opportunities for student affairs professionals to stay current—as Kupo (2014) suggested and as many senior student affairs officers expect (Dickerson et al., 2011). Change is no longer optional, and student affairs professionals must navigate a higher education context with agility.

Creativity as the Medium for Change and Leadership

Puccio, Mance, and Murdock (2011) put forth powerful connections between change, leadership, and creativity. These three concepts are often considered separately, maybe even mutually exclusive, but Puccio et al. (2011) offered an intriguing approach to how creativity bridges leadership and change: "In today's world, stability is temporary at best; at worst, is an illusion. Therefore, successful leadership relies heavily on an individual's ability to effectively respond to change and to proactively drive change—in short, to be creative" (p. 5). Change is part of the experience of every student affairs professional, whether they are a first-year graduate student on a graduate assistantship or an experienced higher education professional leading a sizable division.

One example to this point is Kouzes and Posner's (1995) five leadership practices, which is a common construct taught in many graduate programs. The idea is that effective leaders engage in the following practices: (a) challenge the process; (b) inspire a shared vision; (c) enable others to act; (d) model the way; and (e) encourage the heart. Puccio et al. (2011) suggested that leaders engaged in these practices and activities require some creative process; this could include taking risks, challenging the status quo, or experimenting with new programming or practices. When adopting a creative approach or perspective, Kouzes and Posner's (1995) ethical principles embrace being creative and engaging in innovative practices.

One example of how I use creativity in the classroom is through an "I Am" poem assignment. The course teaches students about theoretical and conceptual frameworks of leadership. Students identify and explore notions of race, gender, and privilege in their own lives, exploring how these factors' influence and intersect with their leadership style and philosophy. In the "I Am" poem assignment, I describe and discuss how artmaking is a valid and important form of expression and ask students to write a poem that integrates how they understand themselves as educational leaders. Students are instructed to begin each stanza with the phrase "I am." Each stanza can address matters of oppression, pride, or privilege. Students can choose to write about their families, educational/schooling experiences, social messages, immigration/migration, economic background, and so on. As an arts-based assignment, the poem serves as a tool for students to express their reflections on their identities.

When I describe this assignment, students' typical questions include, "How long does it have to be?" "Does it have to be in APA Style?" and "Do I have to cite?" I recognize now that this might be because of the parameters we often place on assignments and how students, in turn, expect that guidelines will be in place (e.g., page length, formatting). What I realized through this assignment is the amount of anxiety students experience when they do not have those parameters in place. Not knowing what would be "enough" or "good" brought feelings of worry and unease. I even had students say, "I'm not creative" or "I'm not a poet." This assignment gave students a creative outlet they might not have otherwise had in graduate school. Not having guidelines (other than beginning statements with "I am") forced students to think differently about who they are and represent themselves in a new way. Although it might feel uncomfortable for some students, it pushes them to think differently about themselves—as artists.

Students share their "I Am" poems with their peers, and many students have told me that it is one of their favorite assignments and experiences in the graduate program. Students can work through feelings of unease and connect emotionally with their peers. They can share intimate details of experiences, feelings, and challenges that have shaped who they are as educational leaders. Equally critical is that students recognize that they are indeed creative.

Creativity as a Way to Engage with the ACPA and NASPA
Professional Competencies

Another example of how creativity fits into graduate preparation generally is by seeing how it can be viewed as the common thread across all the ACPA and NASPA (2015) professional competency areas. Puccio et al. (2011) provided rich examples of how innovation can be used in problem solving and in developing a creative mindset. Allowing for creativity to have a space in graduate preparation enables students to think beyond reaching a competency or mastery. In my Introduction to Student Affairs course, I describe how creativity is necessary in assessing and reaching competency in each of the 10 professional competency areas. Creativity affords student affairs professionals to think critically and engage in activities to develop competency.

Adoption of a creative mindset can begin with acknowledging that one is indeed creative. Creativity is not often a lens through which student affairs professionals view and operate. As Puccio et al. (2011) contended, change, leadership, and creativity should not be mutually exclusive; they provided five tenets that can be applied to a higher education context:

1. Creativity is a process that leads to change; deliberate change cannot be achieved without creativity.

2. By deliberately facilitating productive change, leaders help the individuals and organizations they influence grow.

3. Because leaders bring about change, creativity is a core leadership competence.

4. An individual's ability to think creatively and to facilitate creative thinking in others can be enhanced.

5. As individuals develop their creative thinking and master

those factors that promote creativity, they enhance their leadership effectiveness. (p. 289)

With these tenets in mind, I challenge readers to think about how creativity can foster the change that is inevitable in the workplace. Being creative, with the five tenets of Puccio et al. (2011) in mind, can foster the conditions necessary to develop ourselves and the students we serve.

One of the ways I have enabled students to think of themselves as being creative is by allowing them to see the daily ways in which they deal with change. I provide opportunities for them to recognize how they can adapt. I ask them to reflect on their comfort with change, uncertainty, and vagueness. I ask them to think about what is causing their discomfort with change. I ask them to take on new experiences at work or their graduate assistantship site that can stretch them professionally and expose them to new (possibly skill-building) experiences. I want them to realize that being creative is a process that leads to change. Being creative is how they can develop their professional competencies.

Conclusion

As a faculty member committed to preparing student affairs professionals, I no longer resist or deny creativity; it is something I now embrace and welcome. Adopting a creativity lens has helped me provide graduate students with opportunities to reflect on their identities and their practice. Higher education in general—and student affairs in particular—is well positioned to embrace creativity and the inevitable change that comes with it. Embracing creativity engages new realities that are no longer merely possibilities.

Unlock Your Creativity

Make time to stretch for a few minutes each day.

Every morning for one week, take just five minutes and write. You can write about anything; for example, what you are going to accomplish that day, what you are worried about, or what you are excited for the most.

References

ACPA–College Student Educators International & NASPA–Student Affairs Administrators in Higher Education. (2015). *Professional competency areas for student affairs educators.* Retrieved from https://www.naspa.org/images/uploads/main/ACPA_NASPA_Professional_Competencies_FINAL.pdf

Boss, G. J., Linder, C., Martin, J. A., Dean, S. R., & Fitzer, J. R. (2018). Conscientious practice: Post-master's student affairs professionals' perspectives on engaging social justice. *Journal of Student Affairs Research & Practice, 55*(4), 373–385.

Cooper, J., Mitchell, D., Jr., Eckerle, K., & Martin, K. (2016). Addressing perceived skill deficiencies in student affairs graduate preparation programs. *Journal of Student Affairs Research and Practice, 53*(2), 107–117.

Cuyjet, M. J., Longwell-Grice, R., & Molina, E. (2009). Perceptions of new student affairs professionals and their supervisors regarding the application of competencies learned in preparation programs. *Journal of College Student Development, 50*(1), 104–119.

Dickerson, A. M., Hoffman, J. L., Baramee, P. A., Brown, K. F., Vong, L. K., Bresciani, M. J., . . . & Oyler, J. (2011). A comparison of senior student affairs officer and student affairs preparation program faculty expectations of entry-level professional competencies. *Journal of Student Affairs Research and Practice, 48*(4), 463–479.

Eaton, P. W. (2016). The competency-based movement in student affairs: Implications for curriculum and professional development. *Journal of College Student Development, 57*(5), 573–589.

Harrison, L. (2014). How student affairs professionals learn to advocate: A phenomenological study. *Journal of College and Character, 15*(3), 165–178.

Iverson, S. V., & Seher, C. L. (2017). Investigating the development of graduate students' multicultural competence in student affairs professional preparation. *Journal on Excellence in College Teaching, 28*(1), 77–97.

Kouzes, J. M., & Posner, B. Z. (1995). *The leadership challenge: How to make extraordinary things happen in organizations.* San Francisco, CA: Wiley.

Kupo, L. V. (2014). Becoming a scholar-practitioner in student affairs. In G. L. Martin & M. S. Hevel (Eds.), *Research–driven practice in student affairs: Implications from the Wabash National Study of Liberal Arts Education* (New Directions for Student Services, No. 147, pp. 89–98). San Francisco, CA: Jossey-Bass.

Liddell, D. L., Wilson, M. E., Pasquesi, K., Hirschy, A. S., & Boyle, K. M. (2014). Development of professional identity through socialization in graduate school. *Journal of Student Affairs Research and Practice, 51*(1), 69–84.

Muller, K., Grabsch, D., & Moore, L. (2018). Factors influencing student affairs professionals' attainment of professional competencies. *Journal of Student Affairs Research & Practice, 55*(1), 54–64.

Pope, R., & Reynolds, A. (1997). Multicultural competence in student affairs: Integrating multicultural knowledge, awareness, and skills. *Journal of College Student Development, 38*, 266–277.

Puccio, G. J., Mance, M., & Murdock, M. C. (2011). *Creative leadership: Skills that drive change.* Thousand Oaks, CA: Sage.

Renn, K. A., & Jessup-Anger, E. R. (2008). Preparing new professionals: Lessons for graduate preparation programs from the National Study of New Professionals in Student Affairs. *Journal of College Student Development, 49*(4), 319–335.

Smith, L. N., Blixt, A. B., Ellis, S. E., Gill, S. J., & Kruger, K. (2015). *Leading innovation and change: A guide for chief student affairs officers on shaping the future.* Washington, DC: NASPA–Student Affairs Administrators in Higher Education.

8

LEADERSHIP, CREATIVITY, CURIOSITY, AND THE BLANK COMPUTER SCREEN

CISSY PETTY

"You have to be burning with an idea or problem, or a wrong that you want to right. If you're not passionate enough from the start, you'll never stick it out."

—Steve Jobs (Kerpen, 2014, para. 14)

It happens to all of us. Whether it is an annual report, board of trustees presentation, or a TED-like talk, many of us start our preparation by staring at a blank computer screen. As leaders in higher education, we are expected to be innovative and to guide the way to fresh discoveries with and for our students. The blank computer screen is a symbol of either a fresh start or a dreaded beginning; either way, the cursor keeps blinking at us.

This chapters looks at the blank screen as a welcome invitation for synthesizing fresh thoughts that have the capacity to turn into new ideas, concepts, programs, and relationships. Not everyone perceives a blank screen the same way; therefore, we will look at the concepts of creativity and curiosity in the workplace and, as leaders, discover the responsibility and opportunity to encourage innovation in work teams. The question remains: Is it possible that chief among the skills of a leader in higher education is the ability to foster both creativity and curiosity? "The leader's job is not to be the source of ideas but to encourage and champion ideas. Leaders must tap the imagination of employees at all ranks and ask inspiring questions. They also need to help their organizations incorporate diverse perspectives, which spur creative insights and facilitate creative collaboration" (Amabile & Khaire, 2008, para. 18). The creative process must allow for ideation and curiosity, two elements essential to building trust within a group of decision makers.

Defining Creativity and Curiosity

There are countless definitions of creativity and curiosity. For the purposes of this chapter, I use favorites that will resonate with the work we do in higher education. Kenneth Robinson, a British author, speaker, and international advisor on education, defined creativity this way: "There are two concepts to keep in mind: imagination and innovation. Imagination is the root of creativity. It is the ability to bring to mind things that aren't present to our senses. Creativity is putting your imagination to work. It is applied imagination. Innovation is putting new ideas into practice" (MindShift, 2015, para. 3). Similarly, Albert Einstein believed that "imagination is everything. It is the preview of life's coming attractions" (Albert Einstein quotes, 2017, para. 3). Let's look at a few definitions of curiosity and at the intersectionality of creativity and curiosity. Walt Disney described the very essence of being curious when he said, "We keep moving forward, opening new doors, and doing new things, because we're curious and curiosity keeps leading us down new paths" (Smith, 2018, para. 3). Looking at curiosity in a traditional academic way, Zora Neale Hurston (1942) wrote, "Research is formalized curiosity. It is poking and prying with a purpose" (p. 143). The intersectionality of curiosity and creativity helps leaders see new ways to solve problems and can facilitate amazing breakthroughs. The ability to test untried ideas can lead to enhanced programs and staff trust. Chief among the skills leaders need for success is the ability to foster a team's willingness to create, to be curious, and to be unafraid to fail. This kind of leadership brings inspiration to a team and allows for new solutions to old problems.

Curiosity, Creativity, and Leadership

Francesca Gino, an expert on the psychology of organizations, recently published an article in *Harvard Business Review* titled "The Business Case for Curiosity" that details how curiosity improves workers' adaptability and performance. She wrote, "When we are curious, we view tough situations creatively and have less defensive reactions to stress" (Gino, 2018, para. 11). Can you remember a time when you passionately presented an idea that was important to you? The feedback you received from your team members was supportive, but they requested significant changes. The ability to tap into curiosity allows you to encourage others to ask questions without retreating into a disappointed reaction when they do. This skill is essential for leaders and for leadership work teams. Curiosity about people, places, and things allows creativity to grow and encourages us to take risks and try new ideas.

In *Start With Why*, Simon Sinek (2009) brought the "why" question to the forefront of reflective leadership. Searching for "why" is a distinct and thoughtful way to model how to lead and how to deliver results. Sinek explained that everyone knows what they do and how to do it, but few people know *why* they do what they do. Understanding the "why" of student affairs work deepens and underscores its importance. Student affairs professionals have many opportunities to talk with families of first-year students. Our passion for their children's education, health, and wellness is reassuring to them and unveils the "why" of our work. The active pursuit of excellence through leading, teaching, service, and research ensures our capacity to continue to create and reimagine the profession. As leaders we must remain inquisitive not only about our field of study but also about the world around us; we must be able to envision projects and programs in new and resourceful ways. This is easier for some than for others, but all of us have the capacity to be curious and creative; creativity and curiosity are not limited to the artist, writer, performer, or scientist.

In the popular book *Strengths Based Leadership*, Tom Rath and Barry Conchie (2008) wrote about 34 identified strengths. In every strength—whether Strategic or Achiever—there is an element of creativity or curiosity. Research has shown that each of us has all 34 strengths but that we most often use our top 10 strengths—our go-to strengths. Ideation is among the 34 strengths, and people who lead with Ideation tend to be unafraid of new ideas; in fact, they embrace them. These leaders are apt to see connections among a variety of thoughts and ideas. To build trust in your vision, Rath and Conchie (2008) wrote,

> Make things simple. All your ideas and possibilities, and tangents can be confusing to some people. You see the simplicity of the underlying principles, articulate that to others so they

can see it too. The clearer things seem to people, the more certain they can be that you are doing what is right and makes sense. Help people make connections between what is and what can be. (p. 179)

This is especially important to bring a team together around groundbreaking new concepts, new leadership, or new programs.

Creativity and curiosity are particularly important to leaders with strong ideation; however, it is important to build mutually supportive relationships, and people with strong ideation skills tend to rock the boat. Rath and Conchie (2008) encouraged these leaders to also provide the team with a sense of stability:

You are always searching for ways to break from convention and look at things from a new angle. Verbalize the fact that you're not seeking to destroy what is—rather, you want to make things better. You understand that security doesn't come from maintaining the status quo and doing things the way they've always been done; security is about making sure you are prepared for the future. (p. 180)

Leadership should embrace the important role of creativity and curiosity in the workplace.

Sebastian Bailey and Octavius Black (2014), authors of *Mind Gym: Achieve More by Thinking Differently*, presented research on the human ability to use mental shortcuts and operate on autopilot, and the need to learn to challenge assumptions about different aspects of our work. Change is difficult for most people; the ability to use creativity and curiosity is paramount to leadership success. That said, how are curiosity and the creative process supported by leadership, and how might they be stifled?

Creativity and Curiosity Short-Circuited

The following are 10 ways a team can hamper the flow of creativity and curiosity in the workplace.

1. **Fear of being wrong.** Okay, go ahead and say it out loud: "I was wrong." What happened? Nothing. Being wrong is not the end of the world. In fact, after a leader admits fault or admits that something didn't go as planned, the members of the team often feel relief and a willingness to venture forth on their own creative journey. It is okay to fail. Fear of failing or not measuring up to someone else's ideal stifles creativity and curiosity. Remember the old adage: FEAR = False Expectations Appearing Real.

2. **We always do it this way.** If you are a new employee and you are met daily with "No, we do X, not Y, and we've always done it that way," you know it is a spirit killer. New employees have new eyes, new experiences, and a freshness that should be celebrated. Doing things the same old way kills the joy of new discovery. In the right environment and under a supportive and creative leader, staff can invent and reinvent programs and projects.

3. **Staying in your lane.** The idea that you have to work in your own area and not cooperate or collaborate is detrimental to the employee, the team, and the entire institution. The essence of creative power is often captured when people from a variety of areas come together to solve problems. We are so much stronger working together on new ideas and helping them flourish. Collaboration encourages creativity—step out of your comfort zone! We often use the excuse that collaborating takes too much time, and it's easier to do it yourself. This attitude is almost always a mistake and a trust buster.

4. **Too many ideas!** When you are working on a project, you can become so overwhelmed with thoughts and ideas that it can be difficult to focus on a single task. You find yourself evaluating ideas at the same time you are trying to create. Your mind becomes full and it is hard to concentrate. Rather than giving up, take a break. Clear your head, get fresh air, exercise, read a book, or watch a mindless movie, and then return to your project. We all need downtime.

5. **You are not the expert.** Do not let this idea drag your confidence down. You do not have to be an expert in every area to have innovative ideas. Everyone should be invited to participate in finding solutions to issues and creating new practices. Have the confidence to share what you see as possible.

6. **Creativity is a talent.** Many people believe that creativity is only for writers and artists, but this is just not true. The belief that you are not creative is self-imposed. All of us have the potential to draw on inspiration, to see things in a new light, and to discover unexpected solutions to problems.

7. **Being perfect.** This stops the creative process every time. Worrying about not getting something right often keeps things from actually getting started. Think about the times you have started to write a blog or speech and you erase the opening line a dozen times. Sometimes the imperfect idea or random thought that seems totally out of reach ends up being the answer. Sometimes it is all in the flow. Stay curious.

8. **Being too busy.** In her article "How to Train Your Brain to See What Others Don't," Carolyn Gregoire (2017) said that "daydreaming involves a very active brain state that gives the wandering mind the ability to stumble upon sudden and incredible insight" (para. 7). In other words, we must become

daydream believers! Downtime and alone time are important for the creative process. Leaders need to routinely schedule time to create, time to ideate, and time to synthesize.

9. **Not asking questions.** The fear of looking foolish or silly keeps us from involving ourselves more deeply in conversations and asking questions that might lead to better outcomes. When we ask questions, we acknowledge that we are curious and open to learning. "Leading with curiosity rather than authority creates a collaborative learning environment where shared explorations of possible solutions to genuine questions flourish. The process is rewarding for all and the results allow a team to accelerate through the power of the many" (Parsons & Millham, n.d., para. 4).

10. **Groupthink.** Frans Johansson (2006), author of *The Medici Effect*, wrote, "Innovation is more likely when people of different disciplines, backgrounds, and areas of expertise share their thinking." We are accustomed to not bringing up divergent views, because we don't want to make waves. Sometimes it seems easier to "play nice," but a lack of candor does not foster trust in a team. Agreeing just to agree doesn't make us better colleagues.

If you can build a team with curious and creative members, you will have richer discussions and often breakthroughs on difficult issues, processes, and policies.

Flipside: How Leaders Support Creativity and Curiosity

Leadership support for innovative thinking is imperative for success. The role of the creative leader is not to generate all the ideas but to create a culture in which everyone has an opportunity to be inventive and team members are confident of their worth. Leaders can use the following methods to support collaboration and the delivery of innovative ideas.

1. **Create the climate.** You must be supportive of a kind of collaboration—almost like think tanks—in which groups of colleagues regularly meet to share new concepts and ideas. Do not micromanage or feel the need to control the outcome. Build a culture of trust and safety. Lead through your actions.

2. **Set the table.** Ask "Who should be at the table?" Leaders and group members often have go-to people whom they run ideas by for comment. Challenge groupthink by including diverse thoughts, opinions, and styles in ideating and decision-making. Research supports the idea that diverse team members working together, with many different views and experiences, tend to be more creative.

3. **Gather feedback.** In your leadership role, be an active listener and make yourself available to your team for continuous feedback. Feedback is a vital element of staff engagement and continuous improvement. Sam Walton, the founder of Walmart, advised, "Outstanding leaders go out of the way to boost the self-esteem of their personnel. If people believe in themselves, it's amazing what they can accomplish" (Pozin, 2015, para. 11).

4. **Trust your skill set.** Artists, musicians, writers, inventors, and scientists have not cornered the market on creativity and curiosity. Believe in your own creative leadership. Think critically about what you do well. Deepen the "well of learning" at every opportunity, and acknowledge first to yourself and then to others your areas of expertise. Believe in your own worth.

5. **Say "and."** Leaders can support creativity and curiosity by saying "and" instead of "but" in team conversations. Leading

with "but" in a discussion automatically negates the idea offered. To build trust, do not take the leader role in all group meetings; let the conversations flow. There should be very little evaluation when sharing ideas.

6. **Give specific and limited direction.** Great leaders give the members of their team the final destination and allow them to navigate and steer. A team appreciates basic guidelines and goal parameters that give its members room to ideate, create, and deliver results. This is the ultimate of a trusting leader; to let go of the reins means the team together is stronger than any single contributor.

7. **Remember that curiosity did not kill the cat.** Leaders should feel comfortable asking "Why?" and "What would we do if we knew we would not fail?" "Nothing kills curiosity like a risk-averse, play-it-safe leader. To spark creativity, be curious and bring a beginner's mind to the problem," (Forbes Coaches Council, 2017, para. 18). Leaders must be comfortable admitting both the successes and failures of new ideas. Growth comes from trial and error, especially where innovative ideas are cultivated.

8. **Be an active learner.** It is important to stay current in your discipline and to stretch and be curious about other fields that intersect. Spend time reading for growth and pleasure. Challenge yourself in areas in which you know you need improvement, such as writing, speaking, or research. "No one said being a good leader is easy. It takes a lot of energy, focus, and, most of all, a lot of learning" (Fein, 2018, p. 1). Continuous learning is a commitment to yourself and your profession.

9. **Breathe.** Take time for reflection and discernment. If we think we are too busy for downtime, we are not caring for

ourselves. We do not set a good example for the team by putting a premium on business. It has to be okay to sometimes step back so our sense of purpose can become clearer. "Self-reflection is The School of Wisdom" (Gracián, 1992, p. 39). We gain so much more when we can detach long enough for new ideas to come to us. We have stronger teams that are more creative when we realize "reflection is what links our performance to our potential. It is the process of properly unpacking ourselves as leaders for the good of others" (Kail, 2012, para. 3). It is extremely important as creative leaders to know when we have done something wrong and to ask ourselves how we could have done better.

10. **Risk failing.** One thing we should learn from our mistakes is that they are not fatal. "To have no fear of failure does not imply a cavalier attitude or that someone has been given a pass. In fact, it is just the opposite. Courage is what makes the leader" (Burnison, 2011, para. 3). If you are a leader and oversee a team, the team will fail you and you will fail the team. Leaders and teams are not all-knowing. Mistakes happen. People are human. If you are presented with a tough situation, give it your best shot, learn, and move on. You will live to see another day, another win. Be gentle with yourself and others.

Creativity, Curiosity, and Leadership as Art

Max De Pree (1989), in *Leadership Is an Art*, concluded, "Leadership is much more an art, a belief, a condition of the heart, than a set of things to do. The visible signs of artful leadership are expressed, ultimately, in its practice" (p. 148). De Pree reminded us that creativity, curiosity, and leadership are aligned with team trust and integrity. Leaders and artists have a great deal in common: Both use their imaginations to inspire new ways of thinking, feeling, and being. Leading and creating require self-discipline and a curious mind; together, these attributes inspire imagination.

I encourage you to go back over both of the lists in this chapter. Jot down how you felt reading the lists. What resonated with you and why? How will you nurture your creative spirit? As the leader, will you allow time for the members of your team to be curious about the project at hand without steering them to a forgone conclusion? Leadership is actually a creative journey; use your skills often.

As a leader, you have an enormous responsibility and opportunity to nurture and support your organization's drive to be creative and innovative. While it is mission-critical to define organizational goals, initiate strategic planning, and hire for success, it is equally important to foster a diverse, inclusive, and creative environment. And one more thing: Have fun!

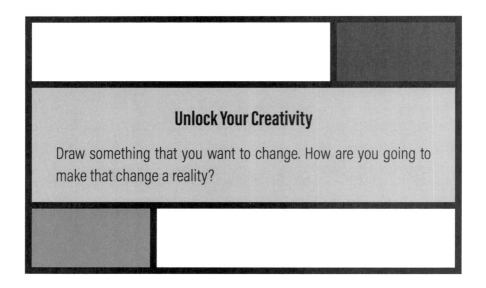

Unlock Your Creativity

Draw something that you want to change. How are you going to make that change a reality?

References

Albert Einstein quotes. (2017). Retrieved from https://beinspiredchannel.com/top-inspiring-albert-einstein-quotes

Amabile, T., & Khaire, M. (2008, October). Creativity and the role of the leader. *Harvard Business Review.* Retrieved from http://www.hbr.org/2008/10/creativity-and-the-role-of-the-leader

Bailey, S., & Black, O. (2014). *Mind gym: Achieve more by thinking differently.* New York, NY: HarperCollins.

Burnison, G. (2011, May 5). If you fear failure, you've already failed. *Forbes.* Retrieved from https://www.fastcompany.com/1751300/if-you-fear-failure-youve-already-failed

De Pree, M. (1989). *Leadership is an art.* New York, NY: Doubleday.

Fein, P. (2018, June 26). The 6 competencies every active leader needs. *Chief Learning Officer.* Retrieved from https://www.chieflearningofficer.com/2016/10/20/6-competencies-every-active-leader-needs

Forbes Coaches Council. (2017, December 21). *15 ways leaders can promote creativity in the workplace* [Blog post]. Retrieved from https://www.forbes.com/sites/forbescoachescouncil/2017/12/21/15-ways-leaders-can-promote-creativity-in-the-workplace/#2968e20d58ef

Gino, F. (2018, December 18). Why curiosity matters. *Harvard Business Review.* Retrieved from https://hbr.org/2018/09/curiosity

Gracián, B. (1992). *The art of worldly wisdom: A pocket oracle* (C. Maurer, Trans.). New York, NY: Doubleday.

Gregoire, C. (2017, December 7). How to train your brain to see what others don't. *Huffington Post.* Retrieved from https://www.huffpost.com/entry/insights-brain_n_3795229

Hurston, Z. N. (1942). *Dust tracks on a road.* New York, NY: Harper Perennial Modern Classics.

Johansson, F. (2006). *The Medici effect: What elephants and epidemics can teach us about innovation.* Boston, MA: Harvard Business School Press.

Kail, E. (2012, March 9). Leadership character: The role of reflection. *The Washington Post.* Retrieved from http://www.washingtonpost.com/blogs/guest-insights/post/leadership-character-the-role-of-reflection/2011/04/04/gIQAdJOr1R_blog.html?utm_term=.a44b5f46d288

Kerpen, D. (2014, March 27). 15 things you need to know about passion. *Inc.* Retrieved from https://www.inc.com/dave-kerpen/15-quotes-on-passion-to-inspire-a-better-life.html

MindShift. (2015, April 22). Sir Ken Robinson: Creativity is in everything, especially teaching. Retrieved from https://www.kqed.org/mindshift/40217/sir-ken-robinson-creativity-is-in-everything-especially-teaching

Parsons, G., & Milham, A. (n.d.). What kind of leader are you? *The Curious Leader.* Retrieved from http://www.thecuriousleader.com

Pozin, I. (2015, September 2). 16 leadership quotes to inspire you to greatness. *Forbes.* Retrieved from https://www.forbes.com/sites/ilyapozin/2014/04/10/16-leadership-quotes-to-inspire-you-to-greatness/#7f38372067ad

Rath, T., & Conchie, B. (2008). *Strengths based leadership: Great leaders, teams, and why people follow.* New York, NY: Gallup Press.

Sinek, S. (2009). *Start with why: How great leaders inspire everyone to take action.* New York, NY: Portfolio.

Smith, J. (2018, October 18). *Creating a culture of curiosity: Why curiosity matters in business* [Blog post]. Retrieved from https://blog.procore.com/creating-a-culture-of-curiosity-why-curiosity-matters-in-business

9

CREATIVE LESSONS IN LEADERSHIP FROM BOTH ENDS OF THE CAREER JOURNEY

FRANK R. LAMAS AND AMANDA STEWART

L eadership—especially creative leadership—presents differently in professionals across all levels of higher education, and how that creativity is practiced can offer inspiration for serving students and institutions more imaginatively. This chapter explores the intersections of how a mid-level professional and a vice president for student affairs and enrollment management see creativity in leadership: One has more than 40 years of experience in the field, and one has 5 years of experience. Here, they share the lessons learned and creative disruptions that have informed their practice.

The examples that follow are from experiences at multiple institutions, in various positions, across a range of divisions of student affairs and will likely be relatable to professionals at all levels. We hope that these insights will inspire deep thinking to support students in a way that is innovative, energizing, and forward looking. A variety of experiences, different stages in careers, and levels of education are present in large organizations, but a shared vision, purpose, and alignment of resources can take any organization from good to great (Collins, 2001).

Dreaming big and making a difference for those served is the ultimate goal of student affairs and higher education. In our fast-paced, ever-changing, and complex world, institutions require creative leaders with passion and courage. Throughout this chapter are questions called "disrupt and reflect." These questions are posed to help you think more creatively about your work—no matter what stage of your career you are in. We also hope that you check out the multimedia resources, which will allow you to explore some of these concepts further.

Both Frank Lamas and Amanda Stewart work at California State University, Fresno. Frank is the vice president of student affairs and enrollment management; Amanda is the coordinator of communications and media for the Division of Student Affairs. Although they work in the same office, at the same institution, in the same division, the paths they took to end up at Fresno State are very dissimilar. They have differing levels of education and have had very different experiences. They are at different stages in their careers.

They see leadership differently.

They see creativity differently.

These are their stories.

This chapter is structured as a dialogue between Amanda and Frank. The conversation is narrated to help readers understand the culture and to keep the story organized.

Part One: Being Creative Means Owning Your Story

As with all stories, it is important to understand where the characters are coming from in order to better situate where they are going. Amanda and Frank begin by talking about their education before college and family backgrounds.

Growing Up

FRANK R. LAMAS: Well, where should we start? The beginning?

AMANDA STEWART: The beginning is always a good place to start. I think a big part of being a creative leader means being brave enough to own your stories, so maybe we should share a bit about our stories.

FRL: I was born in Havana, Cuba. My mom was sick, and we left Cuba to come to the United States when I was 3 years old. None of us in my family spoke English. I learned English from watching TV, from other family members with whom we connected in Syracuse, New York, and from playing outside with other kids in the neighborhood.

AS: I was born in New Jersey. We moved around a lot when I was growing up—Missouri, Colorado, Illinois—and I learned how to make friends very quickly. I have two younger brothers. I always thought I wanted to be a teacher—until I got older and realized that kids have a lot of germs.

FRL: When I started school at age 5, my English was okay, and I had plenty of powerful role models who believed in me: teachers, my parents, family members, and coaches. As I grew up, I became an athlete—basketball, baseball, and track. Sports gave me another space where I belonged. I guess that would be where I first started to understand what a "sense of belonging" means, even though I didn't realize it at the time.

AS: I experienced that with sports, too, a sense of belonging. I'm tall, so I played basketball. I wasn't the best player, but I did it for the community and to feel a part of something. It gave me a space where I didn't feel like such an outsider and so awkward in my own skin. That is so interesting, because both of us are very passionate about fostering a sense of belonging in all students at Fresno State in the division of student affairs at enrollment management. I see belonging being something that is very important to you, Dr. Lamas, as a leader.

FRL: Yes, belonging is so important, and it is integral to student success.

AS: Does anything else stand out to you about your high school years?

FRL: I was fortunate to go to a good high school where I continued to develop leadership and athletic skills. I served on student government, was class president, and was captain of the basketball team.

AS: Wow, you were super involved in high school! I was too shy in high school to be very involved.

FRL: Did anything stand out to you in high school? Foreshadowing your career in student affairs?

AS: I got good grades, was quiet, and kept to myself. So no, not really. [laughs]

From early on in this dialogue, the differences in personalities and styles of these two leaders is evident. Amanda was shy and thought she would end up becoming a teacher; Frank was an athlete. Yet both found belonging through sports.

College

FRL: I am a first-generation college student. I went to college on some athletic scholarship money, and I was the first in my family to receive a college degree.

AS: I am an Iowa State University legacy student. I knew I would go to Iowa State because I grew up in a family of Cyclones: my parents and grandfather attended there, and I knew that was where I would attend as well.

FRL: While I was in college, I decided that education was my calling. I went on to pursue my master's and my PhD.

AS: I don't know if anyone in my family ever expected me to continue my education past college, but they were supportive. At Iowa State, I was very involved. I was a resident assistant and worked in orientation and admissions. Most days, I felt like classes were getting in the way of all of the other things that I felt energized by, like my involvement experiences. It made me feel like I belonged, and when a mentor told me, "You know, you can do this as a career," I decided to go to graduate school. After changing my major 11 times and struggling with "what I wanted to be when I grew up," it felt good to finally have a path.

The Journey

FRL: My 41 years in higher education have taken me on adventures that I am grateful for every day. I started my career as many student affairs professionals do: in residence life. I see higher education as a way of looking at society with the role of creating educated individuals and a workforce. There is an economic impact of higher education. My higher education journey has been more like a marathon than a sprint.

AS: As a marathon runner, I love a good marathon analogy! My higher education journey has been full of hills and windy roads. I have found myself feeling ashamed of those curves and bumps before, until I realized that they've made me stronger. I'll expand more on that later.

FRL: I can relate to those feelings about the bumps. What I've learned is that you have to step up when you are called upon. I took risks and rose to occasions when I was tapped to. When I was a young professional, for example, my vice president was accepted for a prestigious role in a higher education organization. It gave me the opportunity not only to learn but to enhance my skills and get experience. While he was gone, I was responsible for the division. I was fortunate enough to have that experience because I had built a trusting relationship with my vice president at the time. I jumped into the role and started to learn everything that I could so that I could be well versed and one day ready to be a vice president myself.

AS: Did you always know you wanted to be a vice president? And what decisions did you make along the way to get there?

FRL: Yes, becoming a vice president was my goal for a very long time. I always went the extra mile; I always did more than what was required in my job. It was never just about the job but about obtaining and cultivating the skill sets and relationships I could learn from others. It takes creativity to do that, because it requires you to have an open mind when there are doors in front of you. You can't stand in one place if you want to get to where you want to go. You have to own your story and embrace the opportunities that have been given to you.

AS: That makes sense. I have had a rough start to the profession, and I've felt sometimes like I wasn't cut out for this work. I've worked on seven campuses already in my short amount of time in the field. I haven't done a lot of standing in one place. Including graduate school, I had only been in the field for five years, but Fresno State was already my eighth institution.

FRL: Eighth? Wow! How did that happen?

AS: I was laid off from my first role after graduate school. I had only worked there for three months before they announced that the campus was shutting down. The second campus I worked at eliminated the programs that I was hired to recruit for just a few months after I was hired. It has been a bumpy journey, but what it taught me was a lot of resilience and a lot about the kind of leader that I never want to be. Some of the things that I value the most have come from what I've learned from those challenging experiences. I used to internalize a lot of those experiences and felt like there was something wrong with me. Working on different campuses has given me a lens that now I am so thankful for—even though it was really challenging at the time.

Even though they work in the same office, in very close proximity, Frank and Amanda realized in this conversation that there was still a lot they did not know about each other. Being creative in your leadership means taking the time to get to know people for who they truly are.

FRL: One thing that I have learned throughout the years is to always have a vision. I strive to be a leader who not only has a vision but also inspires a shared vision among our team in complex and ever-changing environments.

AS: I can speak to that after working with you for two-and-a-half years. You always have a vision.

FRL: The thing that I have learned is that it's easy to have a vision. Where the magic happens is when you can inspire others to align with and live out your vision until it becomes all of your vision.

AS: How do you do that?

FRL: Forward progress happens in higher education institutions and departments when there is a clear vision. A creative leader understands where the team is headed and aligns resources, people, and funding on a shared vision that is centered on best practices. In order for a vision to be lived out and practiced, resources must be considered as a first step to this process.

AS: People support what they help to create. You have to make your story, their story, until it's our story.

FRL: Exactly. When your organization is living out a vision that benefits those you serve, everyone wins. It is hard to create something extraordinary without a plan, like building a house.

AS: I think I have an example of that. One of the best teams that I've ever been a part of was the leadership of the programming board that I advised in graduate school. My fellow advisor and I were always in sync, and although I had a lot to learn from him, he was able to inspire a shared vision not only in us as leaders but in our students as well. It made everything that we accomplished as a board more powerful. He did it by asking what I thought a lot; I always felt a part of his process.

FRL: I have always been someone who doesn't like to play it safe: Go big or go home.

AS: That's very true. One thing that I notice is that I never feel nervous coming to you with an idea, no matter how wild it may seem. You have a very open mind when it comes to leadership and innovation, which makes it easy for me to come to you with ideas.

Through varying leadership opportunities and experiences at different institutions, Frank and Amanda are able to weave their stories together to offer valuable lessons. A lot of creative leadership stems from listening to one another and creating spaces where people feel comfortable bringing their whole selves into the equation.

Space

AS: I think it's really interesting when leaders use space in creative ways to facilitate learning, collaboration, and leadership. How have you seen space utilized creatively from a leadership perspective in your career?

FRL: When I was at Ithaca College, I first began to see and understand how much facilities impact and shape the environment for students. The spaces that we had there—or did not have—impacted student success, socialization, and learning. These spaces also gave me an appreciation for how I, as a professional, can shape environments in a creative way to impact students and the campus community. In building the new student union on Fresno State's campus, we have been making very intentional decisions about space in that building to cultivate a home-away-from-home experience for students.

Additional Resources

Read: Morgan Harper Nichols Blog

https://morganharpernichols.com/blog

Writer, artist, and musician Morgan Harper Nichols makes her work around people and their stories. She invites people to submit their stories to her website, and she creates art inspired by what they send her.

Watch: Are You Hooked on the Story of Your Struggle?

http://www.oprah.com/own-super-soul-sunday/brene-brown-are-you-hooked-on-the-story-of-your-struggle-video#ixzz60jvoCNql

Brené Brown, research professor at the University of Houston, explains the first phase in every healthy comeback: reckoning. When we fail, we tend to make a story about why we messed up—often based on faulty, biased information. Some of us become addicted to our stories, endlessly looping them in our heads. Ultimately, we must acknowledge what we're feeling in those difficult, confused moments—and be curious enough to figure out why we're feeling it.

Part Two: What Kind of Creative Leader Do You Want to Be?

AS: Much of what I've learned about leadership came from the environments that I've been in, the leaders I've worked for, and the decisions I've seen made at various institutions. As a young professional with a lot to learn, I have found myself soaking in lessons in all of the places I have been in. You have to study what is right in front of you.

FRL: Ha! Do you study me?

AS: Every day! What kind of leaders have you learned creative lessons from?

FRL: I think the creative leaders that I have learned the most from are the ones who aren't afraid to dream big and throw ideas out there to colleagues and their team that might seem far-fetched or out of reach.

Additional Resources

Listen: Know Your Values + Aaron Dignan on Brave New Work

*https://accidentalcreative.com/podcasts/ac/
know-your-values-aaron-dignan-on-brave-new-work*

This episode of *The Accidental Creative* podcast discusses how to establish a decision-making matrix and explores a framework for re-imagining how organizations function in the accelerating and ever-changing marketplace.

Reflect: Build Reflection Into Your Month

https://passionplanner.com/monthly-reflection

Passion Planner is a tool that helps you break down your short and long-term goals and incorporate them into your daily life. It is designed to encourage you to plan for the future, reflect on the past, but most importantly, act on the present.

Part 3: Application of Creative Lessons Learned

Although Frank and Amanda are at very different stages of their leadership journeys, both have applied lessons in leadership in various contexts across their experiences and involvement in higher education organizations.

FRL: I would say, look for new possibilities everywhere and use data and assessment in your dreaming. I set a high bar for goals— both for myself and for my team. Once you, as a creative leader, align your resources with your vision, you can move forward into the dreaming phase of organizational leadership and focus on what might have the highest impact (e.g., programming, resources, facilities) for those whom you serve.

AS: So, that means risk-taking too, right? But how do you know when a risk is too big?

FRL: Dreaming does not just mean dreaming within the bounds of what you think might be possible; it means dreaming bigger than you ever have before. Playing it safe yields mediocre results.

AS: You do set a high bar, but I like working for a leader who sets the bar high. You believe that we can all rise to the occasion. I appreciate that you don't accept the status quo.

FRL: Set a high bar for yourself and your teams, and change your mentality to one that has a big, lasting impact on your organization and on students served. Addressing challenges and opportunities is what helps organizations to go from good to great [Collins, 2001].

AS: I also believe in setting a high bar for myself and others. I think that when we hold ourselves to the highest of standards, others follow suit.

FRL: Over the course of my career I have learned that student affairs professionals can impact change and create environments that facilitate students' sense of belonging, which in turn improves their experience.

AS: It makes our jobs very cool, when you think about it. In how many industries do you get to create and build communities and environments in this way? I think that's a big lesson that I've been learning: the responsibility that we have to create.

FRL: We do have a responsibility to create. Higher education is not going to stop evolving, so we need to learn how to be comfortable evolving with it. Adaptability goes a long way. Our environments are fast paced and ever changing. Creative leaders are adaptable, and they set the tone and direction for the team. Leading by example, with adaptability, goes a long way.

AS: Do you have an example of what those adaptation skills look like in practice?

FRL: I am constantly evolving and adjusting my sails, depending on what is happening in front of me at the time. Being a leader is often a big juggling act, which requires me to adapt all the time. The pace of the leader sets the pace of the pack, and showing your team that you can adapt when new challenges are presented is important leadership modeling. Being adaptable also means that you are not afraid of change—that you can lean into discomfort and the unknown. Change is inevitable; our environments do not remain static. Having the skills to adapt to what's in front of you as well as what is down the road (one to three years and beyond) is important to leadership, organizational health, and well-being.

In my experience, when you work on different campuses and you come in to a new setting, you adapt to the way things are done there. Sometimes, when things are different, that does not mean that it is not a best practice. Another example of adapting is when new leadership comes to the institution that you currently work at, and you need to adapt to the new direction or look for what is next is your career.

AS: I think that listening is a big part of being an adaptive leader. We must listen, learn, and be thoughtful and empathetic—and then decide our direction as a team for how to move forward with what is in front of us. Although change can be difficult, if done right and with listening and empathy, change gives us reasons and courage to move organizations to a great and even better place. We have to all work together.

FRL: Right. I see organizations as very interconnected. I strive to break down silos: Because of finite resources in people and dollars, it's more important than ever that we work together. Also, we must address students' needs in a holistic way; students don't take things in one piece at a time; rather, they process the whole picture. Serving the greater good is the path that I have chosen to take.

AS: Adaptability has been key in my career already. During the years of being laid-off, through campus closures, and during a cross-country move, I found myself questioning everything about higher education, student affairs, and if I chose the path that was right for me. I questioned if I had made a mistake in getting my master's in something so niche like student affairs and if I really did have any transferable skills at all. I doubted myself, the choices I had made, and the field I was in.

FRL: What is something that you did to be more comfortable with all of the questioning and the change?

AS: My involvement outside of my job is what actually led me to land my current role at Fresno State. My educational background is not in marketing, but I learned so much in my involvement in professional organizations. I uncovered the passion that I have for storytelling and using digital tools to build connection. It was my professional organizations that provided an escape from the realities of my job in my first few years out of graduate school. No one really prepares you for what that transition is like from graduate school to the "real world." You finish your master's degree. You realize that even with a master's you are making significantly less (dare I say *half*) of what your friends from college are making in other fields. You spend months in a highly competitive job search only to realize that maybe you accepted the wrong one. You spend two years in a cohort of people with faculty who support you and then all of the sudden that's gone too. You're alone. You're unhappy. You blame yourself— or at least that's what I did. My professional organizations were what kept me connected. I got involved in a few in higher education (National Association for Campus Activities, NASPA–Student Affairs Administrators in Higher Education) as well as one outside of higher education (The Niche Movement). I wrote and reflected often. I blogged regularly for The Student Affairs Collective as well as for my own personal blog. Those experiences kept me engaged and active in the field while I rode out the turbulence in my first few roles.

FRL: Professional organizations have also been immensely important in my career. NASPA has been my professional home, and the connections that I have made through NASPA have propelled me.

Reflection is an important part of creative leadership and also a part of listening and dialoguing with one another.

AS: As you reflect on your career, what are some lessons that you would want to share with newer professionals?

FRL: Sometimes students or newer professionals will come into my office and say, "I want to be you someday." My response is usually something along the lines of: "Do you understand what that means? Do you know the work that you have to do, the time this means away from family, that there is a price to pay?" I don't share that to discourage anyone who has a goal of becoming a vice president but to shed light on the fact that our work isn't always easy.

AS: I think we need to share the truth more often and be more authentic and vulnerable about our experiences. I think we need to talk more about the hard and messy stuff.

FRL: Sometimes that can be hard, but I agree. I think it's hard because a lot of people don't like change. My least favorite thing to hear is, "This is the way that we've always done things." I believe in analyzing environments and considering if the way things are currently being done is truly the best way. I don't like to simply maintain the status quo but to facilitate organized disruption for the betterment of our students and their experiences—even when it's tough.

AS: I also believe that you can learn something from everyone you meet. Being able to thread all of those things that you learn together, to develop your own personal style, is an art form.

FRL: I would say to learn lessons from those who inspire you and also those who can teach you what "not to do" someday. I swore when I was in charge that I was going to do things differently and look at things in a different way. I have stayed on that path. I also keep the "Serenity Prayer" in my office to keep me grounded, especially on the challenging days.

AS: How does the "Serenity Prayer" help you?

FRL: It gives me the strength to understand what I can't change and also the courage to know what I can take on.

AS: I know that I would say that I've observed that you are very comfortable pushing the status quo all across campus, not just in your division. You always strive to be the best and to advocate for student success and the Division of Student Affairs and Enrollment Management across the entire campus. You see what we do in student affairs differently. You draw on your experiences at other institutions and package them all together in a framework that then helps our organization. Your creativity comes from learning, experiences, the journey, a thirst for knowledge, and the way you see organizations and student success.

Conclusion

Creative leadership means thinking about how to pass the baton to the next generation of professionals. How is what you are doing now changing the game for the students and professionals who will follow? Draw from lessons that you learn from your colleagues and other professionals—no matter where they are in their careers, no matter what their stories look like.

Although conventional wisdom may be helpful, as the student affairs field evolves and situations change, leaders need to come to their teams with different ideas and level the playing field for success; this calls for innovative, outside-the-box thinking, which will help transform teams and environments—and ensure that students succeed.

Higher education leaders of the future also must understand changing student populations. This is essential: A cookie-cutter approach will not work in our field. More and more each day, factors such as socioeconomic status, gender, race, and so on influence student success. We need to challenge the thinking of the past and starting planning for the students of today—and the students of the future.

Keep learning. Keep growing.

Unlock Your Creativity

Engage in an activity, exercise, or experience that you don't normally do. Choose someone to whom you don't usually reach out, and discuss change, creativity, and innovation. How did that conversation go and what did you learn?

Reference

Collins, J. (2001). *Good to great*. New York, NY: HarperCollins.

SECTION 2

INTERSECTIONS BETWEEN DIVERSITY, INCLUSION, AND CREATIVE LEADERSHIP

10

IT COMES FROM DEEP WITHIN

Spirituality and the Creative Process

MICHELE C. MURRAY

Twenty years ago, I moved next door to Beth Ann. I was new to the quaint neighborhood of Baltimore rowhouses, but Beth Ann had been born in her home 70 years prior, and it was the only home she had known. Every afternoon Beth Ann would play the baby grand piano that was the centerpiece of her otherwise modest living room. Through the wall we shared, she treated me to an endless string of Carnegie-Hall-worthy performances. Charging anthems, melancholic melodies, and happy little tunes—Beth Ann played them all, though none were pieces I recognized. Intrigued, I asked Beth Ann about her favorite compositions to play. Her response absolutely floored me: "Oh, I don't use sheet music. I sit down and just play what's in my heart." She went on to say, "You know, I'm not a religious woman, but when I sit down to play, I know that God exists. My fingers play the song in my heart like a prayer, and I feel like God is there."

Beth Ann's piano playing was a spiritual experience for her: an expression of her deepest longings for peace and understanding, an outlet for her frustration and heartache, and her "prayer" of thanksgiving. Her honest admission was the first time I had ever thought about creativity as having spiritual dimensions. I moved out of the neighborhood 13 years ago, but that interaction with Beth Ann stays with me; it is the foundation of this chapter.

Over the next few pages, creativity will be explored not simply as a mental process but also as a spiritual one that communicates meaning and purpose and can give rise to interpersonal connection. The concepts of flow, vocation, and generativity will elucidate the spiritual aspects of creativity. Mindfulness, silence, and other spiritual resources can serve as guides when we struggle to be creative. The chapter concludes with the "virtues of creativity."

Connecting the Creative With the Spiritual

"Nothing comes from nothing." So go the lyrics of Richard Rodgers' (1965, side 2, track 4) "Something Good" from the beloved musical *The Sound of Music*. This phrase bucks conventional wisdom that we create "out of thin air." Our cultural lore suggests that not only does something come from nothing but that the best somethings come from nothing. We fool ourselves into believing that creative genius belongs only to those who can make something great out of nothing at all. Recognized for his genius and creativity, Rodgers, along with his longtime collaborator, Oscar Hammerstein, offers us a different perspective: If nothing comes from nothing, then something must come from *something*—but what?

Judeo-Christian believers and nonbelievers alike are familiar with the "creation story" of the Bible, the ultimate something-out-of-nothing narrative. In fantastic fashion, God creates the world we know out of the nothingness of space and time. Perhaps this ancient story gave rise to our modern notion that creation begins with nothing. But even if true, the point of the story is not that God created from nothing; rather, it seems to me, the point is that the created world comes from God's deep longing and love. Like my conversation with Beth Ann so many years ago, the creation story tells me that something comes not from nothing but from the unspoken yearnings of our hearts.

Ultimately, the desires and requests that we harbor—purpose and meaning, justice and fairness, kindness and peace—are spiritual questions. These inquiries and the possibilities they raise stir in our hearts and minds, seeking honest expression. I am reminded of *Black-ish*, the real-to-me ABC sitcom about an upper-middle-class Black family dealing with issues of race, class, gender, and definitions of success in their predominately White surroundings. The concept for the show reportedly springs from the life of its creator, Kenya Barris, and it gives voice to questions and experiences both deeply personal and universal. Although Barris may not describe the process of creating *Black-ish* as a spiritual one, I cannot help but understand the show as an expression of his interior self and the questions that come from his experiences, his observations, and his longings. The show is, in a way, a gift Barris makes of himself that connects the audience to him, to a particular experience of life, and to one another.

To create, to cause something to be that which did not exist before, is a powerful response to the questions that capture our attention and fill our imagination. Our sources of creativity and innovation are "the questions and feelings, which, in their depths, have a life of their own" (Rilke, 1934, p. 27); they come from deep within our inmost being. The ways in which we see, interpret, and interact with the world and those around us give shape to what we create, perhaps imperceptibly. Our inspirations come sometimes from the personal truths we carry, from our lament about our own and others' experiences, and from the hopefulness we feel about a future that exists only in our imaginations. When we are inspired (from the Latin *inspirare*, meaning "to breathe into"; "The Origins of Inspire," n.d., para. 3), we breathe a new idea into existence. Each time we imagine, create, and innovate, we are giving of ourselves and expressing something deep within us; this is recognized as true in our artistic pursuits. I am suggesting that it is just as true when we seek novel solutions to old problems or when we encounter new, uncharted situations.

Across cultures, spirituality is understood and experienced in myriad ways. It has inspired great works of art (think of Michelangelo's *Pieta* or any one of Frida Kahlo's self-portraits); storied monuments (the Great Pyramids of Egypt, India's Taj Mahal, or the Notre Dame Cathedral in Paris); and courageous leaders who have shaped our world (Malala Yousefzai, Martin Luther King Jr., and Mahatma Gandhi). Full disclosure: This interpretation of the origins of creativity and the creative springs from my own spirituality, which is my desire for connection with God, the transcendent, the divine. Informed by my Catholic faith, and heavily influenced by the Ignatian spirituality governing the Jesuit universities for which I have worked for nearly a quarter century, my spirituality connects everything in my life, particularly the longings of my heart, to my understanding of God. Indeed, one of the great tenets of Ignatian spirituality is "finding God in all things"—from the mundane to the sublime (Martin, 2010).

For me, the places I find God are the places I find connection with myself, others, and the world around me; this is the source of creativity for me. Others may find inspiration and transcendence in their connection with the natural world or in the commonalities across cultures and languages. My purpose here is not to sway you to adopt my spiritual understanding but to ask you to consider yours and how it shapes what guides you. How, then, do you understand your spirituality, your inspiration? What are the longings of your heart? Here you may find the source of your own creativity.

Experiencing the Creative as Spiritual

One of the challenges with discussing creativity is that the term is most often associated with the visual, performing, or literary arts. Indeed, the examples of creativity given earlier are mainly artistic in nature. In their book *Creative Confidence*, Tom Kelley and David Kelley (2013) noted that creativity is not the domain of artistic types only; rather, creativity is a resource we all have at our disposal and have carried with us since childhood. Like children, our natural state is one of wonder, of trying new things free from the shackles of convention. Kelley and Kelley (2013) advise that "if you want to be more creative, you just have to be more natural" (p. 6). I have the good fortune of living with a child who is as natural as she can be. So, I asked my 7-year-old daughter what she likes about being creative. She responded as matter-of-factly as 7-year-olds do: "I like using my brain to figure out new things. Even if something doesn't work out the way I saw it in my brain, it can still be good. I can turn a mistake into something new by being creative" (E. Lewers, personal communication, April 7, 2019).

I love her way of understanding her creative process. It is simple, and it is real: problem solving, imagination, possibility. Whether playing make-believe, drawing with crayons, building a blanket fort with friends, or writing a story, my daughter finds solace in forming her thoughts and feelings into something tangible and relatable. I love, too, the freedom she has when she creates and the ways she loses herself in such activities. In these glorious moments of her childhood, I glimpse her own burgeoning spiritual self.

Getting lost in an activity is what positive psychologists call "flow" or "being in the zone." Flow occurs at the point where we exercise our highest levels of skill and talent in service of a challenge worthy of our attention, according to Mihalyi Csikszentmihalyi (1990), who first wrote about the total engagement of flow. In these moments, we are immersed and fully engaged. The flow experience is one of fulfillment and joy—and even a state of ecstasy or feeling beside oneself (Csikszentmihalyi, 1990). This is what my neighbor Beth Ann described when she played her piano: the experience of pouring her inmost self into her music and being so in the moment that she lost track of time. Fulfillment, joy, and ecstasy are experiences usually associated with mystics and other spiritual agents, but Csikszentmihalyi's work attests that this experience of flow is available to any of us when we apply our hard-earned expertise and skill to challenges that capture our imaginations.

Although I am not a musician, like Beth Ann, and goodness knows I am no longer 7 years old, my chosen field of higher education beckons me to be creative and imaginative in the service of students: developing a new perspective on students' changing needs, synthesizing disparate bits of information to see a greater whole, formulating new ways to resolve intractable problems, advancing an institutional effort, forming a cohesive team. In these moments, I resonate with being "in the zone," so focused that I forget to eat or look up from work—only to realize that my bedtime passed hours before. I may be working on a strategic plan or gathering materials for a report, or writing keynote remarks, or working through the latest crisis with trusted colleagues. My experience confirms Csikszentmihalyi's (1990) theory of flow: In using my skills and experience to tackle interesting challenges, I experience fulfillment, joy, and losing myself in time and space. During these moments of flow, time stands still, and my work enters a different dimension. Here I am affirmed that my chosen field holds great meaning for me and gives me a sense of purpose.

Like that of many people, my professional path was not straightforward. I stumbled my way into higher education after taking inventory of what I loved about my work in external affairs for a girls' school and where I felt most fulfilled in my undergraduate years—and, of course, after getting good advice from people who had observed my gifts and talents. At the time, I had no sense of the term *vocation* or that the equation of my gifts and talents in combination with my learned skills, multiplied by my deep passions (Nash & Murray, 2010), could amount to a professional direction. Vocation (from the Latin *vocare,* meaning "to call or summon,"; "Vocare," n.d., para. 1) is famously described by Frederick Buechner (1992) as "the place where your deep gladness and the world's deep hunger meet" (p. 95). For me, the power of education is transformative, and education is among the noblest of professions. It took me a while to learn this about myself, but once I did, I found myself buoyed by the honor of accompanying students on their journeys to become more fully themselves.

In my work I feel privileged that I get to guide conditions for student success, promote greater access and equity, and see the positive effects of my and others' contributions on individual students. The intersection of my vocational talents, skills, and passions with the challenges facing my students and my institution creates that experience of flow—and this confirms that I have specific contributions to make. To live my vocation—to give of myself and to create alongside my team—is to be generative. Not every day is happy, of course, but overall the work itself is joyful for me. Because I feel called into the field of higher education, my experience of the work is a spiritual one, and the joy I derive from it fuels my imagination and creativity.

The creativity I experience is not like one of painting a master-piece, I suppose, but probably more like building a cathedral. A master painter works alone to realize a vision; a cathedral, however, requires the talents and skills of teams of stone masons, carpenters, blacksmiths, architects, engineers, and others who work over years to complete a shared, if not developing, vision. My work builds upon those who came before me and lays the foundation for those who will come after. Each of us uses our time to respond to the students and the conditions in front of us. How I organize a division of student affairs and deploy available resources to be effective in my tenure requires some amount of imagination and creativity. I cannot rely on what my predecessors did because they were responding to different conditions, just as my successors will not replicate what I am doing today. Each of us is the steward of our era, and our collective efforts over time build something beautiful and lasting. The long arc of our work toward student success and development is nothing less than the transformational power of human flourishing.

Locating my place in the history of an institution both grounds and frees me. It grounds me by helping me understand my connection to something larger than myself and my own time. The part of the story I am commissioned to tell must connect in some way to the stories of the past, and there is a reverence to understanding my work as one aspect of a much larger narrative. At the same time, I am free to weave in new story lines and shift conditions to meet the challenges and opportunities that this era presents. The simultaneous experience of being both grounded and free in my work mirrors the influence of Ignatian spirituality in my life: the awareness of God's presence and the freedom to draw myself closer only to that which is more life giving (Martin, 2010). My spirituality, then, invites me to be more authentically myself, which further opens the door to creativity and allows me to be generative.

Restoring Creativity With Spiritual Resources

Reading the previous section might give you the false impression that because I feel called to this work in higher education, and particularly to Jesuit higher education, that every day is filled with creative generativity. I assure you: This is not the case. Like anyone, I go through periods of drought with nothing left in the reserve tank. As I write this chapter, I am in one of those periods now. The wrinkles in the higher education landscape, the complexities of institutional histories, the waves of administrative responsibilities, and the effects of vicarious trauma arising from student and other crises are as much a part of my professional life as are the joy and meaning. Taken one at a time, any of these conditions can exact a heavy toll, but in almost any combination, the effect is utter depletion.

Gratefully, here too I find a relationship between the spiritual and the creative. Under optimal, and even good, conditions, creativity and spirituality are mutually reinforcing energies. Under difficult conditions, however, I find I have no creativity, but I do maintain my spiritual resources. With patience and grace, I can leverage my spiritual strength to revive my creativity.

Recently, a friend called to talk through her challenges managing a large state grant to set up a nonprofit agency. She was trying to keep many plates spinning: community partners, local and state regulations, the needs of the identified population, contractors, providers, her personal life. She was feeling acutely the pressure that if any one plate fell to the ground, not only would it shatter but all the other plates would come crashing down—an enormous load to bear.

She said she called me because she had observed me in high-pressure circumstances and wanted to know how I managed to keep my composure and remain focused. She had perceived me as a calming presence, reassuring others that we would get through whatever difficulties were facing us. Her experience was that we did move past the challenges and land in a better place. (For my part, I remembered the high-pressure situation, but my recollection of the other stuff was vastly different. My friend might have thought I adopted the British World War II motto "Keep calm and carry on," but that was not how I experienced that confusing mess at all.)

I shared with her what a colleague had said to encourage me: "You have all the resources and experience you need to guide you through what today feels like chaos." My most reliable resources during that period, I told her, were the wisdom and contributions of trusted colleagues and mentors and my faith. I reminded her that she has plenty of both—many people whose expertise and support she can rely on as well as a profound spirituality.

A yoga devotee, my friend has spiritual resources that run deep. She is practiced in the art of mindfulness and no stranger to Ignatian spirituality. We spoke about the ways in which she uses her mindful mediation to be present in the moment, to hold at bay the waves of overwhelm that threatened to overtake her. We talked about what we have learned from St. Ignatius and the overlap between mindfulness and his admonition to have a healthy sense of detachment so that we might find ourselves free to do the better thing (Martin, 2010). We agreed that if there is truth in St. Ignatius's tenet that we find God in all things, then surely God was present in the challenging, but near-miraculous, opportunity in which she found herself. I shared what I had learned about finding God in times of trouble—namely, when I am overwhelmed, there's no sense in me trying to find God. Better that I stay still for a moment and let God find me; then, and only then, am I able to forge ahead. Sometimes, I suppose, the most creative thing we can do when we are struggling is slow down, be still for a moment or two, and then courageously put one foot in front of the other.

My friend's mindful meditation allows her to notice her thoughts and feelings but not attach to them. The focus is on breath, continual presence, and actively detaching from the worries that clutter the mind. In this space, new connections emerge and creative solutions find their way to the surface—a paradox, for sure. Pico Iyer (1993) observed this very paradox in his essay on silence:

> We have to earn silence, then, to work for it: to make it not an absence but a presence; not an emptiness but repletion. Silence is something more than just a pause; it is that enchanted place where space is cleared and time is stayed and the horizon itself expands. In silence, we often say, we can hear ourselves think; but what is truer to say is that in silence we can hear ourselves *not* think, and so sink below our selves into a place far deeper than mere thought allows. (p. 74)

In this fast-paced, hyperconnected world, I easily feel the stress and pressure of circumstances beyond my control but for which I have some responsibility. The greater the pressure, the higher the stress, and the quicker my tank runs dry. There is nothing new or creative in my problem-solving. I come up either empty-handed or with solutions that fail to satisfy. Retreating to that place "far deeper than mere thought allows" (Iyer, 1993, p. 74) is like pushing the reset button. Silence, as Iyer (1993) noted, affords immeasurable and profound benefits, and I find these benefits compounded when I seek silence in nature.

Forest bathing, or connecting deeply with nature through our five senses, has become a popular resource. Various articles tout the health benefits of immersing ourselves in and actually noticing nature (see, e.g., Aubrey, 2017; Li, 2018): how the air sounds when it rustles through the tall grasses; how the sunlight dances on the water; how the earth smells rich and loamy after a cleansing rain; how new leaves are tender and cool to the touch and seem to glow with the soft, bright green of new life; how the symmetrical architecture of the spider's web glistens with morning dew. Although I cannot, nor am I qualified to, enumerate the physiological effects of being in nature, I can attest to its restorative quality.

Without knowing that I was dabbling in the Japanese health practice of forest bathing, I have long taken myself on a date with nature, particularly anywhere near the water's edge, when I find I am blocked mentally or struggling with a problem that feels both weighty and intractable. There I recognize myself as small and insignificant against the vast backdrop of the natural world. My perspective changes. My heart rate slows. My breathing becomes more full and gentle. I can hear myself *not* think, in Iyer's (1993) words. It is, for me, a deeply spiritual experience. When I emerge, the problem has not changed, but something in how I am able (or willing) to approach it *has* shifted. Being in nature replenishes my tank, and I am reminded that creative thinking—despite its name—is not simply a cerebral exercise for me but rather a deeply interior process. Perhaps recognizing myself as small in comparison to nature reminds me that I cannot do everything, which somehow frees me to be able to do something. And the something I can do is good. From this point I am able to make meaning of, see patterns in, and make connections between (Parks, 2000) what was previously a jumbled mess of thoughts and reactions.

A silent pause, whether in nature or in a quiet corner, gives me a chance to foreground the ongoing inner dialogue about meaning and purpose, and it quiets—temporarily at least—the concerns that had hijacked my attention. Eventually, even in the midst of great confusion or emptiness, I return to my understanding of my vocation to accompany young people on their transformational journeys to become more fully themselves. With this understanding as my foundation, my tank begins slowly to refill, and imagination and creativity become more accessible.

Establishing the Virtues of Creativity and Innovation

Emerging technologies have caused seismic shifts in many industries. In higher education, online learning causes those of us in student affairs to think differently about how we provide services and support to populations of students who are not on campus. Citing the fast pace of developing technologies and the tendency for those technologies to digitize and automate work that humans have been performing, Hess and Ludwig (2017) made an impassioned plea to shift our mental models. They argued that in today's world, humans should embrace creativity and experimentation, collaboration and learning, and the humility of not knowing. They called their adjusted mental model "NewSmart." The preference here is for the quality of thinking and collaborating, not the depth and breadth of knowledge of facts. Mistakes are opportunities, and ideas do not equate to beliefs (Hess & Ludwig, 2017). NewSmart can fuel creativity and innovation, but it requires operating with a new set of habits.

Several years ago, Larry Smith, Al Blixt, Shannon Ellis, Stephen Gill, and Kevin Kruger (2015) made a compelling argument for innovation and change in student affairs. They outlined the challenges facing higher education, including population and content-delivery trends, and proposed that by incorporating greater flexibility, student affairs would be well positioned to lead innovation on campus. Further, building habits of innovation into the organization would contribute to a sustainable future. Given the enrollment and retention concerns and related budgetary constraints my institution was experiencing at the time, their message resonated, and I was eager to try the ideas Smith et al. suggested. What follows are the lessons I learned alongside my team of outstanding professionals.

For my team and me, changing our mental models and developing habits, rather than episodes, of creativity and innovation was not easy; even more difficult was moving an organization to develop these habits. As professionals (and as human beings, probably), we were conditioned to fear failure, to always have the right answer, and to maintain time-honored systems. Collectively, we saw creative efforts as add-ons (and therefore optional) to our regular work rather than as the work itself. It was difficult for us to let go of systems that we or our predecessors had built for very good reasons, even though the data suggested that those reasons had either changed or no longer existed. The disequilibrium we experienced was the price we paid for moving from old models of recognized and rewarded intelligence to new ways of thinking that I now recognize as Hess and Ludwig's (2017) idea of NewSmart.

If we were to succeed, we would need to develop new habits, or virtues, in our work. By *virtue* I mean principles of excellence that lead to a common good. The new virtues we developed helped us try new approaches without fearing the likely failures we would encounter along the way. Our new virtues helped us individually and as a team become more creative. Embracing and adapting some of the more widely recognized human virtues and then cultivating some to fit our needs, we began to practice what I call the "virtues for creativity and innovation":

- Humility
- Courage
- Humor
- Patience
- Generosity
- Gratitude
- Celebration

Humility. Just as Hess and Ludwig (2017) advised, clearing the space for new and creative thought begins with the ability and willingness to admit ignorance. We learned that when we had the humility to say, "I don't know," we could begin the journey to discover whatever eludes us. Admitting ignorance is not the same thing as saying one cannot or will not learn; rather, having the humility to not know is in itself an invitation to learn and to be open to new, previously unconsidered possibilities. In my organization there was much we did not know. Admitting to one another what we did not know sparked curiosity instead of rebuke, and we were free to try to discover what we did not already but truly wanted to know.

Courage. Different from but related to humility, courage as a virtue of creativity means a willingness to try to new ideas and approaches. Fear of failure was strong in my organization, as I suspect it is in many places. We developed a motto: "Test fast, fail forward." We built failure into our creative processes, and we came to expect it. As long as we were learning from our flops, we did not experience the letdowns as catastrophic failures. Artists have assured me that failure is, indeed, part of any creative process. Why, I wonder, would we expect the workplace to be any different?

Humor. Laughter is a great medicine. Sometimes in the midst of the crises and demands, we can take ourselves too seriously. I know I can, and this was true of my organization as well. (Budget cuts can suck the fun out of any room.) A little lightheartedness went a long way to help us decompress and remind us that we were putting forth our best efforts under trying circumstances.

Patience. Change takes time. This is a hard reality for capable people who are used to achieving tangible and immediate results. But lack of patience can lead to unnecessary frustration. During our team meetings, I often shared a reflection from "Prophets of a Future Not Our Own," a homily delivered by Cardinal Dearden in honor of Archbishop Óscar Romero in 1979:

It helps now and then to step back and take a long view . . .
We plant the seeds that one day will grow.
We water seeds already planted, knowing that they hold future promise.
We lay foundations that will need further development.
We provide yeast that produces far beyond our capabilities.
We cannot do everything, and there is a sense of liberation in realizing that.
This enables us to do something, and to do it very well.
(Untener, 1979)

These words brought comfort and reconciled us to understanding that we may not see the fruit of our labors—or the fruit we do see may not be what we were hoping or expecting. But this does not make our labors fruitless. Patience, coupled with humility, allowed us to do our part and to do it well.

Generosity. Some days it seems as though kindness is in short supply, but a little kindness can go a long way. My team and I recognized early on that if we were to move mountains, we would need to approach one another with a generous spirit. In St. Ignatius's *Spiritual Exercises*, one of his first directives to the retreatant and the spiritual director is to listen generously and to put the best interpretation on what you hear the other person saying (Ignatius & Ganss, 1992). In this team we found that one person's generosity led to generosity in others—and helped us to establish an environment where creativity could emerge.

Gratitude. Positive psychologists contend that practicing gratitude makes a person happier. I do not know if the practice of noticing and appreciating made our team happier, but it did energize us. A particularly creative team member instituted a campaign to recognize contributions from the smallest to the largest. Staff members received a lollipop ring with a "You're a Gem!" note detailing what someone noticed and appreciated about their work. It was a small, but meaningful, gesture. Practicing gratitude helped us focus on what was going well rather than getting overwhelmed and distracted by all that was in front of us.

Celebration. Practicing gratitude also gave rise to the need to celebrate milestones—and celebrate we did! I often used the metaphor of a road trip to describe our innovation efforts. Each goal was like a stop on our journey, and we mapped out many stops between our starting point and our destination. Each time we reached a new stop, we celebrated—sometimes in little ways, like having unexpected tasty treats at a meeting, and sometimes in bigger ways, like a divisional happy hour. Celebrating gave us time to exhale and, importantly, to mark progress.

The virtues of creativity and innovation were particular to the circumstances of that team, but I believe they are also universal. I have been fortunate to be part of other teams that have employed the same habits and can attest that they yield results. If Hess and Ludwig (2017) are correct, we will not solve today's concerns with the strategies we built to respond to yesterday's problems. New ways of thinking and new habits are necessary if we are to discover effective and creative approaches.

Final Words

I began this chapter with the assertion that creativity is a spiritual process as much as it is a mental one. As I close this chapter, I am certain that, for me, creativity is more spiritual than mental. As I alluded earlier, I started this writing project in the midst of exhaustion to the point of near depletion. This is true. I did not know where I would find the words. So, I did exactly what I wrote about in this chapter: I leaned on my spiritual resources. I went for walks in the woods and allowed myself to be in silence. I was reminded of how I derive meaning and purpose. As I tried to convey how I understand my vocation and the source of my inspiration, the words began to flow.

Once again, my purpose in this chapter is not to sway you to adopt my spiritual understanding, but I hope these stories and examples shed light on how your own spiritual understanding may shape what guides you and the longings of your heart. There, I hope, you will find the source of your creativity just as I found mine.

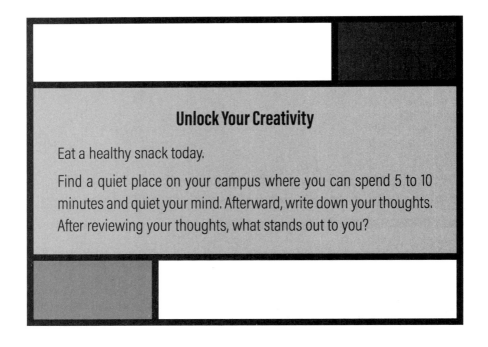

Unlock Your Creativity

Eat a healthy snack today.

Find a quiet place on your campus where you can spend 5 to 10 minutes and quiet your mind. Afterward, write down your thoughts. After reviewing your thoughts, what stands out to you?

References

Aubrey, A. (2017, July 17). Forest bathing: A retreat to nature can boost immunity and mood. *National Public Radio*. Retrieved from https://www.npr.org/sections/health-shots/2017/07/17/536676954/forest-bathing-a-retreat-to-nature-can-boost-immunity-and-mood

Buechner, F. (1992). *Listening to your life: Daily meditations with Frederick Buechner.* New York, NY: HarperCollins.

Csikszentmihalyi, M. (1990). *Flow: The psychology of optimal experience.* New York, NY: Harper & Row.

Hess, E. D., & Ludwig, K. (2017). *Humility is the new smart: Rethinking human excellence in the smart machine age.* Oakland, CA: Barrett-Koehler.

Ignatius, & Ganss, G. E. (1992). *The spiritual exercises of St. Ignatius.* Chicago, IL: Loyola Press.

Iyer, P. (1993). *Falling off the map: Some lonely places of the world.* New York, NY: Vintage.

Kelley, T., & Kelley, D. (2013). *Creative confidence: Unleashing the creative potential within us all.* New York, NY: Penguin Random House.

Li, Q. (2018, May 1). "Forest bathing" is great for your health. Here's how to do it. *Time.* Retrieved from http://time.com/5259602/japanese-forest-bathing

Martin, J. (2010). *The Jesuit guide to (almost) everything: A spirituality for real life.* New York, NY: HarperCollins.

Nash, R. J., & Murray, M. C. (2010). *Helping college students find purpose: The campus guide to meaning-making.* San Francisco, CA: Jossey-Bass.

The origins of 'inspire.' (n.d.) Retrieved from https://www.merriam-webster.com/words-at-play/the-origins-of-inspire

Parks, S. D. (2000). *Big questions, worthy dreams: Mentoring young adults in their search for meaning, purpose, and faith.* San Francisco, CA: Jossey-Bass.

Rilke, R. M. (1934). *Letters to a young poet.* London, England: W. W. Norton & Company, Inc.

Rodgers, R. (1965). Something good. On *The Sound of Music* [Vinyl record]. New York, NY: RCA Victor.

Smith, L. N., Blixt, A. B., Ellis, S. E., Gill, S. J., & Kruger, K. (2015). *Leading innovation and change: A guide for chief student affairs officers on shaping the future.* Washington, DC: NASPA–Student Affairs Administrators in Higher Education.

Untener, K. (1979, October 25). *Prophets of a future not our own.* Retrieved from United States Conference of Catholic Bishops website: http://www.usccb.org/prayer-and-worship/prayers-and-devotions/prayers/prophets-of-a-future-not-our-own.cfm

Vocare. (n.d.). In *The Latin Dictionary.* Retrieved from http://latindictionary.wikidot.com/verb:vocare

11

LEADING CREATIVE AND DIVERSE TEAMS

DOMONIC A. ROLLINS AND KENECHUKWU (K.C.) MMEJE

It's 2020, and we are all tired! Who is *we?* Those of us who are working hard and incessantly to do, be, and embody an inclusive practice in higher education. And *we* have hit the wall—the fourth wall. In theatrical production, breaking the fourth wall is when the actors stop speaking to and engaging with one another and, instead, involve and engage the audience. In other words, the audience members assume a role in the play. When a character breaks the fourth wall, the audience members learn that character's deepest thoughts and true motivations—they become confidants of sorts. Today, regarding diversity and inclusion—in everything from rhetoric to action— breaking the fourth wall is necessary to move beyond the status quo toward real inclusion in how we lead teams specifically and higher education broadly. To break the fourth wall in higher education means to engage, involve, and bring into the change process those who are impacted and served by higher education: students. Breaking the fourth wall in higher education assumes that students have a role, and keeps their voices, concerns, and perspectives at the center.

Why Breaking the Fourth Wall is Necessary

Today's higher education professionals have inherited institutions that are exclusive by design. Any investigation into the history of colleges and universities in the United States attests that they were designed and intended for a select few (Rudolph, 1990). Thus, breaking the fourth wall and leading inclusively in higher education is disruptive to the status quo; it combats the original design. The need for higher education professionals to lead inclusively is greater than ever, and this need requires adaptation and disruption to further bring higher education into the future—with full participation of those who have previously been excluded (Spears & Lawrence, 2003). Currently, several challenges or opportunities create the conditions on many college and university campuses that necessitate inclusive leadership—specifically, changing demographics, demands from marginalized students, and a better understanding of what all students need. Higher education institutions and their "leadership must address multiple demands due to changes in the external environment, faculties, and student demographic population shifts" (Temple & Ylitalo, 2009, p. 277). These challenges compel inclusive leadership as a necessary and adaptive way to serve higher education institutions well.

Changing Demographics in the United States

Higher education is changing. Particularly, there are more diverse students learning in classrooms, faculty teaching these students, and staff running and administering programs and services on college and university campuses. Data from the past 10 years confirm these changes in the composition of higher education (National Center for Education Statistics, 2017). In 2016, students of color composed 48% of undergraduate enrollment; in 1996, students of color composed only 30% of undergraduate enrollment. These demographic shifts in academe reflect broader demographic shifts in the United States. In 2042, it is projected that people of color, across different racial and ethnic groups, will be the numerical majority in the United States—specifically, "Americans who identify themselves as Hispanic, Black, Asian, American Indian, Native Hawaiian, and Pacific Islander will together outnumber non-Hispanic whites" (Roberts, 2008, p. 1). These changes in the racial composition of higher education and the United States necessitate an innovative and creative response to leadership. At base, learning about the needs and expectations of higher education from each of these racial and ethnic groups will go a long way to positively influence their inclusion—an act of breaking the fourth wall.

Alongside changes in the racial makeup in the United States and on college campuses are also growing numbers of LGBTQIA students, religious minorities, and persons with disabilities on campus. In prior years, higher education responded to smaller demographic shifts through a slight adaption and expansion of programs and services. In the 1980s and 1990s, this manifested in the creation of multicultural centers, the hiring of a few faculty and staff of color, and the creation of ethnic studies majors or curricular programs (Stewart, 2011). Such adaptions were slight and took place on the margins of the higher education operation and will be inadequate for future demographic shifts. What will it take to lead tomorrow's college campus? What kinds of adaption will lead to thriving campuses? One answer is: "Leadership practices integrating the strengths of collegial traditions to more postmodern ideas of collaborative and inclusive leadership should be pursued to meet the new challenges" of a changing demographic on colleges campuses (Temple & Ylitalo, 2009, p. 280). This means that higher education leaders must design a student experience that puts students of color, LGBTQIA students, religious minorities, and students with disabilities at the center. Yet this isn't the only challenge for which inclusive leadership is an answer; demands from marginalized students also presents as a leadership challenge requiring redress.

Demands From Marginalized Students

Student activism is as old as colleges and universities themselves. More recently, fall 2015 gave rise to multiple protests at colleges and universities across the United States (Johnston, 2015). As discussed further in chapter 12 of this book, underrepresented students banded together via social media to coordinate massive protests during which they demanded their institutions take meaningful action to address persistent inequities and inequalities in their collegiate experience. These demonstrations caught many colleges and universities by surprise, leaving them scrambling to respond to their students' demands (an example of these demands representing 80 campuses can be found at http://www.thedemands.org). Generally, the demands required that colleges and universities do the following: Improve student diversity by bolstering recruitment and retention efforts; expand the availability of need-based financial aid; diversify faculty and staff; reform the core curriculum to include diverse perspectives; increase academic success and student support services; and enhance access to culturally relevant programs and services. Each demand points to a clear yet innovative principle: Put the needs of underrepresented students at the center, and all students will flourish. Rather than devising solutions to decades-old problems in isolation, colleges and universities must invite historically underrepresented students to dialogue about their needs and enlist their support in implementing meaningful reforms that support student success. Institutions must shift from rhetoric to meaningful action that demonstrates an unwavering commitment to diversity, equity, and inclusion. If met, these demands, like changing demographics, would bring more diverse people to academe.

With the exception of historically Black colleges and universities, tribal colleges, and Hispanic-serving institutions, most colleges and universities have remained predominantly White institutions (PWIs). PWIs have been slow to diversify their student populations. Consequently, underrepresented students enrolled at PWIs often report feelings of isolation, lack of support, and general disengagement (Stewart, 2011). This lack of representation at PWIs sometimes leads these students to feel tokenized by their schools—meaning, their schools are only concerned with portraying a superficial image of diversity and, thus, lack a true commitment to inclusivity. Colleges and universities have faced growing criticism for perpetuating societal inequities via questionable admission practices that constrain access; recent popular admissions scandals are just one example (Bartlett, 2019). More and more, colleges and universities are being challenged to contain the rising costs of attendance and to increase access to higher education, particularly for low-income and historically underrepresented student populations. If PWIs are to become more supportive of underrepresented students and achieve their mission of addressing societal needs, then they must adapt and devise creative ways to increase the enrollment and support of historically underrepresented student populations.

A common theme that emerged from the student protests of 2015 was the need for colleges and universities to diversify their faculty and staff. Students reported that the faculty and staff—but particularly the faculty—were far less diverse than the student populations they served. Students struggled to identify faculty members who understood or could relate to their lived experiences. Furthermore, underrepresented students reported experiencing microaggressions in the classroom from their professors and peers. In addition to highlighting the need for colleges and universities to bolster efforts to recruit and retain faculty of color, students underscored the need for diversity and inclusion training for faculty—specifically, training geared toward equipping participants with the skills to facilitate and engage in conversations across social identity differences. To better serve the needs of all students, and to adjust to changing demographics, colleges and universities must diversify their workforce—particularly faculty and senior leadership (Brewer, 1995).

Often, a college or university's core curriculum is the primary vehicle through which its academic values are promulgated to students. Consequently, many institutions of higher education place considerable emphasis on which courses comprise their core curriculum, and they ensure that all students, regardless of major, demonstrate proficiency in those courses. Unfortunately, underrepresented students at PWIs often lament the noticeable lack of diversity in thought and perspective reflected in universities' core curricula. In fact, among the leading demands from underrepresented students was the need to expand course offerings, particularly the core curriculum. Disrupting the practice of requiring core curricula that do not represent the students who take the classes requires a rethinking of what the Western canon *is* and what *all* students need to know. Again, breaking the fourth wall and, in this example, involving students in shaping a curriculum can be really useful. Students continue to demand the inclusion of ethnic studies courses in the core curriculum, the addition of ethnic studies minors and majors, and an expansion of the perspectives included in history and literature courses beyond Western history and literature. This demand suggests that colleges and universities have been slow to revise their curricula in a manner that reflects the needs and interests of current students—that is, a more diverse student body relative to that of earlier periods. Each of these changes points toward a diversity in representation and experience in higher education that is unprecedented and requires a way of leading that has not always been extant.

Leading Inclusively

What Does It Mean to Lead Inclusively, and Why is It Important?

Today, leading inclusively is more important than ever given the change in demographics that has brought more diversity to both the student body and the workforce of most colleges and universities. Simply put, diverse student bodies and college communities require inclusive leadership. Leading inclusively "is a holistic issue that stems from a mindset, values, and a willingness that must be authentic— it cannot be forced. In so doing, inclusive leadership improves the human condition in that it raises the consciousness of administrators in developing a systematic multicultural world view" (Temple & Ylitalo, 2009, p. 286). The mindset and values that undergird inclusive leadership disrupt the assumed heterogeneity of a group, by operating from a position that difference is always present and welcome. Leading inclusively ensures that people feel that they are treated fairly, their uniqueness is appreciated and valued, they belong, and they have a voice in decision making (Deloitte & Victorian Equal Opportunity and Human Rights Commission, 2013). Principally, leading inclusively is "the step that many educational systems and institutions can take to ensure that all students begin to learn that access to education and belonging is a right, not a privileged status that is earned; and that every person has a contribution to offer the world" (Temple & Ylitalo, 2009, p. 286). Leading inclusively is right to do, and it leverages the benefits that *all* people bring to college and university campuses.

Leading inclusively harnesses and yields the most contributions and benefits from different groups of people. Although research indicates that diverse teams generate innovative solutions, such solutions are not automatic (Thatcher, Jehn, & Zanutto, 2003). The benefits of a diverse team will not harvest themselves; that team's leader must work to ensure that all perspectives, experiences, and voices are heard and included. Doing this well necessitates a habit of mind, a disposition, and a set of behaviors that regularly seeks the contributions of team members. Asking and enacting reflexive questions of oneself and the team can help achieve the benefits of a diverse time. For example: What will my team think of this new decision? How can I solicit and incorporate team members' perspectives? And, where can the contributions of the team be best utilized? Further, a simple act like getting to know your team thoroughly and learning what each member's personal contributions are helps to bring more experiences into the fold, making them central—not peripheral. Ultimately, just like meaningful personal relationships, diverse teams must be cultivated, trained, and developed in order to reap the benefit of the diversity present (Thomas & Ely, 1996).

With the growing diversity in higher education among students, staff, and faculty, it is almost inevitable that campus leaders will find themselves guiding diverse teams (Temple & Ylitalo, 2009). For many such leaders, particularly those working outside of diversity, inclusion, and multicultural areas, leading diverse teams inclusively will be a new idea (Bolman & Deal, 2011). Previously, not much thought was given to leading inclusively, as the assumption was that difference was not present. Notably, areas such as finance, human resources, operations, and information technology have not been diverse in the past (Jackson & O'Callaghan, 2009). Many leaders in these areas have used—and continue to use—a traditional top-down model of leadership, asserting control of unit and department and often acting as sole decision maker for that unit. With increased diversity, these departments will also need to lead inclusively. From the authors' perspectives, newer generations of higher education staff members expect a different kind of leadership. Collaboration, shared decision making, and the addition of various perspectives ground this new expectation.

What Does Leading Inclusively Accomplish?

Leading inclusively ensures that all team members feel a part of decisions, communications, and operations of the team or unit. When done effectively, leading inclusively enhances team functioning because it fosters cohesion. Leading inclusively also boosts morale and encourages retention. In higher education, many people have chosen their jobs because of the mission of the institution and their vocation as an educator. Many can cite meaningful and personal reasons as to why they have embarked on a career in higher education. Recognizing the deep commitment that some staff members have made and including their perspective keeps them involved, engaged, and connected.

What Does It Take to Lead Inclusively?

As senior leaders in higher education, we the authors strive to practice inclusive leadership and create organizational cultures that allow all individuals to feel valued, affirmed, and supported in reaching their full potential. We recognize that inclusive leadership goes against the grain and can be perceived as disruptive to the traditional norms and practices in higher education. Practicing inclusive leadership requires a conscious choice as well as a steadfast commitment to specific behaviors; the next section offers examples of creative and innovative practices.

Inclusive leadership is predicated on self-awareness and an unwavering commitment to harnessing and honoring diversity. Inclusive leaders must be keenly aware of who they are—their dominant and subordinate identities, their values, their conscious and unconscious biases, and their strengths and areas for growth. Beyond simply being self-aware, inclusive leaders must recognize the importance and value of surrounding themselves with an exceptionally qualified diverse team. Inclusive leaders seek teammates who reflect the diversity of the community being served. They select teammates with different viewpoints and teammates who complement their strengths as well as challenge them to develop their growth areas. Such teammates ensure that decisions, outcomes, and results are thoughtful, innovative, and inclusive—groupthink is avoided. Inclusive leaders empower their coworkers to bring their whole selves to their work, and these leaders understand that the team is strengthened when everyone does so. Inclusive leaders ensure that the aforementioned approach to teambuilding is practiced and supported throughout their divisions, departments, and spheres of influence. Practicing inclusive leadership extends beyond the teambuilding process—once a diverse team is built, an inclusive leader must work toward establishing an organizational culture that supports the success of those individuals.

Inclusive leadership is relational and requires investment in people. Inclusive leaders take it upon themselves to foster meaningful relationships rooted in mutual respect and understanding. They take time to know the personal and professional goals of their team members. Furthermore, inclusive leaders actively work to support and advance their staff members' goals via professional development opportunities, regular feedback, counsel, and mentorship. In addition, inclusive leaders demand that the managers they hire provide that same level of support. Inclusive leaders should aim to engage in this manner with all of members of their respective divisions and departments.

Inclusive leadership should also be practiced when making organizational decisions and establishing strategic goals. Organizational decisions often affect most, if not all, staff and have huge implications, so, it is important to invite the input and perspectives of all staff when making such decisions. When making organizational decisions, involve staff at every level and strive to ensure that they understand the implications of the decision and the thought process behind it. Team members greatly appreciate being involved in the organizational decision-making process—even if they disagree with the decision made. This practice supports the inclusion of multiple perspectives and allows staff to feel heard, which results in a greater sense of investment in the organization. A similar approach should be followed when leading strategic planning efforts for a division of student affairs.

Ultimately, inclusive leaders put their staff and team members at the center. Doing so achieves synergy and a connection between inclusivity, innovation, and adaption. By bringing in the voices and experiences of staff, leaders are better able to innovate and adapt; they intimately understand the limits and possibilities of their teams. And—because they have invested in their teams—their teams are willing to invest in the next innovation or adaption necessary for positive change. Ultimately, the return on investing in inclusivity generates the buy-in necessary among teams to produce results in a rapidly changing higher education landscape.

Recommendations for Leaders

Inclusive leadership is leadership for the 21st century. The demographic reality, now and on the horizon, makes clear that the United

States will be more diverse than ever before. Given these changing conditions, higher education leaders must be skilled and prepared to lead a diverse team. There are several recommendations to ensure that a higher education leader's practice is inclusive.

Actively assess and respond to the norms on your team. Inclusive leadership requires attention to the experiences of your team members. Norms, a manifestation of organizational and team culture, are a key way that team members experience their work environment in higher education. Taking stock of the enacted norms by reflecting on them as the team leader and asking your team members how they experience norms, go far to ensure inclusive leadership. Some examples of norms are the way meetings are initiated, customs for lunch or other meal times, and how decisions are made for extra projects or responsibilities. Small instances of exclusion often occur as a result of norms that do not work or embrace all team members.

Evaluate how you make decisions on your team. Decision making is one of the easiest and most evident places to evaluate whether a team is being led inclusively. Often, leaders default to making decisions in a convenient manner that lacks the voices or input of team members who are invested in the choice at hand. Certainly, it is not easy to make all decisions inclusively: Time, confidentiality, and organizational structure often make it hard to always make decisions in an inclusive manner. Notwithstanding these challenges, higher education leaders can begin to articulate to their teams which decisions can be made inclusively and what process they will use to facilitate inclusive decision making. Put another way, transparency in how decisions are made is a key attribute in inclusive leadership, as transparency lets team members understand how a process works and how they relate to that process (Helgesen, 1995).

Make the unwritten rules obvious; document and share processes. A primary way staff experience exclusion in higher education is through informal networks, connections, and influences. In higher education, a person's access to each of these factors is incredibly important; yet, often networks, connections, and influences are established informally, say, over a coffee or other casual means. This is an example of an unwritten rule. Establishing a helpful network at work should not require an individual to get coffee with their manager; rather, one should be able to establish a helpful network through a formal channel, such as asking for it in a one-on-one meeting or regular check-in. Making networks, connections, influences, and other value-added experiences at work accessible through a process that all teams members can undertake and understand is essential to inclusive leadership.

Create and sustain a culture for team members to give feedback about team operations. Ultimately, if they are to feel included, team members must have the opportunity to give feedback on their experience as part of the team. Ask the question: "How are we with one another?" This question allows leaders and team members to reflect critically on team dynamics and culture. Higher education leaders may have great intentions, but without feedback from their team members, they lack the information needed to shift their practice to lead inclusively.

Conclusion

The increasing diversity of colleges and universities, and society in general, requires leaders who are committed to inclusive leadership. Demonstrating a commitment to inclusive leadership requires intentional professional practice that seeks to embrace and involve the perspectives, experiences, and insights of the teams, students, and communities that higher education leaders serve. Without inclusive leaders, colleges and universities will not be equipped to meet the unique needs of a growing population of historically underrepresented students nor will these organizations reach their full operational potential. In the current context, we continue to learn about the needs of students who weren't previously served well by higher education. With this information, we must commit ourselves to creating organizational cultures where inclusive leadership is the norm rather than the exception. Higher education leaders of tomorrow must embrace the imperative to break down the fourth wall; they must place the needs of all students at the center of their work, and work collaboratively with students to ensure college and university campuses are inclusive.

Unlock Your Creativity

Channel your inner organizer and alter your environment by organizing and cleaning your work area. If you are able to do so, consider rearranging your office. If you have a mobile office, reevaluate your files and how you organize your projects. Once completed, reflect on the differences these changes have made in your day-to-day life.

References

Bartlett, T. (2019, March 15). What the admissions scandal reveals about secrecy, privilege, and the nature of merit. *The Chronicle of Higher Education*. Retrieved from https://www.chronicle.com/article/What-the-Admissions-Scandal/245901

Bolman, L. G., & Deal, T. E. (2011). *Reframing organizations: Artistry, choice and leadership*. San Francisco, CA: John Wiley & Sons.

Brewer, M. (1995). Managing diversity: The role of social identities. In S. Jackson & M. Ruderman, (Eds.), *Diversity in workteams* (pp. 131–159). Washington, DC: APA Books.

Deloitte & Victorian Equal Opportunity and Human Rights Commission. (2013, May). *Waiter, is that inclusion in my soup? A new recipe to improve business performance*. Retrieved from https://www2.deloitte.com/content/dam/Deloitte/au/Documents/human-capital/deloitte-au-hc-diversity-inclusion-soup-0513.pdf

Helgesen, S. (1995). *The web of inclusion: A new architecture for building great organizations* New York, NY: Currency/Doubleday.

Jackson, J., & O'Callaghan, E. M. (2009). Special Issue: Ethnic and racial administrative diversity—Understanding work life realities and experiences in higher education. *ASHE Higher Education Report, 35*(3), 1–95.

Johnston, A. (2015, December 11). Student protests, then and now. *The Chronicle of Higher Education*. Retrieved from https://www.chronicle.com/article/Student-Protests-ThenNow/234542

National Center for Education Statistics. (2017). *Status and trends in the education of racial and ethnic groups*. Retrieved from https://nces.ed.gov/pubs2017/2017051.pdf

Roberts, S. (2008, August 14). Minorities in U.S. set to become majority by 2042. *The New York Times*. Retrieved from https://www.nytimes.com/2008/08/14/world/americas/14iht-census.1.15284537.html

Rudolph, F. (1990). *The American college and university: A history*. Athens, GA: University of Georgia Press.

Spears, L. C., & Lawrence, M. (Eds.). (2003). *Focus on leadership: Servant-leadership for the twenty-first century*. San Francisco, CA: Jossey Bass.

Stewart, D. L. (2011). *Multicultural student services on campus: Building bridges, revisioning community*. Sterling, VA: Stylus.

Temple, J. B., & Ylitalo, J. (2009). Promoting inclusive (and dialogic) leadership in higher education institutions. *Tertiary Education and Management, 15*(3), 277–289.

Thatcher, S., Jehn, K., & Zanutto, E. (2003). Cracks in diversity research: The effects of diversity fault lines on conflict and performance. *Group Decision and Negotiation, 12*, 217–241.

Thomas, D., & Ely, R. (1996, September–October). Making differences matter: A new paradigm for managing diversity. *Harvard Business Review, 74*, 79–90.

12

"WE OUT HERE, WE BEEN HERE, WE AIN'T LEAVING, WE ARE LOVED"

Using Creativity in Working With Student Activism and Unrest

BRANDON COMMON AND EILEEN GALVEZ

"If there is no struggle, there is no progress."

—Frederick Douglass, *West India Emancipation Speech at Canandaigua, New York*

In fall 2015, the Intercultural Affairs Council of Yale University prepared a statement that addressed issues of cultural appropriation during Halloween celebrations on campus. Consistent with the mission and values of the council, this action was in many ways expected, considering the occasion. While acknowledging students' free speech rights, the council encouraged members of the Yale community to be thoughtful in their costume decisions. In response to this statement, a lecturer with a courtesy appointment at a residential college of the university openly criticized the statement and encouraged students to be "naughty"—in her public remarks, she referenced her own appropriation of another culture. Many students at Yale, especially women of color, quickly responded to these remarks by exercising their own free speech through leadership and activism. What follows is a portion of a transcript taken from a Halloween e-mail protest video recording that went viral between Yale students and a Yale official (who was the spouse of the lecturer):

ADMINISTRATOR: You would like for me to apologize for hurting your feelings, correct?

STUDENT 1: Yes, I still think that the phrase "hurting feelings" is . . .

ADMINISTRATOR: [interrupts student] Okay, tell me what phrase you want me to use.

STUDENT 1: I don't know, [the response] was an expression of racism.

STUDENT 2: An act of violence!

ADMINISTRATOR: I won't agree with you.

STUDENT 3: We're telling you what it is, and you're saying it's not that way.

STUDENT 1: You keep saying hurt feelings, but I want you to recognize that it goes deeper than feelings; it is an affront to a group of people.

ADMINISTRATOR: I recognize that.

STUDENT 1: Okay great, so understand that you can put it in your own words.

ADMINISTRATOR: So, you want me to say that I apologize, that

I hurt your feelings. [Leans closer to the student] I'm looking at her, and I'm listening very carefully. I know it's deeper than that.

STUDENT 1: So, then apologize! (TheAsianRepublican, 2016, 10:40)

In the weeks after this incident, local and national media amplified and circulated many of the conversations that took place on Yale's campus. What was originally framed as dialogue about the role of free speech on a university campus quickly morphed into a larger discussion about civility and the vales of the community. Marginalized students created a chant to capture the essence of their feelings about their experience at Yale—"We out here, We been here, We ain't leaving, We are loved"—and demanded to be seen and treated as full members of the Yale community, through holding town hall meetings, staging protests, organizing a march (the largest in Yale's history), and providing the president with a set of demands that would help the institution be more responsive to the needs of current and future marginalized students. Student activists issued a deadline for the university to respond to these demands, and what ensued was a communitywide process that involved Yale students, faculty, alumni, and administrators discussing how to improve all facets of the institution in an effort to drastically improve the campus climate for students of color. A process that emerged out of hurt and feelings of invisibility on campus turned into students learning that a dedicated group of individuals can make meaningful and lasting change.

Activism and Higher Education Introduction

In 2015, much of the country took notice as student activists at the University of Missouri (Mizzou) and Yale organized in the aftermath of bias-related incidents on their respective campuses. What began as concerned students gathering to challenge campus leaders to better support institutional values turned into policy changes and the reshaping of expectations nationwide concerning how administrators authentically serve an increasingly diverse student population. The actions of a few dedicated individuals at Mizzou and Yale touched a nerve and gave strength to students nationwide to confront bias-related issues and policies on their own campuses; the Mizzou and Yale student activists essentially created a blueprint for others to follow. Although many of the student activists who led these movements have since graduated, college campuses remain a microcosm of our larger society; as such, there are no signs that activism on campuses will quell (Ndemanu, 2017). As Gonzales (2008) asserted, student activism has always been embedded in the struggle for liberation; therefore, as long as oppression and discrimination exist, so will student activists.

The uptick of student activism on college and university campuses has left many administrators scrambling to meet the needs of their campuses—particularly with respect to matters of inclusion. Recent years have witnessed a rise in nationally distributed white papers and reports as well as regional and national conference presentations and webinars that highlight how college and university administrators can "manage" student activism and unrest. This stance is becoming increasingly problematic, as it ignores systemic issues embedded within the history of American higher education as well as those institutions that have historically benefited from the labor of student activism, such as in the formation of enhanced curricular and cocurricular offerings and identity-based centers (Hoffman & Mitchell, 2016; Horowitz, 1987). Still, as administrators continue to be pressured to make meaningful, lasting, and impactful change rooted in authenticity and respect, we must challenge ourselves and our colleagues to be innovative and creative in how we meet the needs of our 21st-century higher education landscape.

Activism on college and university campuses is not new, but how much and how often the public consumes these happenings is in its infancy if we consider the total history of American higher education. Technology broadly (e.g., Internet) and social media specifically (e.g., Twitter, Facebook, Snapchat) have significantly transformed how activism occurs and how many individuals are aware of it. For example, many members of the public have heard of Emma Sulkowicz, the student at Columbia University who carried a mattress around her campus until her rapist was removed from the institution; or Payton Head, the student body president at Mizzou who was the target of racial and homophobic slurs. Organizations like the Black Liberation Collective, whose purpose is to help student activists across the United States connect so that they can amplify their work, also strengthen networks by exposing larger groups to instances of injustice across the country. Whereas previous historians chronicled the history of higher education through journals, books, and other publications, students today have expanded their creativity and are making history through the creation of videos (e.g., Black Bruins; I, Too, Am Harvard), tweets (e.g., #concernedstudents1950, #BlackLivesMatter), blogs, and social media posts.

What is happening on college and university campuses and how information is distributed is important because higher education is at a pivotal point. Historically, institutions of higher education harbor some of this country's oldest vestiges of racism and White privilege; however, this legacy is in direct conflict with the "now," as the landscape of these establishments is rapidly changing. This evolution of the American college student has put more pressure on leaders to make their campuses welcoming and inclusive. What is more, students are coordinating protests, all in the name of seeking equality. The notion that student protests, especially those ignited by campus climate issues, will fade is simply incorrect.

As campus activism continues its upward trend, colleges and universities alike must not only be responsive but also be proactive and—more important—*creative* in working with students to meet their needs, assist in their development, and support their experience. We, as student affairs professionals, with our experience and training, are uniquely positioned to play a critical role in working in creative and innovative ways with student unrest and activism. Student affairs professionals, due to the ever-changing, intimate nature of our work with student groups, have always had to be willing and able to transform practices in ways that meet students where they are and that address the needs of the moment. This role is critical to institutions, as it could be the difference between an incident being handled "in house" and an incident making national or international news. Still, despite this enormous responsibility, most practitioners do not receive training on how to work with student activists, and what training is available has largely relied on following the status quo. Only recently have many of us discussed how to approach activism on our campuses using diverse approaches. In higher education, change is going to come; for this reason, it is imperative that all higher education professionals participate in dialogue geared at proactively working with student activists. Taking a hands-on approach could mean the difference between campus growth or paralysis in the immediate and long term. This chapter explores the nature of student activism on college and university campuses and discusses ways that practitioners can approach it with creative tactics.

Literature Review

As with most aspects of higher education, activism and unrest on college campuses is not new; in fact, it has existed in some fashion for much of the history of higher education (Gasman, 2013). For example, in describing the early structure of colleges and universities, Rudolph (1990) referenced the sometimes tumultuous relationship between students and their tutors, who often assumed a parental role on campus. Over the past several decades, a breadth of research has attempted to expand our understanding of activism on campus (Astin, 1993; Baird, 1970; Ferguson, 2017; Gasman, 2013; Horowitz, 1987; Rhoads, 1998). Although this research spans multiple institutions and student populations, one theme that cuts across this work is the notion that college students have always sought avenues to have their voices heard. Likewise, how students have chosen to advocate for themselves (e.g., protests, strikes, sit-ins) has in many ways reflected larger societal issues (political and otherwise) happening at the time.

Activism in the 1960s

Much of the research focuses on the 1960s—and for good reason. This decade brought increased access to higher education for marginalized populations, and as the United States debated the basic civil and human rights of African Americans and women, these conversations were concurrently playing out on a smaller scale at institutions of higher education. Although scholars have debated the exact number of campus-based protests that took place during the 1960s (Baird, 1970; Levine & Hirsch, 1991), there remains widespread agreement that the era was "the decade of unrest" for higher education. According to Horowitz (1987), in the 1960s, students at more than 350 colleges and universities across the county declared themselves on strike. Although much national attention focused on the political and antiwar protests at Kent State and the University of California, Berkeley, students nationwide also called for curriculum reform by way of new majors, such as African American and women's studies, as well as racial integration and equality on campus

(Horowitz, 1987). The issues that institutions of higher education faced, paired with a growing student body who leveraged activism to make change, created fertile ground for students to express themselves through demonstrations and other ethical spectacles. By the end of the 1960s, almost a third of all college students reported having participated in a demonstration of some sort, compared with only 19% by the mid-1970s (Levine & Cureton, 1998). The remnants of this activity can be seen today in the form of cultural centers on many campuses as well as majors that examine the experiences of marginalized groups.

Activism in the 1990s

By many scholars' accounts, the 1970s and 1980s saw a relative lull on college and university campuses for student activism (Hurtado, 1992; Rhoads, 1995, 1998; Sidel, 1994). However, the rise in "political correctness" discussions and campus climate issues reignited activism for college students and established what Rhoads (1998) called a "new generation" of student activists. These students entered college with a healthy level of exposure to activism. For example, in 1989, 37% of first-year students had participated in a demonstration of some kind, and by 1993, 25% of undergraduates reported participating in a demonstration (Levine & Cureton, 1998). Rhoads (1998) posited that much of the unrest associated with the 1990s centered on a lack of diversity in many curricula and on campus climate issues for students of color, women, and members of the queer community. On campuses across the country, these issues played out in high-profile ways that shared a common theme: Students were calling for everyone, regardless of identity, to be given equal opportunities to get the best education possible. In this way, Rhoads (1998) asserted that student activism in the 1990s was an exercise in participatory democracy for students.

Student unrest and activism in many ways shaped the overall trajectory of higher education, by inciting changes in policies and practices at many institutions across the country. As higher education continues into the 21st century, one constant remains: Students with minoritized identities feel isolated on college and university campuses. What is different now than in previous years is that students have a larger platform to voice their concerns and thus solicit responses from administrators. Moreover, the activism of the 1990s helped to solidify the importance of marginalized identities in the culture of higher education and made campus climate a topic that had to be taken seriously in the ensuing decades.

Protests and Student Demands

Today, college and university campuses remain environments that foster dialogue and debate about broad political and social issues at the national and international levels. Similarly, some of the content of these debates and reasons for student activism remain the same as they did in the 1960s. In the time since Mizzou and Yale in 2015, the higher education landscape has experienced a wave of resistance and activism from students. One organization, the Black Liberation Collective, collected the demands at 86 colleges and universities during this period. Separately, in a 2017 study analyzing the demands at 73 institutions, the most common wants included expanding faculty of color, offering diversity training, adding mandatory diversity curricular requirements, and recruiting more students of color (Ndemanu, 2017). Other specific demands included the following:

- **University of Missouri:** Meet the demands from 1969 for the betterment of the Black community.
- **Yale University:** Develop racial competence and respect training and accountability systems for all Yale affiliates.

- **New York University:** Make the university more accessible to undocumented students of color.
- **Lewis & Clark College:** Publicly acknowledge that Lewis & Clark College was built upon stolen land through the genocide of indigenous and Native American peoples and that its name honors the lives and deeds of owners of enslaved peoples.
- **The University of North Carolina at Chapel Hill:** Provide gender-nonspecific housing and bathrooms across campus.
- **Vanderbilt University:** Eliminate the inscription of "Confederate" on Memorial Hall as well as the plaque paying homage to the Daughters of the Confederacy. (Black Liberation Collective, n.d.)

All of these demands reflect societal issues that the United States has faced and continues to face. As colleges and universities encourage students to nurture academic thought and exploration, students will continue to enact activism on their campuses as they analyze and deconstruct structures of power at home and on campus.

Challenges in Addressing Student Activism

The Us vs. Them Mentality

In addition to the political and social issues happening in our larger society, racial microaggressions, xenophobia, racial battle fatigue, stereotype threat, nationalism, islamophobia, hypermasculinity, and other issues are prevalent on college and university campuses and directly affect the campus climate and culture (Smith, Allen, & Danley, 2007; Solorzano, Ceja, & Yosso, 2000; Sue et al., 2007). These critical issues not only affect the mental, physical, and emotional health of the students whose identities they marginalize but also influence these students' academic success. Today's students are not content with accepting the status quo; they demand change and, more importantly, are strategic and intentional in how they choose to advocate. The increased willingness of today's students to advocate for themselves has arguably exacerbated the "us vs. them" relationship that exists on many campuses between students and administrators. In many cases this dysfunctional relationship goes both ways: Students view administrators as sometimes inhibiting their ability to make change, while some administrators have an implicit bias against students who refuse to be quiet and accept an unequal collegiate experience. These perceptions can pit students and administrators as adversaries instead of partners. This relationship makes it difficult to build trust between the groups; more important, student affairs administrators do not get the "benefit of the doubt" that we are operating from a student-centered approach when addressing student concerns.

To overcome this hurdle, student affairs professionals must work to welcome students into partnerships with us so that we are not seen as adversaries. For example, if members of the Black Student Union express frustration because their Black Lives Matter posters are continually ripped off walls across campus, this would be a great opportunity to meet with the leadership (in their environment) and discuss options for addressing this issue. This does not mean that we should place the onus on the students to "solve the problem"; rather, we can create an equal partnership so that students view us as true advocates. That said, a word of caution about this approach: We must manage expectations regarding what action will take place.

Working Within Our Sphere of Influence

Many administrators view our roles and responsibilities mainly through the lens of hierarchies in that we have a direct supervisor who has authority and some control over our work. However, in many instances students expect that everyone at the institution is equally responsible for creating a welcoming and inclusive campus climate. Although this is true, we cannot discount our actual sphere of influence. Even though we all have the best intentions to help students, we must have an accurate understanding of the limitations placed on us by our institution, its policies and practices, and the community. Each of us must ask ourselves: How is change made on my campus? What is the power dynamic between senior leadership and the rest of campus? How has my institution historically responded to change? Having realistic answers to these questions does not give us permission to make excuses and not advocate, but it does allow us to be more efficient and effective in accomplishing our goals in student protest situations. In any case, we must be more imaginative in how we build champions for the issues we seek to change. An easy way to foster relationships with existing champions is to take a more thorough assessment of who "shows up" for the programs, panels, and other events that address issues of importance to us. Often, by default, we notice the loud advocates or the "chorus," but are we making it a point to search out the more quiet (yet equally effective) stakeholders in our community? If champions are not readily available, we can cultivate these individuals by leaving our safe spaces (literally and figuratively) and expanding our networks by inviting colleagues to meetings, programs, events, and conversations so that they can become more aware of issues around and on campus. Regardless, it is important that students are made aware that student affairs professionals can always advocate, but we cannot always readily enact change in ways that students want and often need to see. Each situation is different, but it is important to know one's institution before attempting to address potentially volatile student-related situations.

Balancing Student Needs With Institutional Priorities

Most of us entered the field of student affairs because we wanted to work with and support students. We do this by meeting students where they are, while serving as educators via cocurricular experiences. This process naturally lends itself to building strong relationships with students. As these relationships grow, students often begin to see us as their advocates, individuals to whom they can reach out when they feel wronged or when they face obstacles; however, a pitfall to building these strong relationships in times of student protest or unrest is that we cannot forget our role as employees of our institutions. Although many professionals would outwardly say that their employee status and role as a student advocate are intertwined, for some of us, the prospect of placing our careers (and ability to support our families) in jeopardy by being too vocal against our employer is a real fear and concern. We would like to work in a place that matches our personal and professional values, but this might not be the case. In these situations, it is important for us as student affairs professionals to have strong relationships with our direct supervisors and be open and honest about how we can show our activism as professionals. For example, is it okay to participate in the die-in or help lead the Deferred Action for Childhood Arrivals (DACA) march? How much support can be reasonably provided in helping students devise a list of demands that will be sent to senior administrators? These are important questions to consider, because the answers could have a direct impact on whether issues are approached through the lens of an advocate or an employee. How we navigate this process varies largely according to many factors: our position, length of employment at our institution (and subsequent capital built), political acumen, and supervisory relationship, among other factors. Still, regardless of our unique circumstances, we must make students aware of the power that they possess to make change, and we should continually work to build strong student leaders who can advocate for themselves when possible.

But how can we do this? When working with student leaders of color—who often fail to understand their true power—draw on Yosso's (2005) work. Point out the various forms of capital these students possess, which have helped them achieve success, and note that they can leverage this capital in ways that allow them to better advocate for themselves. For example, Yosso (2005) mentioned the idea of navigation capital as the ways in which students of color navigate education systems that were not designed to facilitate their success. Draw attention to how students have already successfully navigated systems, and encourage them to bring this same level of creativity to their current issue. In many cases, students (of all races, ethnicities, etc.) feel more power when administrators show them the power they already possess.

A Creative Approach to Working With Student Activism

In thinking about creative strategies for our work with student activism, it is important that we first view our role as educators working with students to meet their needs and not just seeking to appease their concerns. This is a shift in how many of us were taught to deal with issues that arise on our campuses—as problems that need to be solved instead of opportunities to do what drew us into this profession in the first place (that is, to serve students, educate, and make a difference). A few strategies we can use include embracing activism on our campuses and all that it might entail, working to help set the tone around activism early in students' careers, viewing ourselves as cultural navigators and translators, and challenging the status quo.

Embrace Activism

After a campus finds itself embroiled in a controversy that leads to student activism, administrators often attempt to locate quick solutions that will quell the unrest. In the process, students have been found to view administrators as "gatekeepers, antagonists, supporters, and absentee leaders, but not collaborators" (Hoffman & Mitchell, 2016, p. 279). Even as administrators acknowledge that activism is a right under campus free speech policies, there is a layer of apprehension as to how students will choose to exercise this right.

In 2015, when both Mizzou and Yale found themselves responding to negative racial incidents and climates, each university took a different approach. Administrators at Yale chose to listen, acknowledge faults, and apply recommendations that students were offering. Listening is something that many administrators think they do well, but this is often not the case. In these listening sessions, one-on-one meetings, or random office pop-ins, administrators dropped preconceived notions of what "should be done" in this situation and made themselves totally open to students. Administrators didn't wait for a point to be made so that they could respond; they waited for students to get their points across and then "sat" in their frustration, anger, and, at times, hopelessness to gain empathy. This act might seem basic, but the creativity was in the ability to authentically listen, which allowed administrators to think of ways to meet the students halfway in their demands. For example, if a student said people on campus need to understand the plight of students of color, administrators could interpret this as needing to think of ways to develop a campus culture of education around diversity-related issues that is more pervasive in its implementation. While Yale continues to work on addressing the needs of marginalized students, administrators understood that something powerful, and even special, was at hand as students chanted: "We out here, we been here, we ain't leaving, we are loved."

By the end of that year, applications to Yale surged to the highest in its history, specifically from students of color (Admitted to Yale College, 2016). Conversely, enrollment at Mizzou declined sharply (Hartocollis, 2017). Embracing activism allowed administrators to "lean in" to discomfort and assist students as they developed into civically engaged leaders who reflect the best of the university.

Normalize Activist Actions

Far too frequently when activism takes place on college and university campuses, institutional leaders are quick to overreact and treat the opportunity as a crisis. Instead of operating in a state of emergency, we should work to normalize activism on campuses. We can do this by working to educate others—and ourselves—about the history and current status of activism nationally and on campuses. Specifically, staff should work to see activism as a form of civic engagement and embrace the act of protesting and demonstrating as an exercise of this engagement. For example, when students express the desire to advocate for themselves, when possible, we should approach this conversation with a "yes, and" and not a "no" response in mind (Stewart, 2015). If a student says, "Would it be okay if my Pride Organization plans a program that educates the campus about restroom politics and the transgender community?" our response can be, "Yes, and what if your group worked with [other organization], because they have a shared interest and it would help broaden your audience?" Or if a student approaches us and says, "Can I plan a DACA rally on campus?" our response can be, "Yes, and have you thought about working with the ethnicity, race, and migration studies department to help publicize the event?" When we are proactive in making this form of expression frequent occurrences, we support the needs of students on a deeper level.

Orientation for first-year students is an excellent time to begin to normalize campus activism, through carefully crafted videos and conversations at required meetings or before events. When students first arrive to campus, one of our goals as administrators should be to introduce them to the culture of the institution through social and educational activities. A way to relay the message that the campus is a space that embraces students expressing themselves in different ways is to provide a program that engages first-year students in discourse about the definition of activism, how to be effective with their activism, and what institutional changes have occurred by way of this method of civic engagement.

Embrace Our Roles as Cultural Navigators

In a talk at the University of Illinois at Urbana–Champaign, Terrell Strayhorn (2015) challenged higher education professionals to be "cultural navigators" when assisting students of color in navigating through their collegiate experience. Serving as a cultural navigator involves helping students to understand their campus culture—both the spoken and unspoken rules. It is not a deficit approach toward students; instead, it acknowledges that each institution has its own culture and that if students learn the culture, they will be more successful. The practice of cultural navigation can be adapted to our work with student activism, by treating students as equals and exposing them to information that may aid their efforts. For example, in some cases demands made by students are in the process of being addressed by the institution, but students lack this knowledge. Csikszentmihalyi (1996) pointed out that for individuals to be creative, they must know the rules. How are we educating students about rules so that they can be effective leaders? The idea of helping students navigate through their unrest and activism might seem odd and goes against typical training for practitioners; however, the more information we are willing to provide, the more information we can expect to receive in return. This sharing of knowledge will benefit both sides.

In addition to serving as cultural navigators to students, we must serve as cultural translators to our colleagues and senior-level administrators (if we are not in such a position). When confronted with student activism on our campuses, we bring our implicit biases that impact how we perceive student activists and how we work with them. As champions for students, we can address staff members' preconceived notions of students by serving as cultural translators. This process involves educating colleagues, translating to stakeholders that student activists are students first. We must explain that activism, in most cases, is not meant to be an affront to any one individual but to those institutions that foster environments that maintain structural barriers to the full acceptance of certain groups. It is difficult to hate that which we know; therefore, the job of cultural translator is to help stakeholders know the students at the center of the issue.

Challenge the Status Quo

Higher education's cultural grounding in supremacy continues to fail marginalized students. Even in responding to student demands, student affairs administrators often do so through nonperformative statements—statements that, while enveloped in said commitments to diversity and inclusion, are worded in such a way that lacks concrete action on behalf of the institution and places the onus on marginalized students to better their situation (Ahmed, 2012). An example is when administrators coordinate and promote resilience-building programming: This encourages marginalized students to cope with issues at hand, instead of the institution addressing the persons or conditions that call for the students to be resilient to begin with.

If the issues remain and students decades later are responding similarly, then administrators may need to respond differently. Lessons can be learned from students who challenged the status quo. To include student voices, administrators often employ a shared governance with student governments; however, at many institutions this arrangement ignores the reality that student governments are also institutions of power and may not reflect the campus population. In this instance, it is not innovative to simply include student government in the conversation; instead, administrators can seek out student groups with less institutional authority and provide them with a voice and platform to share their opinions. If certain populations have deemed the campus as unsafe, it is not enough to provide a statement stating the values of the institution; instead, administrators can seek to elevate the voices of marginalized populations through engaging with the local Black Lives Matter chapter at a predominantly White institution, with an LGBTQIA organization, or with first-generation and low-income students who are not able to engage through involvement because they must work their way through school.

As we enter the third decade of the 21ˢᵗ century, racial microaggressions and a plethora of "isms" present within and outside campus communities will continue to offer opportunities for student activism. After a long legacy of student activism in higher education, will students need to keep organizing around the same issues? Will student affairs professionals choose to be on the right side of history and directly address the challenges that run counter to institutional and divisional mission statements that espouse a commitment to diversity and inclusion? Students are the experts of their own experiences, and much of student affairs work stems from the labor that student activists have invested throughout the years to have people on campus to advocate for their needs and safety.

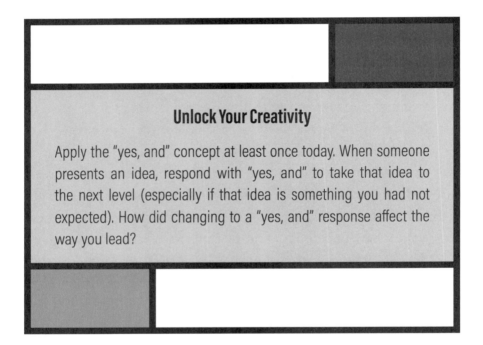

Unlock Your Creativity

Apply the "yes, and" concept at least once today. When someone presents an idea, respond with "yes, and" to take that idea to the next level (especially if that idea is something you had not expected). How did changing to a "yes, and" response affect the way you lead?

References

Admitted to Yale College: 1,972 from largest-ever pool of applicants. (2016, March 31). *Yale News.* Retrieved from https://news.yale.edu/2016/03/31/admitted-yale-college-1972-largest-ever-pool-applicants

Ahmed, S. (2012). *On being included: Racism and diversity in institutional life.* Durham, NC: Duke University Press.

TheAsianRepublican. (2016, September 26). *Yale students berating professor* [Video file]. Retrieved from https://www.youtube.com/watch?v=hiMVx2C5_Wg

Astin, A. W. (1993). Diversity and multiculturalism on the campus: How are students affected? *Change, 25*(1), 44–49.

Baird, L. (1970). Who protests: A study of student activists. In J. Foster & D. Long (Eds.), *Protest! Student activism in America* (pp. 123–133). New York, NY: William Morrow & Company.

Black Liberation Collective. (n.d.). Our demands. Retrieved from http://www.blackliberationcollective.org/our-demands

Csikszentmihalyi, M. (1996). *Creativity: The work and lives of 91 eminent people.* New York, NY: HarperCollins.

Ferguson, R. A. (2017). *We demand: The university and student protests.* Oakland, CA: University of California Press.

Gasman, M. (2013). *The history of U.S. higher education: Methods for understanding the past.* New York, NY: Routledge.

Gonzales, R. G. (2008). Left out but not shut down: Political activism and the undocumented student movement. *Northwestern Journal of Law and Social Policy, 3*(2), 219–239.

Hartocollis, A. (2017, July 9). Long after protests, students shun the University of Missouri. Retrieved from https://www.nytimes.com/2017/07/09/us/university-of-missouri-enrollment-protests-fallout.html

Hoffman, G. D., & Mitchell, T. D. (2016). Making diversity "everyone's business": A discourse analysis of institutional responses to student activism for equity and inclusion. *Journal of Diversity in Higher Education, 9*(3), 277–289.

Horowitz, H. L. (1987). *Campus life: Undergraduate cultures from the end of the eighteenth century to the present.* Chicago, IL: University of Chicago Press.

Hurtado, S. (1992). The campus racial climate: Contexts for conflict. *Journal of Higher Education, 63*(5), 539–569.

Levine, A., & Cureton, J. S. (1998). *When hope and fear collide: A portrait of today's college students.* San Francisco, CA: Jossey-Bass.

Levine, A., & Hirsch, D. (1991). Undergraduates in transition: A new wave of activism on American college campuses. *Higher Education, 22*(2), 119–128.

Ndemanu, M. T. (2017). Antecedents of college campus protests nationwide: Exploring Black student activists' demands. *The Journal of Negro Education, 86*(3), 238–251.

Rhoads, R. A. (1995). The cultural politics of coming out in college: Experiences of male students. *Review of Higher Education, 19*(1), 1–22.

Rhoads, R. A. (1998). *Freedom's web: Student activism in an age of cultural diversity.* Baltimore, MD: Johns Hopkins University Press.

Rudolph, F. (1990). *The American college and university: A history.* Athens, GA: University of Georgia Press.

Sidel, R. (1994). *Battling bias: The struggle for identity and community on college campuses.* New York, NY: Viking.

Smith, W. A., Allen, W. R., & Danley, L. L. (2007). "Assume the position . . . you fit the description" psychosocial experiences and racial battle fatigue among African American male college students. *American Behavioral Scientist, 51*(4), 551–578.

Solorzano, D., Ceja, M., & Yosso, T. (2000). Critical race theory, racial microaggressions, and campus racial climate: The experiences of African American college students. *Journal of Negro Education, 69*(1/2), 60–73.

Stewart, C. (2015). Where creativity intersects with reality: Four recommendations for bringing the creative process into your student activities program. *Campus Activities Programming, 48*(5), 32–38.

Strayhorn, T. L. (2015, March 19). *Cultural navigators and college success* [Video file]. Retrieved from https://mediaspace.illinois.edu/media/Terrell+Strayhorn+-+%22Cultural+Navigat ors+and+College+Student+Success%22/1_u7g18swt

Sue, D. W., Capodilupo, C. M., Torino, G. C., Bucceri, J. M., Holder, A., Nadal, K. L., & Esquilin, M. (2007). Racial microaggressions in everyday life: Implications for clinical practice. *American Psychologist, 62*(4), 271.

Yosso, T. J. (2005). Whose culture has capital? A critical race theory discussion of community cultural wealth. *Race Ethnicity and Education, 8*(1), 69–91.

HARNESSING CULTURAL WEALTH
FOR CREATIVE LEADERSHIP

BRIDGET TURNER KELLY AND NATASHA T. TURMAN

S tudents at colleges and universities across the United States are leading and participating in walk-outs, demonstrations, and protests on issues as diverse as gun safety, police brutality, and immigration reform. Students are looking to leaders in higher education to alter their course from the status quo and act in new ways. Faculty are looking for the same type of creative leadership. Bridget and Natasha, authors of this chapter, entered the academy after experiencing the transformative effect it had on us as students and believing in the mission of higher education to educate the next leaders of society. However, realities in higher education for the past 20 years evidence that status quo leadership will not meet pressing demands, such as the change in demographics from middle- to upper-class White male students to students of color and first-generation and low-income students; market shifts and decreased federal and state funding, which makes the cost of higher education unattainable for most students; and student retention rates at public universities that hover around 60% (National Center for Education Statistics, 2018).

If educators are to meet these and other pressing demands in order to prepare for the future, faculty and staff must transform higher education practice. Such transformation might include teaching higher education professionals to dismantle systems, policies, programs, and practices that are inequitable and to reimagine more inclusive, equitable, and socially just ways to lead. Transformation will take bold, courageous, and creative leadership.

Authors' Positionality

When most people close their eyes and think of a leader, a Black woman is typically not the first person who comes to mind. Historically, in the Western context, leadership frameworks have positioned upper- and middle-class White men and, more recently, White women as the ideal example (Byrd, 2008; Ospina & Foldy, 2009; Parker, 2001, 2005). A recent report by the American Association of University Women noted, "Data from the real-world workforce confirm that black women have faced the steepest climb to leadership of any race/gender group" (Hill, 2016, p. 2).

The scarce presence of the perspectives of women of color in leadership research and scholarship is due to perpetual presumptions that leadership is both gender and race neutral (Byrd, 2008; Parker, 2005; Parker & Ogilvie, 1996). As Turman (2017) suggested, "Viewing leadership as a set of universal constructs, garnered from a select few and generalized to a great many, is not adequate to understanding the leadership experiences of [women of color] within dominant-culture environments" (p. 8). In addition, if educators asked people to close their eyes and picture a creative leader, they might quickly conjure up images of White males such as Elon Musk and Steve Jobs but not as readily think of women of color such as Shirley Chisholm or Sonia Sotomayor. Chisholm's feat of being the first African American woman in Congress in 1968 and the first African American to seek the nomination for president of the United States from one of the two major political parties in 1972 required a high degree of creative leadership. She had no models for how to legislate as a Black woman and had to take legal action to earn the right to give just one speech in her quest for the presidential nomination (Chisholm, 2010). Sotomayor, the first Latina Supreme Court justice, also had no models to follow in serving on the highest court in the United States. Her effective work as an intellectual property litigator and her pro bono work helping AIDS hospices and low-income housing residents receive mortgage insurance garnered the attention of Senator Ted Kennedy, who appointed her to a federal judgeship. Her leadership as a judge led President Barack Obama to nominate her for a position on the U.S. Supreme Court (Sotomayor, 2013). Both creative women leaders of color were motivated to do the work they did because of their minoritized race, class, and gender identities. As Chisholm's and Sotomayor's own works attest, creative leadership often begins with centering ourselves.

As Black women higher education professionals, Bridget and Natasha's perspective on leadership is shaped from their salient intersecting identities, such as race and gender. Natasha and Bridget's experiences as Black women provide cultural capital that enables them to be innovative, creative, and bold in their approach to higher education. Bridget draws strength from the intersection of her salient identities as her marginalized identity as a Black woman interacts with her privileged identities of Christian, heterosexual, cisgender, upper middle class, U.S. citizen, English speaker, and currently able in mind and body. Bridget faces racism and sexism through the power she claims from communities of color and, in particular, women of color.

For Natasha, her identity as a Black woman, cisgender, able-bodied, scholar-practitioner in the field of higher education and student affairs is foundational for her engagement with leadership and research on leadership. She brings 10 years of combined experience as a practitioner, instructor, and researcher. How Natasha understands and practices leadership is in the context of the "irreducibly complex intersections" (Moraga & Anzaldúa, 1981, p. 277) of identity and lived experience. Natasha places concerted effort on engaging in work that disrupts essentialized approaches to leadership that have historically excluded the perspectives and ideas of people like her. This positionality affords her an opportunity to take both a nuanced and critical approach to the study and exploration of leadership phenomena.

As authors, Natasha and Bridget framed this chapter with their positionalities in mind. Natasha and Bridget understand that their interpretations of creative leadership are directly correlated with their identities as Black women and with their personal and professional experiences. They intentionally centered their narratives to elevate the variance in their experiences with leadership and to illustrate the unique challenges and opportunities inherent in being a woman of color doing innovative work. Natasha and Bridget recognize that their experiences are their own and do not offer a universal perspective for other women of color. However, they hope this chapter provides a glimpse into the many ways leadership practices can be reimagined when women of color are the "creators and holders of knowledge" (Turman, 2017, p. 8).

Critical Leadership Is Essential for Innovation

Leadership shapes the very nature of work in higher education, particularly through interactions and commitments. There is no universal definition for it, but universal aspirations exist to practice, develop, and embody leadership. Some view leadership as a position held, others as the commitment to effect change. Although no common definition exists, as critical scholars and authors, Natasha and Bridget situate their understanding of and operationalization of leadership through critical lenses. In doing so, leadership becomes dynamic, liberating, and yes, creative. A critical approach to leadership disrupts normative approaches to leadership practice and development (Dugan & Turman, 2018).

Critical leadership centers the margins and elevates the "experiences of minoritized peoples whose contributions to the leadership literature are all too often co-opted by the dominant narrative or rendered invisible" (Dugan & Turman, 2018, p. 5). Critical leadership enables systems to be examined and places of power to be interrogated and challenged. Whether one's understanding of leadership is rooted in notions of positional power or grounded in activism and social change, a critical lens challenges the status quo and encourages innovative and novel practice to reimagine it—this is creative leadership. In this chapter, Natasha and Bridget narrate case studies that highlight their positionality as women of color and critical leadership as they experienced it in higher education.

Cultural and Leadership Capitals as a Framework

In her seminal work, Yosso (2005) challenged normative assumptions about cultural capital theory (Bourdieu & Passeron, 1977) that perpetuated Whiteness as the status quo and inherently viewed communities of color through deficit lenses. Using critical race theory, Yosso (2005) demonstrated the power in overlaying a critical framework to center the lived experiences of these communities to unearth their historically situated "accumulated assets and resources" (p. 77). She introduced six forms of capital—aspirational, navigational, social, linguistic, familial, and resistant—that served as cultural wealth for communities of color. These forms of capital expanded narrowly defined understandings of wealth and positioned the experiences, knowledge, and abilities unique to communities of color as invaluable assets; assets essential for combating oppression and marginalization.

Yosso's (2005) work disrupted notions about whose knowledge is of value to demonstrate the impactful contributions of communities of color. It is in this vein that this chapter is anchored on creative leadership. The very nature of leadership and the normative assumptions about leadership practice, development, and capacities have left minoritized individuals and communities on the margins in leadership contexts. Who is viewed as a creative leader and which practices or initiatives are labeled as innovative are contingent on who crafts the leadership narrative. Natasha and Bridget were drawn to certain kinds of capital identified by Yosso (i.e., aspirational, navigational, social, and resistant) to illustrate how harnessing cultural assets allows one to engage in creative leadership practice that aligns with one's identities, culture, and lived experiences.

Yosso (2005) defined aspirational capital as the ability to imagine future realities in the midst of opposition and in spite of marginalization. Navigational capital captures the unique skill set used to traverse social spaces not historically intended for communities of color. Social capital reflects the collective of individuals who serve as resources and offer support to help others successfully navigate environments. Finally, resistant capital embodies the skills, insight, and wisdom cultivated in engaging with "oppositional behavior" that combats inequitable practice (Yosso, 2005, p. 80).

This chapter is also framed with emerging leadership scholarship on *leadership capital* for women of color. Turman (2017) introduced adaptive capital, resilient capital, covering capital, and dialectical thinking capital as assets unique to the leadership experiences of women of color engaging in leadership in predominantly White spaces. These leadership assets have proven to be foundational to the leadership practice of women of color.

Turman (2017) defined *adaptive capital* as the ability to evaluate one's surroundings and, if necessary, adjust oneself and one's leadership behaviors to align with the dynamics in that environment. This capital emerges when individuals adopt different leadership styles or find themselves negotiating aspects of their identities through "code-switching and impression management" in leadership contexts (Turman, 2017, p. 223). As a woman of color navigates leadership contexts that may question her presence, ability, competence, and right to be a leader, Turman posited that she harnesses resilient capital, which provides the fortitude she needs to combat marginalization, stereotypes, and othering in leadership spaces. *Covering capital* is defined by Turman as one's ability to *code-switch*, meaning to adjust one's language to present a level of fit and alignment with the norms in that environment. In Turman's (2017) study, the ability to be socially multilinguistic—to "speak the language of the dominant culture" (p. 224)—was essential in the leadership practices of women of color. Everyone code-switches, but Turman (2017) believed that "the social repercussions for not harnessing this skill set for communities of color could be detrimental to their success" (p. 224).

Finally, Turman (2017) introduced dialectical thinking capital as a leadership asset for women of color. Dialectical thinking is the cognitive ability to understand and coexist with divergent and often conflicting ideas (Dugan, 2017). As a capital, dialectical thinking reflects the ability of women of color to "successfully reframe cognitive dissonance within their leadership experiences" (Turman, 2017, p. 225). For example, you can view yourself as a leader even though leadership frameworks have historically excluded the perspectives and experiences of people like you. This asset has informed the strategies women of color use to navigate leadership spaces, as well as the leadership approaches they use.

This chapter applies various kinds of cultural and leadership capital in the case studies presented. The case studies illustrate how harnessing these assets can support creative leadership and, conversely, how not tapping into these assets has the potential to affect leadership efficacy, stifle leadership development, and police leadership practice.

Case Study 1: Withdrawing From Leadership (Bridget)

Resignation and withdrawal are not bold, creative, or innovative leadership choices, but faced with the challenge of staying in a leadership role and fighting the administration of the university, Bridget took the path of least resistance and resigned her role. Three years before Bridget made the decision to step down, hope and passion fueled her desire to lead a graduate program as a tenured faculty member. When she found out that a longtime leader of the graduate program was stepping down and that no one else on the faculty wanted to or could take on the role, Bridget volunteered to be the next positional leader as graduate program director. Initially it was wonderful, as Bridget worked collaboratively with the faculty to understand her new role and thoroughly enjoyed the increased contact with prospective and current students. However, over time, subtle and covert incidents made her question whether she should continue in the role.

First, as Bridget worked on duties assigned to program directors, she discovered that the administrators in the college gave her additional tasks that other directors did not have. Bridget was not sure whether the different treatment she experienced was racism or sexism, or was a reflection of the administration's wanting her to prove herself as the new person. Second, Bridget refused to bend the rules on a decision that the leadership at the university wanted, and the dean reprimanded her. Third, in an era of "do more with less," the dean asked faculty in the graduate program to increase student enrollment, increase class size, and create new programs, all without any new resources or reductions in other areas of work. Bridget and her program faculty complied by almost doubling enrollment, adding multiple sections of courses to accommodate the increased size of the class, and collaborating with another program to create a new degree program. The final straw was when Bridget and her program faculty refused to create yet another new program without added resources, and Bridget accused an administrator in the college of threatening untenured faculty who would not comply with the new demand. Some of the untenured faculty in the graduate program were up for review at the time of this meeting, and Bridget questioned whether the administrator would try to stall or deny tenure to her program faculty unless they complied.

After this incident, the administrators in the college gave Bridget the silent treatment unless communication was absolutely necessary in a formal setting (e.g., program director meeting). Again, as the only Black woman in the graduate program and with no people of color in the administration, Bridget was not sure how racism intersecting with sexism affected the treatment she experienced. During the three years Bridget served as director of this graduate program, she was emotionally stressed because of the tense climate of constantly proving herself; exhausted by the inequitable workload compared with those of other program directors in the college; and unsure of her efficacy in leading, since she had acted against the wishes of the administration by saying no to multiple demands. One morning Bridget took a walk to clear her head and asked herself why she was continuing to serve in this role when it was doing so much internal damage to her. Bridget reasoned that the faculty in the graduate program were now in positions to take on the role, and she resigned at the end of three years. However, staying in the background and choosing not to rock the boat stripped Bridget of her voice and power to lead in a creative manner.

Case Study 1 Analysis: Reclaiming Bridget's Leadership Using Cultural and Leadership Capital

As a tenured faculty member who had led a program at another institution, when the opportunity arose to lead this graduate program, Bridget used aspirational capital to bolster herself, despite the fact that she was new to the university and that no person of color had ever led the program. Bridget envisioned being successful in the role because she knew she could rely on her social capital in the form of relationships she had developed with faculty in the program who knew the institution and the role. The open-door policy of the previous program director had given Bridget the courage to ask for clarity and advice whenever she encountered something new or was unsure about a policy. Bridget also bounced ideas off leaders in her professional and personal circles and asked questions when she needed guidance. Her social capital gave her the confidence to use navigational capital in an academic space that creators of higher education did not design for a Black woman leader. Working in predominantly White universities her whole career had taught Bridget how to use adaptive capital to make her style acceptable to White administrators, who followed hierarchical and authoritative styles. However, she found that the toll adaptive leadership was taking on her body and mind was not sustainable. In addition, integrity is a high value of Bridget's, and when the administration asked her to act in ways that went against her sense of fairness and equity, she used resistant capital.

Perhaps with more practice and knowledge of other kinds of capital Bridget had in her storehouse, she could have navigated the role more successfully. Being creative takes energy and skills that she did not know how to access at the time. For instance, she could have enlisted her social and resistant capital to work creatively as a collective against the oppositional behavior and inequitable practices she observed in the administration. At the time, she was not thinking creatively enough to see how the untenured faculty and she could form a collective and resist the marginalization they faced. Also, Bridget was so emotionally drained that she could not innovate and seek out individuals in positions of power who would help her. In addition, her aspirational capital was depleted to such an extent that she could not imagine a future in which she persevered as program director despite the marginalization she experienced. When Bridget did confront the administration concerning the sexism she experienced, they denied it and brushed aside her claim, further weakening her ability to see herself persevering in the role. Bridget also lacked a command of the language of intersectionality and did not take a step back to look at the whole picture—the racism, sexism, and ageism she was experiencing simultaneously as a Black woman who was younger than the administrative leadership team in the college. Taking full account of her capital and having the energy to use her leadership assets would enable Bridget to be the creative, innovative leader she wanted to be.

Case Study 2: Leading While Contingent (Natasha)

As the academy has grown leaner in the number of tenured and tenure-track (TT) faculty positions available, there has been a significant increase in the number of contingent faculty roles (i.e., nontenured and non-TT full- and part-time positions). Contingent faculty navigated the same academic processes to receive terminal degrees in their fields of study and endured the same academic expectations (e.g., publish, present, teach) to position themselves as viable candidates; however, they have not secured a coveted TT position, whether by personal choice or because of limited options. As Natasha emerged from the last semester of her doctoral degree—having applied, interviewed, and applied some more for TT positions—she found herself entertaining and accepting a contingent faculty position.

As a visiting assistant professor (VAP), Natasha was invited to have a seat at the table with her peers who were tenured or TT faculty members; however, there was a significant difference in how much influence, power, access, and ability to effect change Natasha had. At her institution, Natasha lacked certain rights and privileges customarily afforded to tenured/TT faculty: official voting, promotion, certain kinds of departmental decision making, and access to faculty-specific institutional funding (e.g., teaching and research grants), to name a few. How could Natasha embark upon creative and bold leadership within a finite amount of time? What if the byproduct of her leadership would not benefit her directly? In her role, Natasha did not have promotion and review processes, so the initiatives she implemented might not be actualized for years to come, when she might not be at the institution, given the contingent nature of her position.

When Natasha considered how she wanted to contribute to the academy, how she wanted to be a leader in her field and change the landscape of student affairs and higher education, she thought she would be unable to accomplish this in her role as a VAP. As much as she strove to operate with a critical perspective and situate her understanding of leadership within an "effect change" mindset, she found herself doubting her ability to impact her organization or the students she served because of the lack of power and influence she felt in her new position as a contingent faculty member. Natasha could not fully explore the creative possibilities of her role because she did not believe she had the positional power to have a sustaining impact on the organization. This was a deficit mindset. Natasha was so clouded by the traditional embodiment of leadership and power that she almost missed the inherent power and influence she could have in her role as a VAP. She could ask questions, challenge the status quo, and push new ideas forward that her peers might be hesitant to do given the political nature of departments and higher education organizations. And Natasha discovered that standing on the periphery gave her a better view of the big picture; this vantage point is critical for innovation.

Case Study 2 Analysis: Natasha's Application of Cultural and Leadership Assets for Permanent Impact

As Natasha leaned into this new opportunity, she reminded herself why she entered the field of higher education and student affairs: to center narratives that had historically been on the margins in higher education; to diversify faculty demographics (i.e., increase the number of women of color faculty with her presence); to disrupt normative assumptions about leadership development and practice; and to be at the forefront of changing the landscape of higher education to prepare it for an evolving and dynamic world. To accomplish this, Natasha had to step outside the limitations of her role and lead with a permanent mindset. To operate with a mindset of permanence even though she had a contingency position required dialectical thinking. Dialectical thinking requires that one hold two contrary ideas constant, while still functioning and operating (Dugan, 2017). Natasha used her dialectical capital to hold constant the limited power and time inherent in her formal role and her desire to effect change in her department, to engage in work that would be long-lasting and impactful to the organization.

Natasha used her social capital as an experienced administrator to cultivate relationships across campus and within the division of student life to reignite interest in and support for the program. Early on, she was able to use her knowledge of the field as a practitioner to help her research-focused tenured/TT colleagues see the possibilities of the program when faculty thought outside the box and did not do business as usual. Because Natasha chose to resist the normative assumptions about what it means to be a contingent faculty member, she was able to engage with confidence on such topics as curriculum design and course modifications. As a result, Natasha was able to suggest new approaches to essential program curricula and implement changes that will be felt long after her role expires.

Natasha was given a seat at the table and she harnessed her aspirational capital, choosing to project her voice and ideas in ways that aligned with her future goals, were congruent with her values, and allowed her to fulfill the purposes she set out to accomplish in this field. To make an impact and partake in work that is innovative, educators must not be stifled by the parameters of a position/title or the systems in which that position manifests. As Williamson (1996) proclaimed, "Playing small does not serve the world; there's nothing enlightened about shrinking so that other people won't feel insecure around you" (p. 191). Educators must rely on resistant and resilient capital when faced with challenges. If Natasha had "played small" instead of challenging the limiting nature of her contingent role, she would have missed the opportunity to bring fresh ideas to the program; it would have been a missed opportunity to effect change.

Natasha is grateful that she had supportive colleagues who treated her as their equal, with all the rights and privileges afforded them. Faculty encouragement bolstered her resilient capital, and their presence enriched her social capital.

Implications

The preceding two case studies showed two different ways to use cultural and leadership capital to practice creative leadership. In Bridget and Natasha's positionality statements, they framed this chapter in terms of the very existence of their Black women bodies showing up in historically and still predominantly White and male spaces as being bold and transformative in and of itself. However, presence does not equal creative leadership. Bridget and Natasha's stories show how much energy it takes to fight the status quo and lead in transformative ways. The primary impediment to creative leadership is combative structures and climates that stifle equity, inclusiveness, and critical approaches to leading.

Bridget has many privileged identities that afford her power. In addition to her social identities of power, she has capital from her parents being administrators in higher education, growing up on college campuses, earning her PhD, and working in historically and overwhelmingly White universities. Yet, without knowledge of and practice in all of Yosso's (2005) and Turman's (2017) different kinds of capital, Bridget allowed herself to "play small" and exit the stage. She became a critical scholar after and maybe because of the leadership experiences she had in universities where she knew she could be successful, but at too great a cost.

Bridget did not reveal at the onset that Natasha is her former student. What spurs Bridget and inspires her to lead in new and creative ways is students like Natasha, who expose her to critical scholarship and ways of being that are very different than the theories and models Bridget studied in graduate school. Learning from Natasha's exposure to critical scholarship (particularly on leadership) and watching her create new forms of capital in her research point Bridget in new directions for resources she can draw on to lead.

Transformative Change

Being creative and innovative involves being open to learning and willing to look at alternative theories and frameworks for guidance. If educators want change and leadership that will transform higher education to be more equitable, inclusive, and socially just, faculty, students, and staff need to be exposed to new frameworks and models that center women of color and communities of color. Such critical frameworks allow women and communities of color to be treated as "paradigmatic humans" who "can serve as the source of data . . . to develop theories about the human condition" (Williams, 2001, as cited in Ospina & Foldy, 2009, p. 889).

This chapter shined a light on Yosso's (2005) and Turman's (2017) critical frameworks to offer new ways to view leadership for students, faculty, and administrators who seek to lead in creative, innovative, and critical ways in higher education. As the chapter illustrated, creative, innovative, and critical leadership starts with knowing who you are, being willing to disrupt the status quo, and having a commitment to push forward ideas and initiatives that spark creativity and elicit change. While there is no prescriptive approach to accomplish these goals, educators can assess themselves to determine whether they are embodying critical, innovative leadership. Leadership rooted in a critical perspective recognizes the systems, policies, and barriers that may stifle creativity, silence diverse voices and perspectives, and maintain traditions that are dated and ineffective.

Critical scholars posited that for leadership to be more dynamic, innovative, and diverse, it must be reimagined beyond traditional paradigms and practices and must be anchored by critical frameworks (Dugan, 2017; Kezar, Carducci, & Contreras-McGavin, 2006; Parker, 2001). These critical frameworks acknowledge identity, power, and context within leadership. When educators apply a critical lens to leadership, they can recalibrate the thinking of faculty, students, and staff thinking to shift energy in a direction that challenges oppressive systems and barriers and actively works toward leading in more critical ways. One way to do this is to center diverse ways of knowing and then use those perspectives to solve problems. Or you could work within your sphere of influence to form alliances and partnerships with others to craft an initiative that has never been attempted before. Whatever approach you take, it should be one that invites disruption of leadership as usual and instead welcomes novel and critical approaches to solving the ever-changing issues in higher education.

Unlock Your Creativity

Connect two things that don't typically connect. This could be two colleagues, students, programs, or resources. What were the challenges in connecting the two?

References

Bourdieu, P., & Passeron, J. (1977). *Reproduction in education, society and culture.* London, United Kingsom: Sage.

Byrd, M. (2008). Negotiating new meanings of "leader" and envisioning culturally informed theories for developing African-American women in leadership roles: An interview with Patricia S. Parker. *Human Resource Development International, 11*(1), 101–107.

Chisholm, S. (2010). *Unbossed and unbought: Expanded 40th anniversary edition.* Brooklyn, NY: Take Root Media.

Dugan, J. P. (2017). *Leadership theory: Cultivating critical perspectives.* San Francisco, CA: Jossey-Bass.

Dugan, J. P., & Turman, N. T. (2018). Renewing the vow, changing the commitments: The call to infuse critical perspectives into leadership education. *Concepts and Connections: A Publication for Leadership Educators, 22*(2), 4–8.

Hill, C. (2016). The color of leadership: Barriers, bias, and race. Retrieved from American Association of University Women website: https://www.aauw.org/2016/04/19/color-of-leadership

Kezar, A. J., Carducci, R., & Contreras-McGavin, M. (2006). *Rethinking the "L" word in higher education: The revolution of research on leadership* (ASHE Higher Education Report, Vol. 31, No. 6). New York, NY: Jossey-Bass.

Moraga, C., & Anzaldúa, G. (Eds.). (1981). *This bridge called my back: Writings by radical women of color.* Watertown, MA: Persephone Press.

National Center for Education Statistics. (2018). *The condition of education 2018* (Report No. 2018-144). Retrieved from https://nces.ed.gov/pubs2018/2018144.pdf

Ospina, S., & Foldy, E. (2009). A critical review of race and ethnicity in the leadership literature: Surfacing context, power and the collective dimensions of leadership. *Leadership Quarterly, 20*(6), 876–896.

Parker, P. S. (2001). African American women executives' leadership communication within dominant-culture organizations: (Re)Conceptualizing notions of collaboration and instrumentality. *Management Communication Quarterly, 15*(1), 42–82.

Parker, P. S. (2005). *Race, gender, and leadership: Re-envisioning organizational leadership from the perspectives of African American women executives.* Mahwah, NJ: Lawrence Erlbaum.

Parker, P. S., & Ogilvie, D. T. (1996). Gender, culture, and leadership: Toward a culturally distinct model of African-American women executives' leadership strategies. *Leadership Quarterly, 7*(2), 189–214.

Sotomayor, S. (2013). *My beloved world.* New York, NY: Alfred A. Knopf.

Turman, N. T. (2017). *Centering the margins: Elevating the voices of women of color to critically examine college student leadership* (Doctoral dissertation). Available from ProQuest Database. (Accession No. 10287230)

Williamson, M. (1996). *Return to love: Reflections on the principles of "A Course in Miracles."* New York, NY: HarperOne.

Yosso, T. J. (2005). Whose culture has capital? A critical race theory discussion of community cultural wealth. *Race Ethnicity and Education, 8*(1), 69–91.

14

THE EMERGENCE OF MICRO-INNOVATIONS IN MANAGING COMMUNITY COLLEGE STAKEHOLDERS

STEVE TYRELL

The former notion of higher education as ivory towers on a hill, largely separate from the surrounding communities, is extremely outdated—and likely never has been associated with community colleges. By their names alone, community colleges indicate that these institutions of higher education are more engaged with the larger communities in which they reside and, thus, far from isolated. This strong connection to the larger community means that community college leaders must direct their energies in a variety of ways to support the mutual benefit of a diverse array of stakeholders. The interactions can be complex and contested—and can make solutions somewhat elusive. And yet, it is equally possible in these sometimes difficult arrangements for community college leaders to achieve creative and innovative solutions with these external stakeholders.

Numerous stakeholder groups bound to the community college make up these larger communities. Stakeholders are politicized entities in the context of those interests they wish to protect who also seek to have their needs met by community colleges. Former Speaker of the U.S. House of Representatives Tip O'Neill (1994) said, "All politics is local" (p. xii). A few interpretations of this famous quote exist, but one that resonates here is that all politics are based on personal relationships in which the participants look to foster mutually beneficial outcomes.

Community college leaders understand that local stakeholders, such as legislators and regional workforce development agencies, count on community colleges to support those needs that are intertwined with our institutions. Local stakeholders also want community colleges to avoid, whenever possible, working toward goals that contradict their vested interests. For example, although evidence may attest that it is financially prudent to close an underperforming branch, municipal leaders at that location might see a branch campus closure as working against their interests and not advisable. It would be fair to state that the needs and concerns of local stakeholders connected to community colleges are not always self-evident and clear. For community college leaders in pursuit of new ideas to propel their institutions forward, the cloudiness that sometimes exists with local politics can impede innovation and creativity if these external stakeholders see such novelty impeding on their vested interests. In bountiful times of economic prosperity, community college leaders will be challenged to maintain this delicate balance between supporting stakeholders' needs and steering clear of their protected interests. In times of fiscal constraints, declining enrollments, and public pushback on both publicly funding community colleges and the relevance of higher education overall, this tension between community college leaders and their external stakeholders can be further exacerbated—and creativity is required on everyone's part. At the same time, local stakeholders often face similar economic and social pressures for which community colleges are seeking solutions. It is at this locus of common ground where community colleges and external stakeholders must face their challenges together. In other words, community college leaders are encouraged to run toward the tensions that are expressed by their external stakeholders, not shy away from them. Promoting communication and interaction to find solutions together can be difficult, but it is likely the catalyst necessary to achieve solutions— perhaps even ones that are far more innovative than what might have been produced otherwise.

Economic downturns and social strife unfortunately seem to be more common today than in the past. Thus, more often than not, community college leaders are at the center of a political cauldron of different stakeholders with competing interests. At the risk of being caught between a rock and a hard place, community college leaders look for creative solutions and to innovate with strategies to mitigate institutional challenges. Community college leaders recognize that innovation cannot move forward easily in the absence of strong partnerships and collaboration with their external stakeholders. Because of this strong interconnectedness with external stakeholders, innovation and creative solutions are never arrived at in a "vacuum." Any epiphany that comes from any one individual or stakeholder group will only become a reality when stakeholder support for the new concept or idea outweighs stakeholder concern that such an idea is a threat to vested interests. The politics of a highly contested arena of stakeholders seems to lead community college leaders toward contextualizing novel concepts and initiatives in the form of small incremental moves, or what we might dub *micro-innovations.*

Stakeholder Groups

Community college leaders work with many stakeholder groups in facilitating educational missions. Leaders must consistently maintain a sharp focus on the "local politics" of both internal and external stakeholder groups if they are to carve pathways that lead to change, innovation, and creative outcomes. Internal and external stakeholder groups often have different interests they feel they must protect in order to advance their respective missions. And these interests are often independent and not closely aligned with the mission of the community college.

Internal Stakeholder Groups

Before examining the external stakeholder groups, it is important to acknowledge that several internal stakeholder groups are intimately tied to community college politics and how politics may promote or impede innovation. Although not an exhaustive list, some of the key internal stakeholder groups in community colleges include (a) faculty, with their responsibility to shape curriculum; (b) unions, with their interest to protect and enhance the working conditions of their members; (c) boards of trustees, with their desire to fully meet their fiduciary responsibilities to the institution and represent the region they have been appointed to serve; (d) senior management staff, with their duty to lead strategic initiatives and operational tasks for their institutions; (e) mid-level management staff, with their task to ensure that operations are functioning at full capacity; and (f) auxiliary corporations, with their charge to fulfill specific needs for the community college and any needs not met elsewhere in the organization. And last but not least: Students are internal stakeholders who have a wide array of needs and interests that influence innovation.

External Stakeholders

Leaders at community colleges must also work with a wide variety of external stakeholders. They are organized here into four groups: financial stakeholders, stakeholders of academic credits and credentials, stakeholders of noncredit and nonacademic credentials—workforce focus, and economic development stakeholders.

Financial Stakeholders

External financial stakeholders commit revenue to support the mission of community colleges; some have similar needs and interests, while others are fundamentally different from each other. In some states, community colleges are "sponsored" by a county or municipality, or they are assigned a region to serve. For example, most New York State community colleges have county sponsors that have a statutory financial obligation to fund a portion of the institution's annual operating budget. These county sponsors have a financial investment in the viability and success of their sponsored community college. State governments, another financial stakeholder, often provide funding to community colleges and have a significant number of regulations and provisions that those colleges must meet to continue to receive funding. They also are comprised of state agencies and legislative bodies that have competing interests, which are at times contested at the site of the community college sector.

Students are another source of major financial support, and they are often the greatest source of funding of the three primary revenue sources: tuition, county sponsor, and state government. Although they were listed earlier as an internal stakeholder, until they arrive and begin classes, students are seen as external stakeholders seeking to have their specific needs met—which leads them to select the institution they will eventually attend.

Private donors are a relatively new stakeholder to the community college sector, mostly because, in recent times, philanthropists have turned their attention to the challenges of student access and the need for private dollars to address current gaps in the workforce.

Stakeholders of Academic Credits and Credentials

Community colleges meet many needs for their students. Front and center is the acquisition of an academic credential (often a certificate or associate degree; increasingly more common, some community colleges are also allowed to offer a baccalaureate credential). These academic credentials may be a pathway toward a baccalaureate degree, and four-year institutions are also key stakeholders that receive well-trained community college students who have typically completed the first half of a bachelor's degree. The acquisition of an academic credential may also be a pathway toward employment. For example, an associate degree in nursing can almost immediately result in a graduate getting employment as a registered nurse, due to the nationwide shortage of nurses. Community colleges have also partnered with high schools to offer college credit, often to high school juniors and seniors who enroll in community college courses (usually on the high school site). Described as concurrent enrollment programs, these curricula prepare high school students for college, assist in the accumulation of college credits, and can reduce the number of college courses a high school graduate will need to acquire later in life—and thus reduce the overall college costs for these high school participants. Therefore, school districts and high school parents are additional stakeholders in the community college experience.

Stakeholders of Noncredit and Nonacademic Credentials—Workforce Focus

Beyond the acquisition of an academic credential, community colleges offer a diverse set of noncredit classes. They also can deliver them in short- or long-term durations, and they are geared largely to fulfill a specific workforce training need defined by employers and other workforce development stakeholders. Most regions in any state will have established workforce development boards that are comprised of employers, union representatives (who often coordinate apprenticeship programs), related government agency leaders, industrial development agencies, chambers of commerce, and other entities interested in promoting workforce development. Each entity will have a strong interest in its community colleges to be responsive to its demands and needs. That is *not* to say that each community college is resourced or missioned to be fully responsive to every workforce demand placed on it, but these external stakeholders will often look to community colleges as the first point of contact to meet current unmet workforce training needs.

Employers are an external stakeholder who will often express the most specific needs related to workforce skill sets sought. Employers are often in a competitive environment with other businesses seeking new hires from a limited pool of qualified applicants. This absence of qualified applicants places pressure on community colleges to supply a greater number of qualified applicants to employers—sometimes when the costs associated to operate quality training programs are not cost efficient for the institution. In addition, community colleges may offer additional training to current employees who may wish to "credential up" to support career advancement or to support training into a new career when an individual is the product of downsizing.

Another workforce stakeholder is the boards of cooperative educational services (BOCES), which provide alternative educational programs for high school students seeking technical, applied technology, or vocational careers. Community colleges and BOCES must forge strong partnerships, as students will transition from

BOCES curricula to community college workforce training programs or their academic curricula. Employers rely on these school-to-college pipelines to prepare high school graduates to eventually move into new "middle skills" jobs.

Economic Development Stakeholders

Workforce development is a subset of a larger dimension in the regions that community colleges serve—the greater social, economic, and cultural development of the region. Community colleges are called to serve as gathering points, social-cultural hubs for community members. Community colleges offer their facilities for a range of needs that include hosting meetings and cultural performances for for-profit and nonprofit groups; many such stakeholders rely on community colleges to support their programs and services. This support, in turn, can facilitate community development that has important economic and sociocultural outcomes for the region.

Economic development is certainly varied in scope and takes on multiple forms for community colleges and their external stakeholders. For example, federal granters that wish to promote small business loans in support of job creation will look to community colleges to host incubator or "maker spaces" for these entrepreneurs; in New York State, community colleges are one of several START-UP NY sites to fulfill this purpose. Municipal leaders are another set of external stakeholders. They are committed to restoring their downtown districts into more vibrant places that bring in revenues and enhance the sociocultural fabric of the area. Recently, municipal leaders have sought out community colleges to invest in establishing a campus location or to relocate programs and services downtown so that the community college serves as an anchor in these downtown revitalization efforts.

Innovation in the Community College Sector

Given the variety of external stakeholders and their competing interests (which, again, is not an exhaustive list), a community college leader will need to exercise a considerable amount of creativity in navigating competing needs and interests when considering change or offering an innovative idea. As is perhaps true with most innovations, there are often more cases of failed attempts than successful ones. In the case of community colleges, great ideas for innovation that succeed or fail may not do so solely because of the idea's merit; rather, local politics can block a good idea or an innovation that might have otherwise propelled a community college forward. Couple that dynamic with those competing interests among internal stakeholders and the challenge for community college leaders becomes ever clearer: Any leader who wants to toss a new idea into this constant pressure cooker must do so with the greatest amount of calculated consideration of how it will play out with stakeholders.

With regard to trial and error in innovation, in my experience as a community college president, I have seen most innovative ideas set aside and never get off the ground. The politics of external and internal stakeholders are very strong when the stakes are high and the margins are tight. Vetting new ideas through various stakeholder groups usually feels like running the gauntlet and taking hits from all sides. By the end of the vetting process, the new idea has been reshaped by so many interests that it is no longer recognizable. The question that remains is whether what has been molded and shaped is still viable to advance as an innovation, or has it been so reshaped that it is no longer viable and must be shelved. For all the innovative ideas that have been shelved, some do make it through the gauntlet of competing interests; I will discuss two such examples.

Innovation Through Collaboration (NCCC and PSC)

One of the major challenges most colleges and universities face today is declining revenues. For community colleges, the decline in revenues is often experienced in times of economic prosperity. Students (and their financial supporters) tend to opt for more expensive college choices in these times, and thus community colleges' enrollments—and operating revenues—tend to drop. Some community colleges' enrollments today reflect a decline in the percentage of newly minted high school graduates than perhaps what was present 20 to 30 years ago (Smith, 2018). In New York State, and in particular upstate and rural areas, the percentage of high school graduates has steadily declined over recent years (Arnold, 2019). For small colleges (defined here with a student enrollment below 2,000), the margins for downward swings in enrollment can be challenging if not nearly devastating to an institution's financial stability. For small colleges located in relatively remote areas with low populations, the ability to grow or even sustain enrollment with students in close proximity can be even more challenging.

My institution, North Country Community College (NCCC), is a New York State community college in the six-million-acre Adirondack Park. It is a small, rural, remotely located community college. Paul Smith's College (PSC), a private two- and four-year institution, is the other institution of higher education in Adirondack Park. Both PSC and NCCC have experienced similar enrollment declines, though perhaps for different reasons. In the greater environment of declining enrollments in the region and New York State, the competition for students can be fierce between institutions that are in close proximity. Other external stakeholders for NCCC, such as public comprehensive institutions, may have lowered admissions standards and thus dipped into the pool of prospective students choosing

NCCC. PSC and NCCC share Adirondack Park and generally, from a standpoint of academic program offerings, have some similar programs. PSC is the only baccalaureate degree-granting institution in Adirondack Park. So, the two institutions are immersed in fierce competition with other institutions of higher education but not necessarily with each other. Over the decades the two institutions have coexisted, their relationship has varied. Today, NCCC recruits a large majority of its students within 45 miles of its three campuses, while PSC recruits most of its students from across the northeast region of the United States.

What the two schools have in common is their remote location in New York State. Both colleges have student full-time enrollment equivalents below the 1,200 level. Both have been financially challenged more years than not with declining enrollments. Currently, the senior leaders of both institutions meet regularly to brainstorm how they can work together given their similar challenges and their program differences. Some great ideas have often been set aside as a result of the political pressures that various stakeholders might bring to bear on either or both colleges; again, no epiphany moves forward in a vacuum.

As difficult as it may seem, my advice in these situations is to lean in to the uncomfortable but with a healthy dose of caution. Why? The uncomfortable here is set in the context of stakeholders' vested interests. Each stakeholder group often has many interests it wishes to protect and any one of them may run counter to an innovation proposed to advance a college or its students. A president must discover (as vested interests are not often easy to discern) and then decide how best to respond or even whether to engage the stakeholder regarding this vested interest.

In the community college sector, a multitude of stakeholders with vested interests that can be at cross purposes with each other also further exacerbates this dynamic. It creates a continuous tenuous condition for community colleges, as an entanglement of competing interests can potentially leave leaders opting to take no position or action at all, thus setting the innovative initiative to the side. For example, community college leaders might dance a fine line between the pressure an external entity might exert on an institution to offer a particular academic credential to support local employment needs, and faculty who see the same academic credential as outside the scope of their academic interests and perceive the pressure exerted by the external entity as an affront to their academic freedom. However, leaning in to the uncomfortable requires leaders to find ways to bring stakeholders together and build agreements between competing interests. It is possible then that the initial concept put forth will be molded and perhaps reduced to something lesser than what was initially envisioned—perhaps becoming more like a micro-innovation than major change or full innovation. That said, innovations at this scale can still be valuable, no matter how incrementally small the outcome seems in the end.

Conversely, leaders risk a form of silence if an innovative idea is set to the side once competing vested interests present themselves. For example, setting good ideas to the side versus leaning in to the uncomfortable can also reinforce current expectations and values held by stakeholder groups. If that occurs, further attempts to innovate in these contested environments will be greatly hampered. In today's higher education environment of fiscal pressures and public accountability concerns related to the value of a college credential, no community college leader can afford not to lean in to the uncomfortable—either they move their institutions forward though innovation or they get left behind.

Recently, an innovation emerged out of these discussions and took root. As noted, a significant majority of NCCC graduates are local residents of Adirondack Park. Those NCCC graduates who wish to acquire a baccalaureate degree—and at a cost relatively close to the low price they paid at NCCC—might have to relocate out of the park or drive more than 45 miles to attend a four-year public baccalaureate institution. Of course, they could also pursue a degree online, but many post-traditional-aged NCCC graduates are slightly averse to enrolling in an online program; often these graduates prefer to continue their education in a traditional classroom setting—and ideally in a small classroom of 10 to 20 students, similar to their NCCC experience. Most NCCC graduates end their higher education journeys with their associate degree and remain as local residents in the park.

PSC offers two- and four-year degrees. Like most baccalaureate institutions, it often has smaller classes and more empty seats in the junior- and senior-level courses. The problem for NCCC graduates in transferring to PSC is that NCCC graduates cannot afford to pay the price of a private college education. Although, like many private colleges, PSC offers discounted tuition rates to first-year students, it does not offer discounted rates to most transfer students. Historically, few NCCC graduates have transferred to PSC.

The innovation that emerged from this growing partnership between NCCC and PSC was that PSC agreed to offer all NCCC alumni a discounted tuition rate that was competitive with the New York State tuition rate. Outside the normal PSC discount rate, this opportunity for NCCC alums resulted in no additional operating costs for PSC. PSC was already absorbing the cost to teach upper-division courses to its current students, and there was room in these classes to fill in empty seats with NCCC alumni. A win for PSC!

For NCCC graduates, they could pursue an affordable baccalaureate degree at a high-quality private college. They could continue to experience small class sizes, and they would not have to relocate from their homes in Adirondack Park to obtain this next higher education credential. This new arrangement could generate new revenue for PSC; it also allowed NCCC to market a stronger message to local residents to enroll in NCCC if those residents were contemplating a full four-year college experience. A win for NCCC!

For NCCC, to be able to market a great opportunity for current and future students was a great way to communicate to the region that NCCC was supporting the vested interests of both prospective students and alumni. A win for NCCC! Other external stakeholders from the workforce and economic development sectors applauded the agreement because it reinforced their efforts to "credential up" the local workforce and minimize the concern of a growing exodus out of Adirondack Park among residents who were looking for work or college elsewhere. The innovation was a win for several external stakeholder groups!

One group of stakeholders did express concern: current and former PSC students who didn't like the idea of NCCC graduates paying a tuition rate lower than what some of them paid to attend PSC. In weighing the benefits and concerns expressed with this innovative approach, there were more stakeholder groups benefiting than there were detractors, so the innovation proceeded and was successfully implemented. Innovation emerged after two different institutions facing similar challenges collaborated and created, through trial and error, win-win scenarios.

I should highlight how this innovation came to be and note some of its merits that may not be evident. Leaders at any institution feeling the pressure of increasing operating costs coupled with flat or declining enrollments certainly start thinking out of the box. In this case, a relatively niche small private college collaborating with a community college on articulation agreements is less common than, per se, a public community college partnering with a four-year public baccalaureate institution. In order to fully embrace this 2+2 agreement, both institutions had their senior leaders and admissions staff meet with each other to understand their respective interests. Initial conversations identified specific tasks that had to be clarified and the individuals from each institution who would work together to complete these tasks. It was important that tasks were completed at a level that ensured both institution's interests were fully being met. Any new marketing strategy had to reflect messaging and branding that blended both institutional brands without (a) creating a new brand, or more importantly, (b) emphasizing the brand of one institution over the other. They also met to learn each institution's recruitment processes so that both teams could effectively promote the academic offerings of the other institution to their student prospects. So, what might be a micro-innovation in this initiative? NCCC is marketing a regional/nationally focused private college in its backyard, and PSC is marketing a local community college with a very narrow geographic market to its broader and far more expansive recruitment region.

Another micro-innovation emerged out of careful discussions and mutual understanding of some of the sensitivities that needed to be honored in this agreement. For example, both colleges recognized that PSC could not, at the onset of its recruitment pitch to student prospects, promote NCCC in its recruitment markets and, thus, undercut its efforts to recruit its first-year class. However, PSC's senior leaders suggested the power of the partnership could create an important exception, wherein a PSC recruiter might sell the NCCC option to one of its first-year prospects under a set of prescribed conditions. Let's assume for the moment that many private colleges are discounting tuition and fees down to what is near the cost of the comprehensive public baccalaureate institution. And let's assume that the cost to attend a two-year community college is still lower than the comprehensive public baccalaureate institution. But what if, then, the private college's discounted tuition rate isn't low enough still for some first-year prospects?

Some private-college prospects reside close to a fiscal breaking point where financial aid packaging, discounted tuition, and scholarships still fall short of their needs. However, for some of these students, the lower cost to attend the community college next door with a partnership with the private college might be the financial difference in how they will be able to eventually attend the private college—albeit at a time span much later than when NCCC alumni initially completed their associate degree. From a student access standpoint, this innovative agreement was an opportunity for some first-year prospects on the financial margin far outside the community college's geographic region to achieve their dream of attending a private college of their choice. This micro-innovation benefits the students and both institutions. This possibility—for a PSC first-year prospect struggling financially to attend the private college—is as meaningful and powerful as the 2+2 agreement described earlier for NCCC alumni attending PSC at a cost near the state tuition rate.

Innovation Through Partnerships (NCCC and PBI) versus the Status Quo

Higher education has reified how some systems in various sectors of public higher education work with each other. For example, a high school student applies to a public comprehensive college in New York State 100 miles from the student's home. The public baccalaureate institution (PBI) determines that the applicant does not meet its minimum admissions standard. The applicant is advised to attend a community college and then reapply to the baccalaureate institution after a semester or year of successful academic performance. The applicant opts to stay home and attend a local community college. This scenario plays out repeatedly in higher education and is the status quo. As a neighbor to a comprehensive institution, NCCC can provide the coursework such an applicant needs; however, the applicant does not want to attend the community college—the applicant wants to attend the baccalaureate institution, and nowhere else, in this upstate region.

It is very common for a four-year institution to set up satellite operations on a community college campus, but it is rare to see the reverse. NCCC and PBI leaders proposed to do exactly that: NCCC would accept applicants into NCCC associate degree programs but deliver those programs on the PBI campus. Applicants would take NCCC classes at PBI, reside in PBI residence halls, and be fully integrated into the social-cultural-academic fabric of PBI campus life. In essence, those students would be members of PBI's community in every way except for who teaches courses and who provides academic advising and tutoring.

When NCCC and PBI looked at the enrollment potential—and thus the revenue potential—it was significant. Hundreds of downstate, urban-based applicants were being turned away from the baccalaureate institution because they could not quite meet the admissions criteria. NCCC, similar to other community colleges, was successful in helping its students overcome the challenges they faced, whether academic or nonacademic, in moving through its programs. NCCC faculty and academic support services have been very effective with engaging students, building their confidence and their academic skills required to complete the rigors of a higher education credential. NCCC was prepared to offer the same level of support services at PBI. In addition, many applicants in this pool were underrepresented students. The opportunity to give these students access to higher education—something they are often denied—and at the campus of their choice was very appealing to them. The program included these applicants as new NCCC students living and integrating into the residence halls of PBI.

This innovative concept has not yet launched. Before the program can move forward, other stakeholders must be engaged. Clearly, the program as proposed is a win for both institutions and for the students it would bring to the North Country region. But there are interests among other external stakeholders that must also be ironed out. Another college, a public agricultural and technology institution (referred to as CA&T) in close proximity to PBI, wants to join the partnership and could bring some added benefits to the overall experience for these students; however, as noted earlier, adding another external stakeholder (such as CA&T) that could be a direct participant in delivering the program magnifies the complexity. Attending to these complexities can be challenging for all three potential partners and negotiations continue.

County sponsors are very interested in how this new program as proposed may impact their required financial contribution—a matter that must also be discussed and addressed if this concept is to move forward. State agencies, too, are interested in how this program could greatly increase college access to New York State residents, particularly those who have been largely underrepresented in academe. At the same time, state representatives must attend to the impact that current state regulations (some untouched in decades) might have on blocking this innovative concept simply because those regulations are no longer relevant or have outlived their intended purposes. Additional vested interests are also in the mix, and it is unknown if this innovative approach will fully move forward. But it does speak to the fact that innovation sometimes occurs when state agencies and public colleges are willing to look past the status quo.

Recommendations for Leaders

Community college leaders know that to effect innovation, we must think creatively with our stakeholder partners. Those common structures that define our work can become so taken for granted that we cannot see the merit in challenging them. There may be many other entrenched organizational structures that community college leaders and stakeholders will likely need to question—especially in the face of declining enrollments and shrinking public support. We know that consumers (students and employers) want community colleges to develop custom-designed credentials that better support workforce needs. The traditional method for instruction delivery in a traditional weekday, semester design is rapidly losing its attractiveness to consumers, and there are calls for new delivery systems that challenge the status quo. Community colleges that fail to innovate will likely be at risk of survival. Workforce and market demands are shifting at light-year speed. The adage I shared earlier that institutions of higher education are slow to change still holds true: Higher education cultures move slower than external stakeholders when it comes to change and innovation. Internal stakeholders are largely comfortable with this pace, but external stakeholders are impatient with community college leaders' interest to protect this aspect of institutional culture.

In light of these external forces, can community colleges survive if they do not innovate or change at a pace that external forces demand? The pressures of local politics and internal stakeholders' interests mean that no community college leader can navigate innovation and change in calm waters today.

Innovation is not likely to occur or succeed as a result of a single epiphany that is implemented as policy thereafter. Where vested interests vie for space, innovation requires the painstaking time of collaboration with other interested parties. There is a growing sentiment among institutions of higher education that innovation requires more collaboration—rather than competition—with one another. If nothing else, this sentiment would reduce some of the pressures and perhaps provide a few more openings for innovation to be realized.

There are no easy pathways for community college leaders. We must be willing to take calculated risks and push and mold innovation. Too much is at stake for students, institutions, and all stakeholders. We must be prepared to fail more often than succeed when we move forward with innovation. Unfortunately, the general public has far less patience for leaders to fail; however, waiting for the perfect innovation to align or, worse, to fail to innovate at all may, in fact, exact a cost that no community college can afford to pay. It may also require institutional leaders not only to look to innovate with stakeholders with competing ideas but also to spend additional time with stakeholders discussing the innovation process itself. Specifically, stakeholders and the public would benefit from a better understanding of the intrinsic merit of risk-taking through innovation—and why failures along the way reveal a collective need to learn together from mistakes and setbacks. These lessons may be as valuable as the successes.

Unlock Your Creativity

Attend a local performance, art walk, production, or event beyond the place you work. Share what you experienced with your colleagues, friends, and students. Did that experience change the way you think?

References

Arnold, C. (2019, February 14). Is New York's population decline impacting college enrollment? SUNY says yes. *Democrat & Chronicle*. Retrieved from https://www.democratandchronicle.com/story/news/politics/albany/2019/02/14/nys-population-loss-impacting-suny-enrollment/2679066002

O'Neill, T. (1994). *All politics is local, and other rules of the game.* New York, NY: Times Books.

Smith, A. A. (2018, June 21). No bottom yet in 2-year college enrollments. *Inside Higher Ed*. Retrieved from https://www.insidehighered.com/news/2018/06/21/community-college-enrollment-rates-expected-keep-falling

15

THE END IS JUST THE BEGINNING

ROBERT D. KELLY AND COLIN STEWART

Innovative and creative leadership is not easy. New ideas, imaginative programs, and visionary services are difficult to establish in the face of growing concern and even disdain for higher education. Yet the demand from the public for higher education to be different from what it used to be and do more with less continues to grow. It is with this sense of urgency that this book was written. This volume offers a conceptual framework for leaders to get on the path to more inspired practice. The numerous examples of innovation and creativity presented in the preceding chapters just scratch the surface of what is possible for higher education.

Conditions Matter

Colleges and universities (and those who lead them) are sometimes criticized for not moving as fast as their counterparts in business. However, higher education has been enormously successful precisely because it has been methodical and meticulous in its innovative and creative spurts. Strategic leaders often use their strategic plans to incorporate meaningful change throughout the institution. However, before those thoughtful leaders make such dramatic shifts, they consider the following when making decisions: language, customs, values, traditions, etiquette, rules, regulations, policies, and politics.

The benefits of the work student affairs professionals and faculty do in higher education are profound. Research has shown that advanced study beyond high school improves an individual's quality of life (Rugaber, 2017). Compared with high school graduates, college graduates have longer life spans, have better health care, enjoy more stable employment, are more likely to participate in community service, and are happier (Rugaber, 2017). Although higher education is not going to go away, it must change and evolve. Higher education also needs leaders who can recognize when conditions are ripe for disruptive transformation and who are capable of navigating those changes.

Forces Internal and External to Education Are Calling for Change

Change will occur because of expectations from students, parents, and donors, and to align with government regulations and compliance. Similarly, changing student demographics, rising costs, personalized and digitized learning, the increasingly complex role of technology in student life, and the expansion of continuing education will necessitate the evolution of the higher education industry. Further, institutional closures, mergers, and consolidations will encourage transformation—even revolution. Regardless of the causes, leaders will need to be both adaptive to change and proactive in preparing, planning, and executing thoughtful change.

Institutions must become more affordable, accessible, relatable, and—most of all—relevant in an increasingly competitive market. Creative and thoughtful change is necessary for higher education to stay relevant. Increasing tuition rates, growing student debt, changes in compliance and regulation, daunting academic bureaucracy, and certain members of the academy holding on to past memories pose challenges that require innovative and creative leadership.

So, Now What?

This book argues that creative and innovative leadership should not be about one person but, rather, should focus on every level of an organization. In some cases, changing practice will require disrupting the status quo, but hope thrives. Most faculty, staff, and administrators are willing to try new things when the environment is conducive.

After reading this book, you might come away feeling intimidated or daunted by the variety of factors, both internal and external, that stifle innovative and creative leadership. However, the challenges and opportunities explored provide an opportunity for you to reflect on and analyze what you know, think, assume, and hope for in your institutional environment. This will allow you, as a leader, to create a culture in which staff, administrators, and faculty can take chances and innovation can grow.

As this book has made clear, innovative and creative leadership is present in higher education, and leaders must have an understanding of the landscape and tools at their disposal to aid in navigating choppy and turbulent waters. Kelley and Kelley (2013) wrote that "karaoke confidence" is an environment where one "feels the genuine support of the audience, the karaoke singer is encouraged to sing again, getting a bit better next time" (p. 183). It is this assembly choir that students, faculty, and staff deserve.

The future of higher education is filled with exciting possibilities, and, contrary to what many people believe, the industry is changing rapidly. Institutions are creating new majors, minors, and opportunities for interdisciplinary study. High-impact practices such as study abroad, internships, residential learning communities, equity and inclusion experiences, experiential learning and research, first-year transition courses, fourth-year capstone experiences, and community-based education are making a difference at many colleges and universities.

Converting lessons learned into action will not necessarily be easy; it will take trial and error. It will require leaders to remember why they started doing this work in the beginning. It will mandate partnering with others to tear down walls and be transparent, open, and optimistic about future goals, objectives, and plans. Every leader who works with others accepts that learning, growth, and grace are a critical part of the process. Gonzalez, Ching, White, and Kelly (2018) noted that leaders need resources and time, the opportunity to be allowed to experiment, to be open, and to owning that we may not know everything. This will require leaders to absorb information, incubate and reflect upon programs, and test divergent ideas.

Figure 15.1 provides a framework that may help leaders navigate through uncharted systems and networks. This model is based on a DNA double helix. However, innovative and creative leadership is not an innate or fixed trait. Rather, anyone can engage in creative and innovative leadership, but it requires practice. Nevertheless, executives and managers are becoming increasingly unwilling to take chances because the stakes of managing resources are so high. Now, more than ever, leaders need to carefully examine their environments, including how to expand connections, build diverse teams, secure resources and budgets, blast through barriers, collaborate with supervisees and supervisors, cultivate relationships and navigate political frameworks, prepare and create plans for the "X" factors, and invite disruptions to get the work done.

Figure 15.1. Creative and Innovative Leadership Model

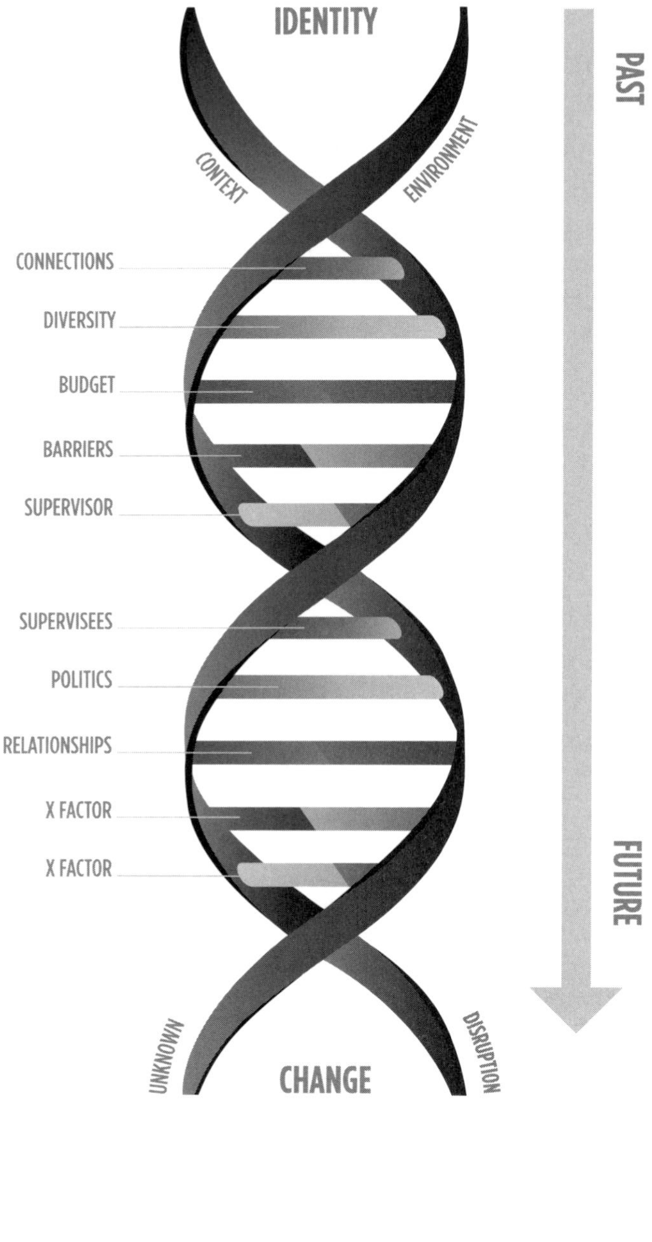

Imagine for a moment a child throwing away the LEGO instruction booklet and imagining a new design. Or a writer taking hold of a blank notepad and creating. It is this freeing spirit that college and university leaders must be able to access. Although higher education has come a long way by means of current practices and processes, the system might go even further by creating new and different structures. Leaders must not shy away from being more fearless in approaching and encouraging disruption to current ways of thinking.

Implications for Practice

Although change can be difficult, there are numerous examples of higher education professionals "building the plane while they are flying it." When leaders take this approach, they must expect and in some cases anticipate failure. Google actually encourages its employees to fail and rewards them for it. The company believes that the more they know how to fail, the more productive they can ultimately become (Blueprint Creative, 2018). Higher education has accountability, metrics, and outcomes that it must achieve. Therefore, failure is something that is often feared, but that culture can change if leaders redefine failure and invite it to become a part of the process. Leaders must learn from failure and get better at failing and accepting the failure of others.

It is also imperative that higher education adapt to the digitized economy. In particular, institutional leaders should be conscious of the digital student life experience. For example, colleges and universities have seen the rise of eSports (competitive video gaming) programs. Although not the first to create an eSports program, California State University, Fresno, launched its program in fall 2019. The process of developing the program required creative and innovative leadership. Fresno State carefully examined its internal and external environment through focus groups, research, and consultation with students, staff, faculty, and numerous other institutions. Fresno State formed an advisory board comprising students, staff from multiple divisions, faculty, and community members. The advisory board was mindful of gender, age, race, ethnicity, and ability as its member's navigated politics and barriers.

While the team was thoughtful and strategic, almost every milestone included some unknown factor that required creative and innovative leadership to create a program that was student centered, customized for the specific campus, and created opportunities for expansion and growth. By utilizing creative and innovative leadership, Fresno State moved beyond launching just one team, but two varsity eSports teams in the first year. This program also launched during a time when partners within information technology were impacted, and this required the team to develop creative solutions that could be efficiently and effectively implemented. The program also sparked willingness from others to contribute to the program by creating an additional shoutcaster (i.e., game commentator) program and bold connections to other gaming and community platforms. The eSports program has implications for enrollment, the university brand, and the digital student experience.

Recommendations for Research

As indicated in earlier chapters, discussions of creative and innovative research raise more thoughtful questions than produce cookie-cutter solutions. There are numerous opportunities to engage in further exploration on this topic in higher education. The following questions invite opportunities for future research: Why do new professionals and faculty conform in higher education? What sparks colleges and universities to begin to assess student leaving, involvement, and development and initiate high-impact practices? What unique case studies on creative and innovative practices and leaders are available? Does innovation and creativity differ by industry? Are lessons applicable across industries? What creative collaborations enhance student success? What are examples of failures that yielded unexpected and exciting results? What are the long-term effects of disruption? These topics also invite new and innovative approaches to conduct research. The field must be bold not just in the questions asked, but also in the ways they are answered.

Rob's Reflection

Recently, a colleague asked how I might encourage disruptive transformation among faculty, staff, and administrators with whom I work. To be honest, I don't urge disruption from everyone, nor do I want to. First, not everyone is comfortable sharing thoughts and ideas. Some people perceive innovation and creativity as a distraction from the important work of the day. Others see efforts for creative leadership as directed guidance and view these moments as freeing and full of possibility. Higher education needs people to not only challenge ideas but also support those who are spearheading innovations and serving as trailblazers. Not everyone needs to push new ways of thinking and doing. Higher education has been successful because of its ability to balance multiple perspectives. However, the environment must be cultivated and nurtured so that innovative faculty and creative administrators can appropriately and methodically revolutionize and transform higher education for student success.

I once asked a mentor to share with me her favorite job. I wanted to know where she felt the most joy, and the most free to create. She told me it was her first job out of graduate school as a residential hall director. She was able to work most closely with students, hearing their hopes, their dreams, their fears, and their concerns. It was in this first job where she was most in touch with her reason for being in higher education. She recalled the number of times she took educated risks, tried new ways of connecting, and shared her ideas and thoughts without fear of ridicule. Now, as a university president, she recognizes how measured she is in every public setting, and she wants to lead differently to encourage transformation.

Colin's Reflection

Creative and innovative leadership is not just about providing additional dollars for an institution to be creative; it's about building a campus culture where everyone has the ability to tap into their creative practice to provide the best student experience. You should expect that the process of developing an innovative and creative culture will not be perfect, and anticipate failure and resistance along the way. Playing the devil's advocate can be useful, but bringing creative solutions to every challenge can be a game changer. The grind of higher education professionals will be daunting at times, but the investments in innovation will start to add up. You will know the tide has turned when more colleagues step up in unexpected ways to advance student success. Innovation and creativity should not be an afterthought, but rather a part of key leaders' job descriptions. Especially those areas of campus that are contributing to student success.

Everyone can learn how to be creative and innovative, even if they don't use these skills every day. Learning to disrupt one's process is a critical part of becoming a creative and innovative leader. Everyone can be creative or innovative in some way, shape, or form; the right environment just needs to exist for that to occur. The challenge is how to take those creative and innovative skills and learn how to apply them to your own unique leadership style. You are encouraged to infuse the various concepts and models from this book into your own unique practice.

Although creative and innovative leadership is a critical need for student affairs, leaders must also be careful to not always be looking at the "next thing" or building something "new" because they are trying to fill a void that is taking place within their current role. It is remarkable when leaders can collaboratively create new facilities, traditions, programs, resources, and courses and then empower others to take on those responsibilities. However, there is a delicate balance between creation and sustainability of the work. Creative and innovative leaders must be strategic about the long-term impact of revolutionary ideas. In order to empower rather than overwhelm your team by taking on too much for the sake of being "new," be thoughtful about expanding new programs, services, budgets, and human resources.

Yes, And

The future of higher education is bright because of a willingness among brave faculty and administrators to restore, reconstruct, and revitalize. These creative and innovative leaders are taking informed chances and educated guesses. Although higher education is solidly based on the past, who knows what "X" factors the future holds? As the field marches toward an exciting and uncharted future, it is important to encourage an ethos of "yes, and"—to not simply show up, but to listen with a full heart and add to the next chapter of the story. As a higher education leader, you must remember the past while carving out a new pathway, and embrace opportunities that invite transformational learning. Unlock your inner creativity not just for yourself but also for the ones you lead and teach. Fully honor your identity, your students, and what might be possible for and with others to develop environments that harness creative energy. Embrace your community and disrupt your practice to become a creative and innovative leader.

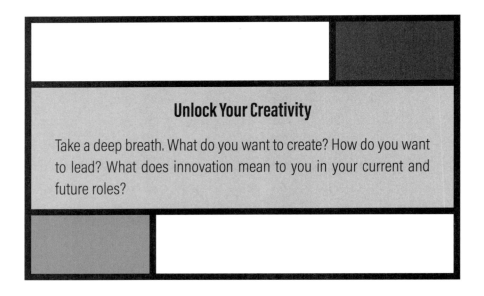

Unlock Your Creativity

Take a deep breath. What do you want to create? How do you want to lead? What does innovation mean to you in your current and future roles?

References

Blueprint Creative. (2018, January 8). Why Google rewards its employees for failing [Blog post]. Retrieved from https://blueprintcreativeinc.com/why-google-rewards-its-employees-for-failing

Gonzalez, A., Ching, D. M., White, L., & Kelly, R. D. (Eds.). (2018). *Transformational encounters: Shaping diverse college and university leaders.* Washington, DC: NASPA–Student Affairs Administrators in Higher Education.

Kelley, D., & Kelley, T. (2013). *Creative confidence: Unleashing the creative potential within us all.* New York, NY: Crown Publishing.

Rugaber, C. S. (2017, January 12). Pay gap between college grads and everyone else at a record. *USA Today.* Retrieved from https://www.usatoday.com/story/money/2017/01/12/pay-gap-between-college-grads-and-everyone-else-record/96493348

THE AUTHORS

Robert D. Kelly is a higher education scholar-practitioner. Currently, he is the university vice president and special assistant to the president at Loyola University Maryland, his alma mater. He provides counsel for the president and coordinates initiatives across the institution in support of the strategic plan and institutional objectives and his research focuses on areas of administrative ethical decision making in higher education, transforming the college environment for student and institutional success and higher education leadership.

Colin Stewart is an adaptive scholar-practitioner who currently serves with the student life team at California State University, Fresno, as the associate dean of student involvement. He has been formed at institutions that are small, large, public, private, domestic and international, which explains why he is deeply committed to student success, innovation, inclusion, and belonging. His current research and expertise center on creative and innovative leadership.

Brandon Common is assistant vice president for student affairs at Illinois Wesleyan University. Prior to this position, he held roles in several student affairs functional areas including residential life, diversity and inclusion, and fraternity and sorority affairs.

Eileen Galvez is a scholar-practitioner. She is currently an assistant dean at Yale University and working on her PhD in higher education leadership through Colorado State University. Her research is on free speech and higher education administrators of color.

Anna Gonzalez is vice president of student affairs and dean of students at Harvey Mudd College. She is also a faculty member and program director for the Student Affairs and Educational Justice program at the Claremont Graduate University. Her most recent publication is the edited book *Transformational Encounters: Shaping Diverse College and University Leaders* (NASPA, 2018).

Susana Hernández is an associate professor in the higher education, administration, and leadership pathway and the chair of the Department of Educational Leadership at California State University, Fresno. She also coordinates the higher education administration and leadership degree pathway. Her published work has examined in-state resident tuition policies that affect undocumented students as well as how federal policy discursively shapes Latinx/a/o educational opportunity and equity. She is currently examining how colleges and universities designated as Hispanic-serving institutions embed Hispanic-servingness into their policies and practices.

Bridget Turner Kelly is an associate professor and director of the Higher Education, Student Affairs, and International Education Policy program at the University of Maryland. Her research focuses on marginalized groups in historically White universities, preparing socially just educators, and utilizing visual research methods. Kelly serves as executive editor of the *Journal of Student Affairs Research and Practice* and is committed to publishing innovative and equitable research in student affairs.

Ann Marie Klotz is vice president of student success at The New School in New York City. Prior to her current role, she served in various positions within student affairs for the past 18 years, most prominently in housing and residence life. She is a frequent speaker, trainer, and consultant.

Frank R. Lamas currently serves as the vice president for the division of student affairs and enrollment management at California State University, Fresno, with thirty plus years of extensive experience as a higher education leader and faculty member. He is responsible for organizing, directing, and managing the resources of the division to meet the needs of students, the university, and the surrounding community. In 2016 he was named a Pillar of the Profession by NASPA–Student Affairs Administrators in Higher Education, and in March 2018 received the NASPA Fred Turner award for higher education lifetime achievements/accomplishments.

Patrick Love is vice president for student affairs and director of the Student Affairs Administration graduate program at Springfield College. His career in higher education has spanned managerial work in student affairs, academic affairs, and as a professor in college student affairs at institutions including Bowling Green State University, Rutgers University, New York University, and Kent State University. His areas of scholarship include organizational culture and innovation, leadership and management issues in student affairs, and applying theory to practice.

Kenechukwu (K.C.) Mmeje has over 15 years of progressive experience in student affairs at various colleges and universities. In his current role as vice president for student affairs at Southern Methodist University (SMU), he provides leadership and strategic vision for a comprehensive student affairs division comprised of residence life and student housing, student health and counseling services, campus recreation, student conduct and community standards, student involvement, fraternity and sorority life, Office of the Dean of Students, Office of the Student Experience, Office of Social Change and Intercultural Engagement, and the Women and LGBT Center, to name a few.

Art Munin serves as associate vice chancellor and dean of students at the University of Wisconsin Oshkosh. He has written and coedited several books including *Keep Calm and Call the Dean of Students* (Stylus, 2019), *The Diversity Consultant Cookbook: Preparing for the Challenge* (Stylus, 2019), and *Color by Number: Understanding Racism through Facts and Stats on Children* (Stylus 2012).

Michele C. Murray serves as vice president for student affairs and dean of students at the College of the Holy Cross. She provides leadership for integrating students' intellectual, spiritual, and emotional development, ensuring a vibrant campus life, and delivering excellent services and programs for all students. Having served Jesuit higher education for 24 years, Murray has coauthored two books and authored numerous chapters and articles. She has served on professional boards, including NASPA–Student Affairs Administrators in Higher Education and the Jesuit Association of Student Personnel Administrators.

Vijay Pendakur serves as the Robert W. and Elizabeth C. Staley Dean of Students at Cornell University. Prior to this appointment, he worked on campuswide student success initiatives for underserved populations as an associate vice president for student affairs at California State University, Fullerton. He is editor of the recent book *Closing the Opportunity Gap: Identity-Conscious Strategies for Retention and Student Success* (Stylus, 2016) as well as numerous chapters on racial identity development, critical leadership pedagogy, and student affairs administration.

M.L. "Cissy" Petty serves on the president's leadership team of The George Washington University, as vice president for student affairs and dean of students. She is known for her strategic leadership, thoughtful approach to student affairs and passion for issues of diversity and equality. She has a reputation for ensuring all students feel a deep connection and a sense of belonging to their college experience. Recognized nationally as a thought leader in higher education, she is a proven change agent who uses assessment and strategic planning to implement institutional priorities. She presents extensively on issues of leadership, culture, and collaboration.

Domonic A. Rollins is director of diversity, equity and inclusion at The Dalton School located in New York City. In this role, he provides leadership and oversight to develop a comprehensive diversity, equity and inclusion strategy that supports the fundamental Dalton principle that diverse beliefs, ethnicities, cultures, and lifestyles are a critical underpinning of a successful education in today's global society. At The Dalton School, Rollins provides direction for committees and affinity groups charged with DEI work; collaborate with the K–12 teachers and academic leaders to institute a culturally relevant equity pedagogy in the classrooms and; serve as a mentor for faculty, staff, students, and parents on issues of social justice, diversity, equity, and inclusiveness.

Amanda Stewart is coordinator of marketing and communications for the Division of Student Affairs and Enrollment Management at California State University, Fresno. In this role, she serves as a digital community builder and student affairs storyteller.

Natasha T. Turman is director of the Women in Science and Engineering Residence Program at the University of Michigan. As a critical scholar-practitioner and researcher, Turman has worked in the field of higher education student affairs for 11 years in a variety of areas including leadership studies, student activities, residential life, and multicultural affairs and most recently as visiting assistant professor at Miami University in the Student Affairs in Higher Education program.

Steve Tyrell serves as a consultant for colleges struggling with enrollment, political challenges and budget constraints. He develops comprehensive turnaround plans to support future fiscal, enrollment and political viability. He previously served 7 years as a president of a community college and 29 years prior as a student affairs educator and student services administrator.

Joseph P. Zolner is an adjunct lecturer on education at the Harvard Graduate School of Education (HGSE). From 1999 to 2018, he served as senior director of the Harvard Institutes for Higher Education, a role responsible for the quality, relevance, and variety of executive education programs offered by HGSE for the higher education community. He serves as educational chair for three professional development programs at HGSE: the Management Development Program, Leadership Institute for Academic Librarians, and Contemporary Challenges in Library Leadership.

INDEX

Figures and tables are indicated by "f" and "t" following the page numbers.

A

Academic freedom, 30, 250
Accessibility
  activism and, 205
  change management for, 32
  community colleges and, 255–256
  costs prohibiting, xi–xii
  funding decreases and, 222
  hiring practices and, 109
  inclusivity and, 189–190
  legislation expanding, 22
  Millennium Scholars Program and, 36
  philanthropy and, 244
The Accidental Creative (podcast), 152
Accounting, 29
ACPA, 118, 120–122, 125–126
Activism
  challenges in addressing, 208–212
  contemporary demands of, 207–208
  creative strategies to work with, 14, 203, 204, 212–218
  curricular change and, 202, 205–207, 234
  diversity and, 186–189, 202, 207

higher education's history of, 201–207
  inclusivity and, 186–189, 202
  marginalized students and, 184, 186–189
  normalization of, 214–215
  traditional practices and, 27, 33, 191
  at Yale University, 199–202
Adaptability and adaptation
  creativity and, 154–155, 158
  curiosity and, 131
  higher education and, xi, xii, 185, 187, 263, 267–268
  leadership and, 7, 154–155, 184, 193, 227, 230–231, 263
  students and, 5, 126
Adaptive capital, 227, 230–231
Administrators. *See also* Higher education; Organizational culture; Student affairs
  activism and, 202, 207, 209–215
  at community colleges, 242
  creativity prioritized by, 5
  cultural navigation for, 216–217, 229
  curricular reform and, 28
  four frames of leadership and, 56
  high stakes for, 265

inclusive leadership and, 189, 202
search committees and, 100–101
standards for creativity among, 8
transformational learning and,
    53–54
Admissions
    community colleges and, 248–
        249, 254–256
    development of standards for,
        22, 26
    diversity and, 187
    institutional traditions and, 27
Advertising job opportunities, 95–
    100, 111–112
Advocacy and social justice work,
    118–122. *See also* Activism
African American students. *See*
    Marginalized students and
    identities; Race and racism
African American studies, 205–206
American Association of University
    Professors, 30
American Association of University
    Women, 222
American Council on Education, 30
American Management Association, 5
Art and artistic pursuits, 115, 124,
    132, 135–140, 166, 167, 177
Artificial Intelligence (AI), x, 50
Aspirational capital, 226–227,
    230, 231
Assessment and evaluation
    adaptive capital and, 227
    as competency area, 120
    of costs in higher education, 20
    of creativity, 7, 8
    of critical leadership, 236–237

idea generation and, 138
inclusivity and, 194
transformational learning and,
    48, 51
Association of American Colleges and
    Universities, 30
Athletics, 145–147

B

Baer, J., 6
Bailey, Sebastian, 133
Barris, Kenya, 165
Batten, Greg, 67
Baumol's cost disease, 30
Belonging. *See* Inclusivity
Berger, Jennifer Garvey, 45n2
Bible, 165
Bill and Melinda Gates
    Foundation, 36
Black, Octavius, 133
Black-ish (TV show), 165
Black Liberation Collective, 203, 207
Black Lives Matter, 217
Black students and faculty, 25, 185,
    207–209, 222–224, 228–235.
    See also Marginalized students
    and identities; Race and racism;
    Students and faculty of color
Blank screens, 129–130
Blixt, A. B., 4, 175
Boards of cooperative educational
    services (BOCES), 245–246
Boards of trustees, 31, 242
Bolman, L. G., 55–56
Bonchek, M., 49
Bookstores, 33

Boss, G. J., 119

Brainstorming. *See* Ideation and idea generation

Bravery. *See* Courage

Breath. *See* Mindfulness

Brown, Brené, 151

Buddhists and Buddhism, 49

Buechner, Frederick, 169

Burger, Edward, 48

Burstiness, 62, 71–72, 262

C

California Master Plan for Higher Education (1960), 32

California State University, 144, 146, 155–156, 267–268

Casap, Jaime, ix–xii

Catholicism, 166

Celebrating success, 80–81, 179

Chamarro-Premuzic, T., 55

Change management
  culture of no and, 80, 85, 87
  empathy and, 155
  innovation and, 31–37
  leadership and, 31–34, 56–57, 123, 125, 133
  status quo and, 157
  transformation of individuals and, 43

Ching, D. M., 264

Chisholm, Shirley, 223

Christensen, Chris, 51–52

Code-switching, 227

Cole, Johnetta, 19

Collaboration
  activism and, 213–214

change management and, 32–33, 80

community college innovations and, 248–254, 258

curiosity and, 136

diverse perspectives from, 130, 134, 190, 191

divisional/departmental, 80, 86, 134, 268

higher education developing, xi

idea generation and, 137

NewSmart model and, 175

screening matrices for, 102, 103*f*

transformational learning and, 47*f*, 50, 52–53, 152, 157–158

Common, Brandon, 14, 199

Community colleges
  collaboration and, 248–254, 258
  credits and credentials at, 244
  economic development and, 246
  funding for, 243–244
  innovation in, 241, 242, 247–254, 257–258
  local politics impacting, 240–242
  partnerships for, 254–256
  stakeholders in, 239–246, 249–250, 256–257
  workforce focus of, 244–246

Competencies
  ACPA and NASPA areas of, 120–122, 125–126
  creativity and, 4, 7–8, 119–122, 125–126
  graduate preparation and, 117–118
  informational learning and, 46
  leadership and, 54–55
  screening matrices and, 103*f*

transformational learning and, 50
Compliance, 29, 263
Computer science, 27–28
Conchie, Barry, 132–133
Confederate landmarks, removal of, 27, 33
Contingent faculty, 231–235
Cooper, J., 117–118
Cornell University, 96–98
Corporate sector, 92–93, 242, 245
Costs
    accessibility and, xi–xii
    as barrier to change, 28–30, 78–79, 262–263
    diversity and, 187
    of innovation, 26, 86
Courage, 31–37, 139, 144, 145, 176–177
Covering capital, 227
Creation story, 165
Creativity. *See also* Exercises for creativity; Ideation and idea generation; Innovation; Inspiration; Leadership; Spirituality
    activism and, 203, 204, 212–218
    adaptability and, 154–155, 158
    apps for, 83
    biases against, 7–8
    competency areas and, 120–122, 125–126
    critical leadership and, 225, 231, 235
    cultivating environments for, 62, 65–72, 130, 136–140
    curiosity and, 130–133, 139–140, 157
    definitions for, 130–131

diffusion and, 7
flow and, 168–169
graduate preparation programs and, 115–116, 122–126
importance in higher education, 3–5
inclusivity and, 192–195
music and, 61–62, 72, 163–164
organizational culture and, xi, 4, 5, 16, 134–140, 144
owning your story and, 145–151
as responsibility, 154, 267, 270–271
restoration of, 171–174
risk-taking and, 153–154
stress and, 70
virtues of, 175–180
Critical leadership, 225, 232–233
Critical thinking, xi, 22, 23, 25, 48, 50
Csikszentmihalyi, Mihalyi, 6, 168–169, 215
Cultural appropriation, 199–201
Cultural capital/wealth, 15, 225–228, 236–237
Cultural centers, 185, 206
Cultural navigators, 215–216
"Culture of fear," 76–78
"Culture of no," 76, 78–81, 85, 134–138. *See also* Organizational culture
Culture wars, 21, 31
Curiosity
    cultivation of, 130, 136–139
    definitions for, 130–131
    humility and, 177
    leadership and, 130–133, 136–140
    workplace impediments to, 134–136

Curriculum and curricular change
activism and, 202, 205–207, 234
barriers to, 27–28
change management for, 33–34
diversity and, 185, 188–189
future orientation for, 34–35
historical innovations in, x, 23
for professional development,
51, 121

D

Daydreaming, 135–136
Deadlines, 70
Deal, T. E., 55–56
Dean, S. R., 119
Dearden, John Francis, 177–178
Deliberately developmental
organization (DDO) thinking, 57
Departments
collaboration across, 80, 86,
134, 268
curricular reform and, 28
diversity of, 190–191
higher education's development
of, 24
De Pree, Max, 139
DeVry University, 25
Dialectical thinking capital, 227–
228, 233–234
Diffusion, 7
Digitalization economy, x–xii, 5. *See
also* Technologies
Dignan, Aaron, 152
Dino, R. N., 6
Disney, Walt, 131
Disney experience, 54

Disruptive transformation
activism and, 221–222
digitalization economy and, xi
inclusivity and, 184
leadership and, 8–9, 143, 235–
237, 262–267, 269–271
tradition vs., 20–21
vocation and, 169
Diversity
activism and, 186–189, 202, 207
collaboration and, 130, 134,
190, 191
as competency area, 121–122
curricular innovation and, 188–
189, 202, 205–206
faculty and, 184–188, 207
higher education and, 184–189,
194–196, 237
hiring practices and, 96–100,
108, 111
historical growth of, 25
innovation and, 136, 137, 190–
192, 269
nationalism and, 14
PWIs and, 187–188
Division of Student Affairs at New
York Institute of Technology
(NYIT), 75–76
Doody, Tony, 82
Douglass, Frederick, 199
Drucker, Peter, 21
Dubois, W.E.B, 24–25

E

Eaton, P. W., 120–121
Eckerle, K., 117–118

Economic development and community colleges, 246
Eighth graders, 34–35
Einstein, Albert, 48, 52, 130
Elastic thinking, 49, 52, 58
Eliot, Charles William, 23
Ellis, S. E., 4, 175
Emotional intelligence, 50, 52
Employment models, 21
Enrollment
    community colleges and, 248–249, 252, 255, 257
    curriculum and, 28
    decline in, 25
    diversity and, 185, 187
    eSports and, 268
    future orientation for, 35, 175
    presidents' tenure and, 31
eSports, 267–268
Evaluation. See Assessment and evaluation
Exercises for creativity, 16, 37, 59, 73, 87, 113, 127, 140, 159, 180, 196, 218, 237, 259, 272
Expertise and specialization, 24, 49, 135, 136

F

Facebook, 98, 203
Facilities and maintenance, 29, 86, 150–151
Faculty. See also Tenure
    activism and, 221–222
    community colleges and, 242, 250
    contingent roles and, 231–235
    costs of, 29–30
    curricular reform and, 20, 24, 28, 35
    diversity and, 184–188, 207
    of graduate programs for higher education professions, 115–116, 122
    institutional traditions and, 27
    transformational learning and, 53–54
Failures
    competing stakeholders and, 247
    creativity and, 62, 175, 177, 267
    elastic thinking and, 49
    fear of, 131, 134, 138, 139, 176
    idea generation from, 83
    lack of purpose and, 64–65
    leadership and, 71, 72, 258, 267
    reckoning with, 151
Faith. See Spirituality and faith
Fear, 85, 131, 134, 136, 138, 139, 176
    "culture of fear," 76–78
Feedback, 33, 137, 195
Fenn, Dan, 44
Financial aid, 186, 254
Financial stakeholders in community colleges, 243–244
Finkelstein, S., 49
Fitzer, J. R., 119
Fleming, A., 57
Flow of creativity and curiosity, 13, 135, 164, 168–169, 180
Folt, Carol, 31, 33–34
Forest bathing, 173–174
For-profit colleges, 25
Four frames of leadership, 55–56
Free speech, 199–201
Free writing, 83

Fresno State, 144, 146, 155–156, 267–268

Funding streams for higher education, 29–30, 222, 243–244

G

Gallos, J. V., 55

Galvez, Eileen, 14, 199

Gandhi, Mahatma, 36

Gay students. *See* LGBTQIA students

Generosity, 176, 178

G.I. Bill (1944), 22

Gill, S. J., 4, 175

Gilman, Daniel Coit, 23

Gilmore, T. N., 58

Gino, Francesca, 131

Gladwell, Malcolm, 72

Glassdoor, 89

Golden Circle, 63, 63*f*

Gonzales, R. G., 202

Gonzalez, Anna, 10, 19, 264

Google, 267

Graduate programs for higher education professions
  creativity and, 120–126
  deficiencies in, 118
  leadership case study in, 228–231
  overview of, 115–120
  professional competencies and, 120–122, 125

Grant, Adam, 62

Gratitude, 178–179

Gregoire, Carolyn, 135

Groupthink, 136, 137, 192

H

Habits and habit forming, 80, 175–177, 179, 190

Hammerstein, Oscar, 164

Harrison, L., 118

Harter, J., 110

Harvard Institutes for Higher Education (HIHE), 41–42, 44–45, 50, 55–57

Head, Payton, 203

Helsing, D., 57

Hernández, Susana, 12, 115

Hess, E. D., 50, 175, 176

Higher education. *See also* Curriculum and curricular change; Hiring practices; Student affairs
  activism's history in, 201–207
  barriers to change in, 26–30, 184
  career perspectives on, 147–151, 169
  community colleges and, 244
  criticisms of, ix–xi, 19–22, 24–25
  demographics of, ix, 184–186, 221–222
  diffusion of ideas in, 7, 9
  as equalizing factor, 20
  failure and, 267
  graduate preparation for professions in, 115, 117
  inclusivity and, 183–184
  leadership transforming, 30–34, 36–37
  reform in field of, 4–5, 21–25, 31, 36–37, 149–150, 221–222, 257–258, 262–264, 269–272
  standards for creativity in, 8, 122–

124, 168–169
  student activism and, 184, 186–189
  student affairs' role in, 4, 175, 262
HIHE (Harvard Institutes for Higher
  Education), 41–42, 44–45, 50, 55–
  57
Hiring practices
  challenges of, 89–91
  creativity prioritized in, 5
  diversity and, 96–100, 108, 111
  inclusivity and, 192–193
  job descriptions in, 91–93
  offers of employment in, 91,
    94, 109–110
  onboarding and, 90, 110–111
  on-campus interviews in, 90–91,
    97–98, 105, 107–109, 112
  phone interviews in, 90, 92, 94,
    104–105, 107
  promotion and advertisement in,
    93, 95–100, 111–112
  reference checks in, 94, 105–106,
    109, 112
  relocation and, 97, 107, 109–
    111, 148–149
  screening matrices in, 101–
    102, 103f
  search committees in, 93, 94, 100–102
  student involvement in, 101,
    106–107, 111
  timelines for, 93–94, 110, 112
Historically Black colleges and
  universities, 25
Horowitz, H. L., 205
Human resources, 29, 95, 120,
  190–191
Humility, 27, 34, 50, 52, 58, 175–178

Humor, 177
Hurston, Zora Neale, 131
Hypermasculinity, 208

I

"I Am" poetry assignment, 123–124
Ideation and idea generation, 81–86,
  130, 132–133, 135–138, 150
Ignatian spirituality, 166, 170,
  172, 178
Immunity to change (ITC)
  framework, 56–57. See also
  Change management
Inclusivity
  activism and, 186–189, 202
  acts of courage for, 33–34
  benefits of, 191
  leadership and, 184–186,
    189–196, 235
  sports and, 145–147
  student affairs and, 147, 154,
    183–184, 264
Industrialization, 24
Inequality. See Accessibility;
  Activism; Inclusivity; Marginalized
  students and identities; Race and
  racism; Sexism
Information. See also Feedback;
  Internet and Internet access
  as commodity readily available, xi
  cultural navigation and, 215–216
  synthesizing, 168
Informational learning, xi, 45–52,
  47t, 58
Information technology (IT), 190–
  191, 268

Inhibitions and creativity, 68, 70–71
Innovation
    activism and, 186–187
    building cultures of, 75–76,
      81–87, 140, 270–272
    community colleges and, 241, 242,
      247–254, 257–258
    competency areas and, 125–126
    courage in leadership and, 31–34,
      36–37, 139
    cultural capital theory and, 226
    definitions and background, 6–9,
      76, 130
    diffusion and, 7
    diversity and, 136, 137, 190–
      192, 269
    fear and, 77, 138
    future orientation for, 34–35
    hiring practices and, 104, 106, 107
    importance in higher
      education, 3–5
    inclusivity and, 192–195
    NewSmart model and, 175
    organizational culture and, 11,
      75–76, 81–87, 134–140,
      177–179, 263–267, 270–272
    spirituality and, 165–166
    traditions vs., 20–21, 26–27,
      33, 35–36
    unlearning/undoing and, 49, 53,
      58, 76–81
    women of color and, 224, 234
Inspiration
    career perspectives for, 143–144
    from colleagues, 157
    creativity and, 62, 135, 140
    leadership and, 130, 131, 140,
      149–150, 261
    purpose and, 64–65, 123, 149–
      150
    spirituality and, 166–167
    transformational learning and, 46
Instagram, 98
Institutional culture. *See*
    Organizational culture
Intercultural Affairs Council of Yale
    University, 199–201
Internet and Internet access, x, xii,
    35–36, 203. *See also* Technologies
Interviewing candidates, 90–92, 94,
    97–98, 104–105, 107–109, 112
Introspection. *See* Exercises for
    creativity; Personal development
Iowa State University, 147
Islamophobia, 208
ITC (Immunity to change)
    framework, 56–57. *See also*
    Change management
Iverson, S. V., 121
Iyer, Pico, 173, 174

J

Jessup-Anger, E. R., 117
Job postings and descriptions, 91–
    93, 95–100
Jobs, Steve, 26, 129
Johansson, Frans, 139
Johnson, Spencer, 31
John-Steiner, V., 7
Josselson, R., 9

K

Kaleidoscope thinking, 42–43
Kanter, R. M., 42–43
Kaufman, J. C., 6
Kegan, Robert, 45n2, 53, 56
Kelley, David, 167, 264
Kelley, Tom, 167, 264
Kelly, Bridget, 14–15, 221
Kelly, Robert, 3, 15, 261, 264
Kennedy, Ted, 223
Kent State University, 205
Kerr, Clark, 32
Klotz, Ann Marie, 11–12, 89
Kotter, John, 31
Kouzes, J. M., 123
Kruger, Kevin, 4, 116, 175
Kupo, L. V., 119, 122

L

Lahey, L. L., 56
Lamas, Frank, 13, 143
Land grant institutions, 24, 28–29
Leadership
    activism and, 186–189
    adaptability and, 7, 154–155, 184,
        193, 227, 230–231, 263
    as art, 138–140
    change management and, 31–34,
        56–57, 123, 125
    community colleges and, 247, 250,
        252–253, 258
    as competency area, 120
    contingent faculty and (Turman
        case study), 231–235
    courage and, 30–31, 32–34

creative burstiness and, 70–72
creativity as medium for, 123–
    124, 153–159
critical lenses on, 225, 232–
    233, 236–237
culture of innovation and, 80, 87
curiosity and, 130–133, 136–140
fear and, 77–79
five practices for, 123
four frames for, 55–56
future orientation for, 34–35
hiring practices and, 104, 111–112
humility and, 50, 58
inclusivity and, 184–186, 189–
    196, 235
legacy of, 158
purpose and, 64–65
stress management and, 69–70
tradition and, 20–21, 185–186
transformational learning for,
    42–43, 45, 48, 51, 54–58
vision and, 8, 32, 123, 132–133,
    144, 149–150, 153
visual model for, 264–265, 266f
withdrawing from (Kelly case
    study), 228–231
women of color and, 222–
    224, 227–228
Leadership capital, 227–228, 236–
    237
Learning. See
    Transformational learning
Lewis & Clark College, 208
LGBTQIA students, 82, 97, 122, 185,
    186, 206, 217
Liberal arts, 22–25, 27–28
Linder, C., 119

LinkedIn, 98

Listening, 104, 155, 213–214

Love, Patrick, 11, 75

Low-income students. *See* Poverty
and low-income populations

Ludwig, K., 50, 175, 176

M

Macklemore and Ryan Lewis: *Ten
Thousand Hours,* 72

Majors and courses. *See* Curriculum
and curricular change

Mance, M., 7, 123

Marginalized students and identities
activism and, 184, 186–189, 201,
202, 205–207, 213–214
amplifying creativity of, 14
challenges facing, 208–209, 216–
217
community colleges and, 255–256
intersectionality and, 223–224
leadership and, 226–228, 231, 233

Marketing, 155–156, 253. *See also*
Advertising job opportunities

Martin, J. A., 119

Martin, K., 117–118

Meditation, 27, 164, 172–173

Meetings, environments for, 65–69,
177–178, 194, 209

Mentors, 118. *See also* Networks
and networking

Mezirow, Jack, 48–49

Microaggressions, 188, 208, 217

Micro-innovations, 15, 241,
250, 253–254

Millennium Scholars Program, 36

Miller, M. L., 57

Milton, J., 35

Mindfulness, 27, 164, 172–173

Mind maps, 83

Minorities. *See* Marginalized students
and identities; Race and racism;
specific minority groups

Mitchell, D., 117–118

Mizzou (University of Missouri),
201–202, 207, 213–214

Mlodinow, L., 49

Mmeje, K. C., 13, 183

Moran, S., 7

Morgan Harper Nichols Blog, 151

Morrill Acts (1862, 1890), 22,
24, 28–29

Multicultural centers, 185, 206

Multicultural Competence for
Student Affairs-Preliminary 2
Scale, 121

Multiculturalism. *See* Diversity

Munin, Art, 11, 61

Murdock, M. C., 7, 123

Murray, Michele, 13, 163

Music and creativity, 61–62, 72, 163–
164

N

National Association for Campus
Activities, 156

National Association of Student
Personnel Administrators
(NASPA), 116, 118, 120–122,
125–126, 156

Nationalism, 14, 208

Native and indigenous peoples, 185,

208. *See also* Marginalized students and identities; Race and racism

Networks and networking, 42, 97, 115, 118, 148, 195, 203, 210. *See also* Collaboration

NewSmart model, 175, 176

New York Institute of Technology (NYIT)
   building culture of innovation at, 75–76, 81–87
   undoing anti-innovation elements at, 76–81

New York State community colleges, 243, 256

New York University, 208

The Niche Movement, 156

Nichols, Morgan Harper, 151

No Child Left Behind, x

Norms. *See* Status quo; Traditions

North Country Community College (NCCC), 248–256

Nursing degrees, 244

O

Obama, Barack, 223

Offers of employment, 91, 94, 109–110

Ohio State University, 29

Onboarding, 90, 110–112

On-campus interviews. *See* Interviewing candidates

O'Neill, Tip, 240

Online learning and degree programs, 25, 31–32, 35–36, 251

Organizational culture
   activism and, 209–212

anti-innovation elements in, 76–81, 134–136

building innovation in, 11, 75–76, 81–87, 134–140, 177–179, 263–267, 270–272

change management and, 32–34

as competency area, 120

creativity and, xi, 4, 5, 16, 65–70, 134–140, 144

curiosity and, 131

hiring and, 91, 106, 112

inclusivity in, 191–196

purpose in, 63–65, 132, 139, 140, 144, 264

traditions in, 26–31

transformational learning and, 47

unlearning and undoing in, 49, 53, 58, 76–81, 85, 176

Orientation for first-year students, 147, 215

Outcomes
   peer-to-peer collaboration for, 52–54, 58
   personal development and, 58
   professional development and, 45, 51–52, 54, 58
   for students, 32

P

Passion Planner, 152

Patience, 177–178

Paul Smith's College (PSC), 248–254

PBI (Public baccalaureate institutions), 254–256

Peer-to-peer collaboration, 52–53, 58, 79–81

Pendakur, Vijay, 12, 89

People of color. *See* Students and faculty of color

Perfectionism, 71, 135, 258, 270

Personal development
  career perspectives on, 156–158
  centering self in, 9, 223
  as competency area, 120
  graduate programs and, 117, 125–126
  "I Am" poetry assignment and, 123–124
  immunity to change framework and, 56–57
  inclusivity and, 14, 190, 192
  Passion Planner as tool for, 152
  professional development and, 43, 45, 58, 71, 138
  reflection as, 138–139
  self-trust and, 137
  spirituality and, 170, 174
  transformational learning for, 48, 53, 56–58

Petty, Cissy, 12, 129

Pitch Days, 84, 86

The Placement Exchange (TPE), 99

Political correctness, 206

Pope, R., 121

Posner, B. Z., 123

Poverty and low-income populations, ix, 187, 217, 222, 223

Predominantly White institutions (PWIs), 187–188, 217, 235

Presidents of colleges and universities, 30–31, 77, 78

Price, Alan C., 31

Professional development
  creativity prioritized in, 4–5
  graduate preparation and, 117
  HIHE and, 41–42
  inclusivity and, 192–193
  as leadership, 71
  peer collaboration in, 52–53, 58
  personal development and, 43, 45, 58, 71, 138
  transformational learning and, 43, 45–46, 51–55

Promoting job opportunities, 95–100, 111–112

Protests. *See* Activism

PSC (Paul Smith's College), 248–254

Public baccalaureate institutions (PBI), 254–256

Puccio, G. J., 7, 123, 126

Purpose
  inclusivity and, 191
  spirituality and, 165, 180
  in student affairs, 63–65, 132, 139, 140, 144, 264

PWIs (Predominantly White institutions), 187–188, 217, 235

Q

Qualifications. *See* Job postings and descriptions

Queer communities. *See* LGBTQIA students; Marginalized students and identities

R

Race and racism. *See also* Activism; Diversity; Marginalized students

and identities; Students and faculty of color
  activism against, 199–203, 205–208, 217–218
  cultural wealth and, 15
  higher education and, 203, 235
  traditional practices and, 34
  women of color and, 224, 228–230
Race to the Top, x
Rath, Tom, 110, 132–133
Recruitment, 90, 92–93, 111–112, 186, 188, 207, 253
Reference checks, 94, 105–106, 109, 112
Reflection. *See* Personal development
Religion. *See* Spirituality and faith
Relocation and hiring, 97, 107, 109–111, 148–149
Renn, K. A., 117
Research
  as competency area, 120
  curiosity and, 131
  experiential, 264
  as focus of higher education, 22–24
  recommendations for, 268–269
  tenure and, 234
Residence life, 147, 264, 270
Resilient capital, 227, 234–235
Resistance to change and innovation, 80. *See also* "Culture of no"
Resistant capital, 226–227, 231, 234
Résumé screening, 101–102, 103*f*
Retention, 64, 106, 108, 175, 186, 188, 222
Reverse reference check, 106

Reynolds, A., 121
Rhoads, R. A., 206
Risks and risk-taking
  career perspectives on, 148
  courage and, 33–34
  curiosity and, 131, 138
  failure and, 139
  impacts of, 153–154, 258
  innovation and, 21, 72, 77–78
  safe spaces for, 68, 70–71
Robinson, Kenneth, 130
Rodgers, Richard, 164
Rogers, E. M., 7
Rollins, Domonic A., 13–14, 183
Rudolph, F., 205

S

Sabbaticals, 35
Safe spaces
  creativity in, 62, 70–71, 137, 150–151
  spheres of influence outside of, 210
  for students, 218
  for transformational learning, 45, 53
Save-the-date hiring announcements, 93, 95, 96*f*, 98
Scholar–practitioner identity, 119, 224
Schwartz, T., 43
Screening matrices, 101–102, 103*f*
Search committees, 93, 94, 100–102
Seating at meetings, 66–67
Seher, C. L., 121
Self-exploration. *See* Personal development

Serenity Prayer, 157

Sexism, 15, 224, 229–231

Shared governance, 21, 27–28, 217

Sharing success, 80–81, 179

Shea, G. P., 58

Sinek, Simon, 63–65, 132

Singer, J. L., 5

Smith, K. K., 58

Smith, L. N., 4, 175

Snapchat, 203

Social capital, 226–227, 230, 231, 234–235

Social justice work, 118–122. *See also* Activism

Social media, 65, 93, 95, 97–100, 186, 203

Social mobility, 25–26

Society for Human Resource Management (SHRM), 89

Sotomayor, Sonia, 223

Specialization and expertise, 24, 49, 135, 136

Spheres of influence, 209–210

Spirituality and faith
    campus support for, 82
    connecting creativity with, 164–167, 179–180
    creativity restored through, 171–175
    experiencing creativity as, 167–170
    music and, 163–164
    virtues and, 175–179

Sports and athletics, 145–147

Staff. *See* Facilities and maintenance; Faculty; Organizational culture

Stakeholders in community

colleges, 239–246
    complexity of innovation and, 256–257
    external, 243–246
    internal, 242

Standing strong, 80–81

Start with Why, 63–65, 132

Statues dedicated to Confederacy, 27, 33

Status quo
    activism and, 204, 216–218, 221
    community colleges and, 256
    critical leadership and, 225, 233, 235–237
    cultural capital theory and, 225–226
    disruption of, 72, 78, 81, 157–158, 184, 263
    inclusivity and, 194

STEM-based disciplines, 27–28

Stewart, Amanda, 13, 143

Stewart, Colin, 3, 261

Strayhorn, Terrell, 215

Stress, 69–70, 78, 171–173

Student affairs. *See also* Higher education; Hiring practices; Leadership; Organizational culture
    activism and, 204, 209–218, 221
    advent of, 24, 26, 35
    advocacy/social justice work as preparation for, 118–122
    career perspectives on, 143–151, 153–154, 157–158, 170, 269–271
    competencies and creativity in, 116, 120–122
    costs of, 29, 30, 155, 171

expectations of, 32
four frames of leadership and, 56
graduate preparation for, 115–118
hiring questions for, 104
inclusivity and, 147, 154, 183–
 184, 264
institutional priorities and, 211
NYIT as case study for, 75–86
purpose in, 63–65, 132, 139, 140,
 144, 264
relocation and, 97, 107, 109–111
The Student Affairs Collective, 156
Student debt, 263
Students. *See also specific categories
 of students*
 activism and, 184, 186–189, 199–
  208
 campus climate affecting, 208–209
 community colleges and, 242,
  243, 248
 curricular development and, 24
 demographics and, 184–
  186, 262–263
 faculty and, 30, 115
 future orientation for, 34–35, 158
 in hiring processes, 101, 106–
  107, 111
 inclusive centering of, 183–184,
  196, 203
 institutional traditions and, 26–27
 professional preparedness of, 5, 22,
  116, 126
 shared governance and, 21, 27–
  28, 217
 social justice theory and, 119
Students and faculty of color. *See
 also* Black students and faculty;

Marginalized students and
 identities; Race and racism
 activism and, 188, 200–201, 206–
  208, 212–215
 cultural capital theory and, 225–
  228
 demographics and, 185–
  186, 221–222
 diversity and, 25
 leadership case studies of, 228–
  235
 transformative change and, 236–
  237
Sulkowicz, Emma, 203

T

Talent tracking, 100
Teaching, 51–52, 66–69. *See also*
 Transformational learning
Technologies. *See also* Information
 technology (IT)
 activism and, 203
 as competency area, 120
 costs of, 29
 higher education adapting to, xi–
  xii, 5, 175, 262–263, 267–268
 online degree programs and,
  25, 175
TED talks, 83
Temporary housing. *See* Relocation
 and hiring
Tenure
 contingent faculty and, 231–232
 institutional change and, 26, 29,
  30, 35
 of presidents of colleges and

universities, 30–31

The Placement Exchange (TPE), 99

Thompson, L., 68

Timelines for hiring, 93–94, 110, 112

Tokenization, 187

Traditions
  inclusivity and, 185–186, 191–192
  innovation vs., 20–21, 26–27, 33, 35–36
  transformational thinking questioning, 49

Transformation. *See* Disruptive transformation

Transformational learning
  collaboration and, 47*f,* 50, 52–53, 152, 157–158
  creativity from, 42–43
  defined, 46–47, 49
  informational learning compared to, xi, 45–52, 47*t,* 58
  optimal conditions for, 53–58
  professional development and, 43, 45

Transparency, 194–195

Trump, Donald, educational initiatives of, 22

Trust, 139–140

Turman, Natasha, 15, 221

Twitter, 98, 203

2+2 agreement, 252–254

Tyrell, Steve, 15, 239

U

Unions and community colleges, 242, 245

University of California, 32, 205

University of Illinois, 27, 29

University of Missouri (Mizzou), 201–202, 207, 213–214

University of Montana, 28

University of North Carolina at Chapel Hill, 208

University of North Dakota, 27

University of Phoenix, 25

University of Wisconsin, 29

Unlearning and undoing, 49, 53, 58, 76–81, 85

Unrest. *See* Activism

V

Vanderbilt University, 208

Virtues for creativity, 175–179

Vision
  change management and, 32–33
  communication of, 64–65
  creativity and, 170
  hiring practices and, 101
  leadership and, 8, 32, 123, 132–133, 144, 149–150, 153

Vocation, 164, 169, 171, 174, 191

W

Wagner, T., 5

Walker, Scott, 29

Walton, Sam, 137

Washington, Booker T., 24–25

Washington State University (Pullman), 28

Web meeting interviews and applications, 104–105

Western canon, 188–189

White, L., 264

Whiteness and White privilege, 203,
    225–226, 230
Williamson, M., 234
Wilson, Daniel, 48
Women
    activism and, 200, 205–206
    critical leadership and, 222–224,
        227–228, 233, 235, 236
    diversity and, 25
    leadership case studies of, 228–
        235
Women's colleges, 25
Work environments. *See*
    Organizational culture
Workforce training, 244–246,
    252, 257

X

Xenophobia, 208

Y

Yale University, 27, 199–202,
    207, 213–214
Yerkes-Dodson Law, 69, 69*f*
"Yes, and" approach, 137–138, 214,
    218, 271–272
Yosso, T. J., 15, 225–226, 235
YouTube, 99

Z

Zolner, Joe, 10–11, 41